THE TRAGEDY OF

Hamlet,

PRINCE OF DENMARK

EDITED BY
George Lyman Kittredge

Revised by Irving Ribner

William Shakespeare

THE TRAGEDY OF

Hamlet,

PRINCE OF DENMARK

XEROX

XEROX COLLEGE PUBLISHING

LEXINGTON, MASSACHUSETTS • TORONTO

PREFACE

The New Kittredge Shakespeares

The publication of George Lyman Kittredge's *Complete Works of Shakespeare* in 1936 was a landmark in Shakespeare scholarship. The teacher who for almost half a century had dominated and shaped the direction of Shakespearean study in America produced what was recognized widely as the finest edition of Shakespeare up to his time. In the preface to this edition Kittredge indicated his editorial principles; these allowed a paramount authority to the Folio of 1623 and countenanced few departures from it while, at the same time, refusing to "canonize the heedless type-setters of the Elizabethan printing house." Kittredge's work was marked by a judicious conservatism and a common sense rarely found in equal measure in earlier editors of Shakespeare. In the thirty-odd years which have gone by since the appearance of this monumental volume, however, considerable advances have been made in the establishment of Shakespeare's text, and our body of knowledge about the dates, sources, and general historical background of Shakespeare's plays has vastly increased. The present revision is designed to apply this new knowledge to Kittredge's work so that it may have as much value to the student and general reader of today as it had to those of thirty years ago.

Before his death Kittredge had issued, in addition to *The Complete Works,* separate editions of sixteen of the plays, each copiously annotated. Some of the notes were unusually elaborate, but they interpreted Shakespeare's language with a fullness and precision attained by few other commentators, for Kittredge had few equals in his intimate knowledge of Elizabethan English. In freshly annotating the plays I have, accordingly, tried to use

v

Kittredge's own notes as fully as space would permit. Where I have repeated his distinctive language or recorded his characteristic critical opinions, I have followed the note with the symbol [K]; where Kittredge's definition of a term can be found in essentially the same words in other editions, I have not used the identifying symbol. Every annotator draws upon the full body of the notes of earlier editors, and to give credit for every note is impossible. Notes have been placed at page bottoms.

The brief introductions which Kittredge wrote for the plays have been replaced by new ones, for what seemed like indisputable fact some thirty years ago often appears today to be much more uncertain, and many new issues of which Kittredge was not aware have been raised in recent criticism. The new introductions seek to present what are now generally agreed to be basic facts about the plays and to give some indications of the directions which modern criticism has taken, although specific analyses of individual plays are avoided.

Such great authority attaches to Kittredge's text that it has not frequently — and never lightly — been departed from. Where changes have been made, they have usually involved the restoration of copy-text readings now generally accepted in place of the emendations of eighteenth- and nineteenth-century editors of which Kittredge, in spite of his extraordinary conservatism in this regard, sometimes too easily approved. Only rarely has an emendation been adopted in the present revision which was not also adopted by Kittredge. All departures from the copy-texts are indicated in the notes, emendations followed by the names of the editors by whom they were first proposed. Wherever Kittredge's text has been departed from for any reason, his reading is given in the notes. Modern spelling has in a few instances been substituted for Elizabethan forms which are mere spelling variations but which Kittredge nevertheless retained. His punctuation has not been altered except in a few very rare instances.

The system of recording elisions and contractions which Kittredge explained in his introduction to *The Complete Works* has been retained, as has his method of preserving to the fullest the copy-text stage directions, with all additions to them enclosed within square brackets. Although modern editors recog-

nize the vagueness of the place settings of Elizabethan plays and
are reluctant to include the place designations so favoured by
eighteenth- and nineteenth-century editors, much historical interest nevertheless attaches to these, and Kittredge's place designations accordingly have been retained between square brackets.
Kittredge's attempt to retain the line numbering of the Globe
text, which resulted in considerable irregularity in prose passages,
has been abandoned, and the lines of each play have been freshly
numbered. Kittredge's act and scene divisions have been retained,
as has his practice of surrounding by square brackets those divisions which are not in the copy-texts.

The *New Kittredge Shakespeares* include individual editions of
each of the plays, the sonnets, and the minor poems, and a new
edition of *The Complete Works* in a single volume. A comprehensive introduction to Shakespeare's life, times, and theatrical
milieu is available both as a separate volume and as an introduction to *The Complete Works*.

IRVING RIBNER

INTRODUCTION

The Tragedy of Hamlet

◇◇◇◇◇
◇◇◇◇◇ Shakespeare's *Hamlet* poses more problems than any
◇◇◇◇◇ other play he wrote. These include the text of the play,
its date, its sources, and — what has intrigued the imaginations of
mankind perhaps more than any other question in the world's
literature — the character of the hero and the nature of his tragedy. The play was entered in the Stationers' Register by James
Roberts on July 26, 1602, but Roberts did not print it until 1604.
In the meantime, in 1603, there appeared a garbled version (Q¹)
printed for Nicholas Ling and John Trundell and usually called
the Bad Quarto. Exactly how it came into being we are not sure,
but it seems almost certainly to have been reconstructed from
memory by a group of actors who had either performed in the
play themselves or seen it on the stage. While it is based clearly
upon Shakespeare's play, it is affected also by memory of an
earlier version of the Hamlet story which we know was on the
stage before 1589. The Q¹ text of Hamlet has been studied most
thoroughly by G. I. Duthie, *The "Bad" Quarto of Hamlet* (Cambridge University Press, 1941).

In 1604/5 an authorized version of the play (Q²) appeared.
It was printed by James Roberts for Nicholas Ling, the publisher
of Q¹, some agreement apparently having been reached between
them. Some copies bear the date 1604 on their title pages and
some 1605. We may be virtually certain that this version was
printed from Shakespeare's own manuscript (foul papers), and it
is the most authoritative text that we have, but it is unfortunately
marred by a large number of printers' errors and omissions. It
also shows signs of contamination by the Bad Quarto, which appears to have been referred to during the course of composition,

possibly because Shakespeare's manuscript was defective. It formed the basis of a third quarto (Q³) printed in 1611, and this in turn served as copy for a fourth quarto (Q⁴), undated but printed sometime before 1623. Neither of these texts has any authority.

The version of *Hamlet* which appeared in the folio of 1623 (F¹) derives from a manuscript version different from that behind Q². It omits more than two hundred lines (recorded in the notes), and at the same time it supplies at least five authentic passages omitted from Q²: II.ii.235–65 ("Let . . . attended"), 329–52; IV.v.159–61; V.i.30–5 ("Why . . . without arms"); V.ii.68–80. Although it has been the subject of much debate, it is now generally agreed that the F¹ text was set from the theatre prompt-book being used at the time the folio was printed, or from a transcript of it, as argued by J. D. Wilson, *The Manuscript of Shakespeare's Hamlet* (Cambridge University Press, 1934). Harold Jenkins has shown in an important article in *Studies in Bibliography*, XIII (1960), 31–47, that the F¹ text incorporates a great many changes and additions made by actors during some twenty years of stage production. It does, however, correct Q² in numerous instances, and where the two texts present readings equally meaningful, F¹ is sometimes preferable. Q² must furnish the text of the play, with reliance upon F¹ only where it is clearly superior. There are no act or scene divisions in Q¹ or Q²; there is some inaccurate division in the first two acts of F¹. The act and scene divisions of the present edition are those of the Globe text. All significant departures from Q² are recorded in the notes. Variants are far too numerous to be listed fully.

DATE

As to the date of *Hamlet* there is no reliable external evidence of any kind. A reference to the play which Gabriel Harvey made in the margin of Speght's edition of Chaucer could have been placed there almost any time after 1598, when that edition was published. That the play must be later than 1598 is suggested also by the failure of Francis Meres to mention it in his *Palladis Tamia,* entered in the Stationers' Register in that year, and it is confirmed by the reference to the companies of child actors and the Wars of the Theatres (II.ii.319–52), which could not have been made before 1598, when the Children of the Chapel Royal began to act at Blackfriars. This allusion would suggest a date between 1599 and 1601 when the childrens' companies had become so popular as to seriously challenge the adult companies and force some of them to leave London for tours of the provinces. Most scholars are thus inclined, with stylistic criteria also in mind, to date the play in 1600 or 1601, the Stationers' Register entry of July 26, 1602, furnishing an absolute terminal limit.

THE HAMLET STORY

The story of Hamlet is told for the first time in the Latin *Historia Danica* of Saxo Grammaticus, a Danish historian who between 1180 and 1208 gathered together into a comprehensive history of his country not only authentic historical fact but also the ancient legends and folk traditions of his Northern Europe. Hamlet (or Amlethus, as Saxo calls him) belongs in this latter category. We may find traces of him as a legendary hero as far back as the tenth century. Snorri Sturlason, a contemporary of Saxo, around 1230 prepared a kind of handbook of the art of poetry called the *Skaldskapar-màl.* Among the fragments of earlier poetry which he reproduced was one by the tenth-century bard and explorer Snæbjorn, who speaks metaphorically of a region of the sea as a giant mill which in ages past had ground the meal of Amloþi.

The story of Amlethus, as it is told in the third and fourth books of Saxo's *Historia* is a long and brutal account, covering a period of many years, of a struggle between powerful adversaries. Horwendil, Governor of Jutland, who has married Gerutha, daughter of the King of Denmark, is openly murdered by his brother Fengon, who seizes the throne and marries Gerutha. Amlethus, the son of Horwendil, is a mere boy at the time. He grows up determined to avenge his father's death. Being completely in his uncle's power, he pretends madness for self-protection, but his madness hides a superhuman cunning. When his uncle suspects that Amlethus may not really be mad, he devises a series of attempts to entrap him, all of which Amlethus by superior cunning is able to evade. These tricks include what are to be the core of the story as it came down to Shakespeare's play: a woman enjoined to seduce him so that he may betray himself through love, a courtier secreted in his mother's room so as to kill him unawares, and two false friends to accompany him to an intended death in England. Amlethus is always able to outwit his adversaries. After marrying the English king's daughter, he returns to Denmark, gets the courtiers drunk in the great hall of the palace, causes them all to be secured on the floor with a net he has devised for the purpose, and then sets the hall afire, killing them all. His uncle, who has escaped the hall, Amlethus kills with his own sword. After making a speech to the people, he ascends the throne himself and rules for some years. Later he returns to England, marries again, is betrayed by his second wife and killed in battle with another uncle.

Saxo's account was slightly amplified and somewhat moralized by François de Belleforest who, beginning in 1565, began to publish a series of tragic prose stories called *Histoires tragiques*. In the fifth series, published in 1576, he included the story of Hamlet, and it appeared again when Belleforest's collected stories were published in 1582. An English version, *The Hystorie of Hamblet*, printed by Thomas Pavier in 1608, was translated from this edition. Belleforest adds little of significance to Saxo's account other than the suggestion that Gerutha and Fengon had committed adultery before the murder of Horwendil, that Hamlet suffered from melancholy, and that he had been the lover of the woman engaged to entrap him.

THE UR-HAMLET

While it is possible that Shakespeare may have read the story in the French of Belleforest, we are fairly certain that his primary source was an old play on the subject of Hamlet which may go back to the beginning of the 1580's, although our earliest reference to it is in Thomas Nashe's Epistle prefixed to Robert Greene's *Menaphon,* published in 1589: "English *Seneca* read by Candle light yeelds many good sentences . . . and if you intreat him faire in a frostie morning, hee will afford you whole

Hamlets, I should say handfuls of Tragicall speeches." Phillip Henslowe recorded in his *Diary* a performance of this play on June 11, 1594, and Thomas Lodge referred to it in his *Wits Miserie, and the Worlds Madnesse* (1596): "As pale as the Visard of ye ghost which cried so miserably at ye Theator, like an oister wife, *Hamlet, reuenge.*"

It is likely that in this play Shakespeare found the suggestions for some of those elements which are so strikingly absent from Belleforest's account: the ghost, the play within the play, the duel, Laertes, and Fortinbras. It seems certain that it was the kind of Senecan revenge play popular in the 1580's, of which Thomas Kyd's *The Spanish Tragedy* provides perhaps our best extant example. Since *The Spanish Tragedy* includes a ghost, a play within the play, and other features we may find in *Hamlet,* Kyd has usually been considered to have been the author of the *Ur-Hamlet.* This is by no means certain, although it is supported also by Nashe's allusion to "the Kidde in Aesop" in the passage in which he mentions the old play.

Various attempts have been made to reconstruct the *Ur-Hamlet.* Since the Bad Quarto contains certain elements which are in Belleforest but not in Shakespeare's play, these have been assumed to be *Ur-Hamlet* details which the Q¹ reporter or reporters remembered from the old play. Most use, however, has been made of a German play, *Der Bestrafte Brudermord (Fratricide Punished),* first printed in 1781 from a manuscript dated 1710 which has now disappeared. We know that from 1586 onward bands of English actors had travelled in Germany. It has been assumed that sometime before 1600 a troupe of inferior English actors performed a Hamlet play somewhere in Germany. The play fell into the hands of German actors who translated it into their own language, and finally, through at least two manuscript transcriptions, made its way into the printed version which has survived. The German play is entirely too different from Shakespeare's to have been based upon it, but it may well have been based upon an abbreviated version of the *Ur-Hamlet.* Polonius is called in it Corambis, as he is also in the Bad Quarto. There is a prologue which strongly resembles that of *The Spanish Tragedy* and which may well have been based upon the prologue to the *Ur-Hamlet.*

The chief importance of *Der Bestrafte Brudermord* is for the example it furnishes us of the kind of crude material with which Shakespeare probably began and out of which he fashioned one of the most highly intellectual works in the theatre of the world.

THE PROBLEM OF INTERPRETATION

Hamlet has generated probably more critical controversy than any other play ever written. Nineteenth-century romantic critics tended to concentrate upon the personality of the hero, often removing him from his context in the play, and treating him as though he were a real person, the victim of some strange psychological disorder. Such critics were countered perhaps most effectively by G. L. Kittredge in the introduction which he wrote to his 1939 edition of the play. Kittredge was concerned with *Hamlet* as a play rather than as a psychological case study, and he dealt at length with the historic questions of Hamlet's supposed procrastination, his age, and the nature of Claudius as an adversary. Kittredge's criticism, of course, represents only one limited point of view, and no student of the play should fail to consult also the essays by A. C. Bradley in *Shakespearean Tragedy* (London: Macmillan, 1904), by Harley Granville-Barker in *Prefaces to Shakespeare* (Princeton University Press, 1946), and G. Wilson Knight in *The Wheel of Fire* (New York: Oxford University Press, 1930). The most thorough exploration of all of the play's problems is John Dover Wilson's *What Happens in Hamlet* (Cambridge University Press, 1935). Because of its great historical interest, Kittredge's introduction is reproduced without alteration in the following paragraphs:

[HAMLET'S DELAY]

Both in Shakespeare and in Belleforest we have a story of necessarily deferred revenge, but the situation at the outset is not the same, and the ground of the necessity differs accordingly. In the old tale the murder is no secret; but the avenger is helpless, a mere boy in his uncle's power. In the drama, on the other hand, the murder is suspected by no one until the Ghost reveals

it. But this is "spectral evidence." Hamlet believes that the apparition is indeed the ghost of his father and that it has told the
truth. Yet it may be a demon in his father's shape, tempting him
to kill an innocent man. This doubt as to the ambiguous apparition accords with ancient doctrine and was perfectly intelligible
to any Elizabethan audience. Disregard of Hamlet's dilemma has
led to misinterpretation of his character, as if he were a pro-
crastinator, a vain dreamer, an impulsive creature of feeble will.
But Shakespeare has done his best to enforce the imperative
scruple as to the apparition. It inspires aud dictates Horatio's
challenge (I.i.46*ff*); it is implicit in Bernardo's assent (line 109);
it is manifest in Hamlet's declared resolution (I.ii.244–6); and it
finds solemn utterance when he adjures the Ghost to speak
(I.iv.40*ff*). Nothing could be clearer, in this regard, than Horatio's
warning (I.iv.69*ff*). All this leads up to Hamlet's soliloquy at the
end of Act II:

> The spirit that I have seen
> May be a devil; and the devil hath power
> T' assume a pleasing shape; yea, and perhaps
> Out of my weakness and my melancholy,
> As he is very potent with such spirits,
> Abuses me to damn me. I'll have grounds
> More relative than this.

And the substance of this soliloquy is repeated and enforced
when Hamlet explains to Horatio the purpose of the play within
the play (III.ii.73–85). Hamlet cannot act upon mere spectral
evidence. The testimony of the Ghost must somehow be corrob-
orated. The murderer must be forced to testify against himself.
Then, and not till then, will action be possible for a reasonable
man. "The play's the thing!" Significant, too, is the fact that the
calm and philosophic Horatio — Hamlet's sole confidant as to
the Ghost's revelation — accepts the crucial experiment as necessary, and agrees with Hamlet that its success is conclusive
(III.ii.85–7, 275–8).

   The necessity for some device like the play within the play is
due to the failure of Hamlet's assumed madness to achieve its

purpose. In the old saga and in Belleforest, Hamlet feigns madness for self-protection. It is made perfectly clear that the King
can kill him at any moment, and that he refrains only because
he cannot satisfy himself that the boy is in his right mind. He
tries to entrap him into some act that will prove his sanity, but
in vain. Hamlet is too shrewd for him and carries through his
pretence of insanity until at last he finds the moment for a terrible revenge. Thus his pretended madness, like the deferred
vengeance, was an essential element in the saga and the old play.
How the old play accounted for it, it is idle to conjecture. In
Shakespeare's drama, however, Hamlet's motive for acting the
madman is obvious. We speak unguardedly in the presence of
children and madmen, for we take it for granted that they will
not listen or will not understand; and so the King or the Queen
(for Hamlet does not know that his mother is ignorant of her
husband's crime) may say something that will afford the evidence
needed to confirm the testimony of the Ghost. The device is
adopted on the spur of the moment (I.v.169*ff*), and, once adopted,
it must be maintained. But it is unsuccessful. The King is always
on his guard, and the Queen is not an accomplice.

The earliest moment at which Hamlet is justified in striking
the blow does not come until the end of the third scene of the
third act — or, in other words, until Shakespeare's play is more
than half finished. It is the moment when Hamlet finds his uncle
at prayer (III.iii.73):

> Now might I do it pat, now he is praying;
> And now I'll do 't.

Now, for the first time, Claudius is off his guard, and his attitude
of prayer confirms the evidence — already strong enough — that
he is guilty.

Obviously, up to this point, we must acquit Hamlet of procrastination. He had adopted the device of madness on the instant, immediately after the Ghost's revelation; and, when this
failed as a detective agency, he had utilized the first opportunity
for a further test — the play within the play. Note the prompti-
tude of his action in this regard. No sooner had he heard the

players' declamation and observed its emotional effect than his plan was formed. When the players appear at Elsinore he is at his wit's end for evidence. Partly from love of the drama (for the actors are old favourites), partly to distract his mind from a hideous and hitherto insoluble problem, he calls for a "taste of their quality." The emotional effect of the Pyrrhus declamation — both upon the player and upon himself — suggests a device which he instantly puts into action. The interval between the appearance of the Ghost and the arrival of the players is hardly more than a couple of months.

The sight of the King on his knees gives the finishing touch to the testimony of "The Mousetrap." Now, then, at this the first usable opportunity, is Hamlet, if ever, in the mood to kill the King. Yet this is the one moment when it is impossible for any-one but an assassin to strike. This would be true if Shakespeare had merely introduced the King in the attitude of prayer. How much stronger is the case when our very souls have been shaken by the terrific mental and spiritual struggle through which Claudius has just passed — when (for the first time) our sympa-thies (if we are human) have gone out to the man whom we have hitherto regarded with abhorrence. The strenuous avenger Laertes would not have hesitated to plunge his sword into the King's back as heartily and instinctively as a bulldog bites. But such an act is not in accord with Hamlet's nature and education. This does not mean that he is a born weakling or that he has learned inertia at the university. For we must accept the vale-dictory tribute of young Fortinbras — the pattern of vigorous soldiership — when he declares that Hamlet "was likely, had he been put on, to have prov'd most royal" (V.ii.384–5). Hamlet cannot butcher a defenceless man. Nor would such an act accord with the emotional mood of the audience at this juncture. It is a dramatic, a moral, almost a physical impossibility.

Shakespeare is face to face with an exacting problem. He has brought his two main personages together in such a way that it is impossible for Hamlet to strike, though the opportunity is ideal, and though it is, in theory, his sacred duty to kill his uncle as soon as he can. How is he to extricate his characters from the situation in which he has deliberately involved them?

Manifestly it is out of the question for Hamlet to give the real reason for sheathing his sword; for that would be to make him repudiate the traditional code to which he still subscribes, though he has outgrown its literal savagery. The only excuse or pretext for inaction now must consist in his persuading himself that, after all, the moment is *not* favourable; and there is but one way in which he can so persuade himself — by proving that, if he strikes now, his vengeance will be ineffectual. Hence we have the diabolical outburst which prompted Dr. Johnson's famous comment: "This speech, in which Hamlet is not content with taking blood for blood, but contrives damnation for the man that he would punish, is too horrible to be read or to be uttered."

But these diabolical sentiments are not Hamlet's sentiments. He does not really postpone his uncle's death in order that he may consign him to perdition. The speech is merely a pretext for delay. The problem is not, "Why does Hamlet entertain such infernal sentiments?" but rather, "How happens it that such a pretext occurs to him?" And the answer is obvious: Because the views in question accord with an old-established convention with regard to adequate revenge. With this convention the Elizabethan audience was familiar, and it made allowance accordingly; for language means only what it is meant to mean by the speaker and what it is understood to mean by the hearer. Examples in abundance establish the convention. Thus in *2 Henry VI* (IV.x. 83-5), when that mild and almost idyllic character Alexander Iden, "a poor esquire of Kent that loves his king," kills the rebel Cade, he expresses himself in just such terms:

> Die, damned wretch, the curse of her that bare thee!
> And as I thrust thy body in with my sword,
> So wish I, I might thrust thy soul to hell!

And it assumes idiomatic guise when Ancient Pistol curses Captain Fluellen: "Die and be damn'd! and figo for thy friendship!" (*Henry V*, III.iv.60).

The delay is not for long. The moment comes in the very next scene, when Hamlet is nerved to strike and when (if his sword had found the victim it aimed at) neither he — nor even we, his modern judges — could have felt the slightest scruple. And then he acts with decision. It is in his mother's chamber, when he thrusts his sword through the arras and kills Polonius, mistaking him for the King. This is the turning point of the tragedy. The King, who knows now that Hamlet means to kill him, lays his plans accordingly. There is no moment until the very end of the play when Hamlet has Claudius at his mercy. Both before Hamlet's embarkation for England, and after his return, Claudius is well guarded and Hamlet is under surveillance. And finally, when vengeance comes, it involves the avenger as well as the criminal. And this is well, for nothing could so completely justify Hamlet as the situation at the end of the tragedy. He kills the King in hot blood — as it were in a hand-to-hand struggle — and, in this melee, he acts, to all intents and purposes, in self-defence, for Claudius (by the trick of the poisoned rapier and the poisoned drink) has struck the first blow.

[HAMLET'S AGE]

How old is Shakespeare's Hamlet? Specific evidence is supplied by the Sexton (V.i.130ff). In reply to Hamlet's question, "How long has thou been a grave-maker?" he declares that he "came to't that day that our last king Hamlet overcame Fortinbras"; and he adds, "It was the very day that young Hamlet was born," and "I have been sexton here, man and boy, thirty years." In support of this reckoning, we have his date for the burial of Yorick: "This skull hath lien you i' th' earth three-and-twenty years." And Yorick had borne Hamlet "on his back a thousand times." On the fallacious principle that "figures won't lie," the grave-digger's evidence has been accepted by some critics, despite its flat contradiction of the testimony of Laertes and Ophelia (both of whom describe Hamlet as a very young man), of the King, and of Hamlet himself. Evidently he cannot be more than twenty years of age when the play begins, and the whole action of the drama occupies only two or three months. "Revision" has been suggested to explain the gross inconsistency. But such revision cannot have been Shakespeare's, unless he had lost his memory in the interval; and, if it was an actor's or a manager's revision, we may safely ignore it. Misprint or miscopying is a more plausible guess. Such errors are common in numerals, as every proofreader knows; and they were particularly easy in Shakespeare's day, when Roman numerals were often used. It is comforting to find in the First Quarto "this dozen year" instead of "three-and-twenty";

> Looke you, heres a scull hath bin here this dozen yeare,
> Let me see, I euer since our last king *Hamlet*
> Slew *Fortenbrasse* in combat

[KING CLAUDIUS]

King Claudius is a character that repays careful study. It is a mistake to regard him as a usurper. In Hamlet's Denmark, as in Macbeth's Scotland, the crown was elective within the limits of the royal family, and there was nothing against the law in Claudius's taking advantage of his nephew's absence to bring about his own election. Nowhere in the play is the question of usurpation raised. The nearest approach to such an idea comes in Hamlet's passionate outburst to his mother (III.iv.98–101):

> A vice of kings;
> A cutpurse of the empire and the rule,
> That from a shelf the precious diadem stole
> And put it in his pocket!

And this ambiguous evidence is vacated by his words to Horatio when he is setting forth, with relentless logic, the "perfect conscience" of his vengeful plan (V.ii.64*ff*):

> He that hath kill'd my king, and whor'd my mother;
> Popp'd in between th' election and my hopes;
> Thrown out his angle for my proper life,
> And with such coz'nage.

Hamlet's deliberate use of the term *election,* and of *my hopes* instead of *my rights,* is decisive. The council of nobles has elected Claudius, and no Dane questions his title. This fact, indeed, is implied when, in his first speech from the throne (I.ii.1*ff*), he thanks the councillors for their aid and comfort. Claudius has wronged his nephew by excluding him from the succession, but the wrong was effected in strict accordance with legal procedure.

King Claudius is a superb figure — almost as great a dramatic creation as Hamlet himself. His intellectual powers are of the highest order. He is eloquent — formal when formality is appropriate (as in the speech from the throne), graciously familiar when familiarity is in place (as in his treatment of the family of Polonius), persuasive to an almost superhuman degree (as in his manipulation of the insurgent Laertes) — always and everywhere a model of royal dignity. His courage is manifested, under the most terrifying circumstances, when the mob breaks into the palace. His self-control when the dumb show enacts his secret crime before his eyes is nothing less than marvellous. It was no accident that Shakespeare gave him that phrase which has become the ultimate pronouncement of the divine right of monarchy: "Such divinity doth hedge a king."

Intellectually, then, we must admit Claudius to as high a rank as Hamlet himself. What are we to say of him morally? On this point there is danger of misinterpretation. Claudius is often regarded as a moral monster — selfish, calculating, passionless — subtle and cold as a serpent. From such an error we are rescued by one of the supreme passages in all Shakespeare — the King's soliloquy after "The Mousetrap" has caught his conscience (III.iii.36*ff*):

> O, my offence is rank, it smells to heaven;
> It hath the primal eldest curse upon't,
> A brother's murder!

In this soliloquy Claudius unlocks his soul. It reveals him not only as passionately remorseful — with a heart in no wise cauterized by crime — but as so clear-sighted, so pitiless in the analysis of his own offences and of the motives that actuated them, that he cannot juggle with his conscience.

> What form of prayer
> Can serve my turn? "Forgive me my foul murder"?

> That cannot be; since I am still possess'd
> Of those effects for which I did the murder —
> My crown, mine own ambition, and my queen.

His crime was a crime of passion. "My queen" is the acme of the climax. So she was in the Ghost's revelation to Hamlet (I.v.74–5):

> Thus was I, sleeping, by a brother's hand
> Of life, of crown, of queen, at once dispatch'd.

To neglect or undervalue Claudius destroys the balance of the tragedy. On the stage, for generations, his lines were cut unmercifully, and his role was assigned to an inferior actor, so that he became the typical melodramatic villain, who frowns and mouths and struts and beats the air. And Hamlet has suffered accordingly, and has too often been conceived as a pathetic creature of high imagination but feeble will. Otherwise, why did he not abolish this ineffectual obstacle with a sweep of the arm? Of late, however, managers and actors have done better in this regard, but the prejudice lingers. Of Shakespeare's intent there can be no doubt. The play is a contest between two great opponents. This Hamlet understands; and he expresses the truth in his words to Horatio (V.ii.61–2), which might well be a summarizing motto for the play:

> the pass and fell incensed points
> Of mighty opposites.

THE TRAGEDY OF

Hamlet,

PRINCE OF DENMARK

CLAUDIUS, *King of Denmark.*
HAMLET, *son to the former, and nephew to the present King.*
POLONIUS, *Lord Chamberlain.*
HORATIO, *friend to* HAMLET.
LAERTES, *son to* POLONIUS.
VOLTEMAND,
CORNELIUS,
ROSENCRANTZ,   } *courtiers.*
GUILDENSTERN,
OSRIC,
A Gentleman,
A Priest.
MARCELLUS, } *officers.*
BERNARDO,
FRANCISCO, *a soldier.*
REYNALDO, *servant to* POLONIUS.
Players.
Two Clowns, gravediggers.
FORTINBRAS, *Prince of Norway.*
A Norwegian Captain.
English Ambassadors.

GERTRUDE, *Queen of Denmark, mother to* HAMLET.
OPHELIA, *daughter to* POLONIUS.

Ghost of HAMLET's *Father.*

Lords, Ladies, Officers, Soldiers, Sailors, Messengers, Attendants.

SCENE. — *Elsinore.*]

Act One

<><><><><><><><><><><><><><><><><><><><><><><><><><><><><><><><><>

SCENE I.
[Elsinore. A Platform before the Castle.]

Enter two Sentinels — [first,] Francisco, [who paces up and down at his post; then] Bernardo, [who approaches him].

BER.	Who's there?
FRAN.	Nay, answer me. Stand and unfold yourself.
BER.	Long live the King!
FRAN.	Bernardo?
BER.	He.
FRAN.	You come most carefully upon your hour.
BER.	'Tis now struck twelve. Get thee to bed, Francisco.
FRAN.	For this relief much thanks. 'Tis bitter cold, And I am sick at heart.
BER.	Have you had quiet guard?

5

I.I. 2 *Nay, answer me* "Me" is emphatic. Bernardo, in hailing Francisco, instinctively uses the sentinel's formula. Francisco, with a touch of humour, suggests that it is rather his business to ask this question of Bernardo than Bernardo's to ask it of him [K]. *unfold* disclose. 3 *Long live the King* Not, apparently, the watchword or countersign but merely a customary exclamation. Francisco, who is expecting Bernardo, recognizes his voice [K]. If it is the watchword, as some editors have suggested, it is highly ironical in the light of what the play is to reveal about the King. 9 *sick at heart* depressed, in low spirits.

1

FRAN.   Not a mouse stirring.   10

BER.   Well, good night.
        If you do meet Horatio and Marcellus,
        The rivals of my watch, bid them make haste.

                   Enter Horatio *and* Marcellus.

FRAN.   I think I hear them. Stand, ho! Who is there?

HOR.   Friends to this ground.

MAR.   And liegemen to the Dane.   15

FRAN.   Give you good night.

MAR.   O, farewell, honest soldier.
        Who hath reliev'd you?

FRAN.   Bernardo hath my place.
        Give you good night.   *Exit.*

MAR.   Holla, Bernardo!

BER.   Say —
        What, is Horatio there?

HOR.   A piece of him.

BER.   Welcome, Horatio. Welcome, good Marcellus.   20

HOR.   What, has this thing appear'd again to-night?

BER.   I have seen nothing.

MAR.   Horatio says 'tis but our fantasy,
        And will not let belief take hold of him
        Touching this dreaded sight, twice seen of us.   25
        Therefore I have entreated him along,
        With us to watch the minutes of this night,

---

13 *rivals* partners, sharers.   15 *the Dane* the King of Denmark.   16 *soldier* Q¹,
F¹; Q²: "souldiers."   19 *A piece of him* A mildly humorous affirmative [K]. Perhaps he means that since he does not believe in ghosts only his body, not his
mind, is present.   21 *What . . . to-night* Q²; Q¹, F¹, K give the line to Marcellus.
The mocking tone of incredulity is far more appropriate to Horatio and supports
the Q² ascription.   23 *fantasy* imagination.   26 *along* to come along. Ellipsis of
a verb of motion is very common [K].   29 *approve* prove the trustworthiness of.
speak to it They have not ventured to speak to the Ghost, for it was thought
dangerous to address an apparition, except in due form [K]. As a scholar Horatio
would be familiar with such matters.   33 *have two nights* Q²; F¹, K: "two nights
have."   36 *pole* North or Pole star.   42 *Thou art a scholar* Commonly but

    That, if again this apparition come,
    He may approve our eyes and speak to it.
HOR. Tush, tush, 'twill not appear.

BER.   Sit down awhile,   30
    And let us once again assail your ears,
    That are so fortified against our story,
    What we have two nights seen.

HOR.   Well, sit we down,
    And let us hear Bernardo speak of this.

BER. Last night of all,   35
    When yond same star that's westward from the pole
    Had made his course t' illume that part of heaven
    Where now it burns, Marcellus and myself,
    The bell then beating one —

        Enter Ghost.

MAR. Peace! break thee off! Look where it comes again!   40

BER. In the same figure, like the King that's dead.

MAR. Thou art a scholar; speak to it, Horatio.

BER. Looks 'a not like the King? Mark it, Horatio.

HOR. Most like. It harrows me with fear and wonder.

BER. It would be spoke to.

MAR.   Speak to it, Horatio.   45

HOR. What art thou that usurp'st this time of night
    Together with that fair and warlike form
    In which the majesty of buried Denmark

---

erroneously explained in accordance with DOUCE'S note, "that the exorcisms of troublesome spirits were usually performed in Latin." Horatio is not asked to drive away the apparition, but to question it, in order to discover what it is and why it appears. To accost the spirit was hazardous, for it might be a demon. Horatio, as a scholar, knows how to address the apparition in the right way, so as neither to offend it nor to subject himself to any evil influence. His language is formal and solemn, but he uses no Latin and utters no exorcism. See also lines 126–39 [K]. 43 *'a not* he not — a common colloquialism (Q²; F¹, K: "it not"). 45 *Speak to it* Q²; Q¹, F¹, K: "Question it." 48 *buried Denmark* the buried King of Denmark.

Did sometimes march? By heaven I charge thee speak!

MAR.   It is offended.

BER.   See, it stalks away!   50

HOR.   Stay! Speak, speak! I charge thee speak!   *Exit* Ghost.

MAR.   'Tis gone and will not answer.

BER.   How now, Horatio? You tremble and look pale.
          Is not this something more than fantasy?
          What think you on't?   55

HOR.   Before my God, I might not this believe
          Without the sensible and true avouch
          Of mine own eyes.

MAR.   Is it not like the King?

HOR.   As thou art to thyself.
          Such was the very armour he had on   60
          When he th' ambitious Norway combated.
          So frown'd he once when, in an angry parle,
          He smote the sledded Polacks on the ice.
          'Tis strange.

MAR.   Thus twice before, and jump at this dead hour, 65
          With martial stalk hath he gone by our watch.

HOR.   In what particular thought to work I know not;
          But, in the gross and scope of mine opinion,
          This bodes some strange eruption to our state.

MAR.   Good now, sit down, and tell me he that knows, 70

---

49 *sometimes* formerly.   56 *might* could.   57-8 *the sensible . . . own eyes* the
testimony of my own eyes, which is a matter of the senses and must be true [K].
61 *Norway* King of Norway.   62 *parle* conference before battle.   63 *sledded
Polacks* the Polanders, who ride in sledges [K] (MALONE; Q²: "sleaded Pollax": F¹:
"sledded Pollax"). Some have suggested a "pole-axe weighted with lead," but
MALONE's reading and explanation are usually accepted.   65 *jump* precisely.   68
in the gross . . . opinion in the general view or range of my opinion (as opposed
to my precise thought) [K].   *mine* Q²; F¹, K: "my."   69 *eruption to* sudden
calamity in.   72 *toils the subject* makes the subjects toil.   73 *cast* casting (F¹; Q²:
"cost").   74 *foreign mart* dealing with foreign countries; negotiations abroad [K].
75 *impress* Shipcarpenters were impressed (conscripted) in time of war [K].   77

Why this same strict and most observant watch
So nightly toils the subject of the land,
And why such daily cast of brazen cannon
And foreign mart for implements of war;
Why such impress of shipwrights, whose sore task   75
Does not divide the Sunday from the week.
What might be toward, that this sweaty haste
Doth make the night joint-labourer with the day?
Who is't that can inform me?

HOR.   That can I.
At least, the whisper goes so. Our last king,   80
Whose image even but now appear'd to us,
Was, as you know, by Fortinbras of Norway,
Thereto prick'd on by a most emulate pride,
Dar'd to the combat; in which our valiant Hamlet
(For so this side of our known world esteem'd him)   85
Did slay this Fortinbras; who, by a seal'd compact,
Well ratified by law and heraldry,
Did forfeit, with his life, all those his lands
Which he stood seiz'd of, to the conqueror;
Against the which a moiety competent   90
Was gaged by our king; which had return'd
To the inheritance of Fortinbras,
Had he been vanquisher, as, by the same comart
And carriage of the article design'd,
His fell to Hamlet. Now, sir, young Fortinbras,   95
Of unimproved mettle hot and full,
Hath in the skirts of Norway, here and there,

---

toward in preparation.   81 image exact likeness.   83 emulate pride pride of
rivalry; a proud desire to rival him [K].   87 law and heraldry heraldic law, i.e. a
decree made and ratified by the heralds of both countries; equivalent to what we
call "international law" [K]. Shakespeare wishes to emphasize the absolute legality
of the forfeiture of the lands in question (Q²: "heraldy," an old form of the
noun).   89 seiz'd possessed (a legal term).   90 a moiety competent an adequate
portion (of his own lands). "Moiety" was not confined to the sense of "half"
[K].   91 gaged pledged, staked.   had would have.   92 inheritance possession.   93 comart mutual bargain (Q²; F¹: "Cou'nant" has been preferred by
some editors).   94 carriage . . . design'd the purport of the agreement drawn up
[K].   carriage what it carries, its tenour.   96 unimproved unused, untested.

      Shark'd up a list of lawless resolutes,
      For food and diet, to some enterprise
      That hath a stomach in't; which is no other,   100
      As it doth well appear unto our state,
      But to recover of us, by strong hand
      And terms compulsatory, those foresaid lands
      So by his father lost; and this, I take it,
      Is the main motive of our preparations,   105
      The source of this our watch, and the chief head
      Of this post-haste and romage in the land.

BER.   I think it be no other but e'en so.
      Well may it sort that this portentous figure
      Comes armed through our watch, so like the King   110
      That was and is the question of these wars.

HOR.   A mote it is to trouble the mind's eye.
      In the most high and palmy state of Rome,
      A little ere the mightiest Julius fell,
      The graves stood tenantless, and the sheeted dead   115
      Did squeak and gibber in the Roman streets;
      As stars with trains of fire, and dews of blood,
      Disasters in the sun; and the moist star
      Upon whose influence Neptune's empire stands
      Was sick almost to doomsday with eclipse.   120
      And even the like precurse of fear'd events,

---

98 *Shark'd up* swept up quickly and without discrimination. *lawless* Q²; F¹: "Land-lesse." *resolutes* bravoes, desperadoes. 100 *stomach* opportunity to show valour. 105 *motive* moving cause. 106 *head* source. 107 *romage* intense general activity [K]. 108-25 *I think . . . countrymen* Q²; not in F¹. 109 *Well may it sort* it may well be in accord with this state of things [K]. 112 *mote* a speck of dust. 113 *palmy* flourishing, triumphant [K]. 115 *sheeted* in shrouds. 116 *squeak* Alluding to the horribly thin and strident voice ascribed to spectres [K]. 117 *As stars . . . blood* A line seems to have been omitted previous to this one. Its substance would be that prodigies appeared in the skies. That unnatural phenomena preceded the death of Cæsar was reported by Plutarch. 118 *Disasters* threatening signs. "Disasters" in its astrological sense includes any threatening phenomena in the heavenly bodies [K]. *moist star* the moon. 119 *Upon . . . stands* by whose influence the sea is controlled (in its tides) [K]. 120 *to doomsday* That eclipses would herald the ending of the world was widely believed. Several eclipses occurred in England between 1598 and 1603. 121 *precurse* advance indication. *fear'd* ALEXANDER; Q²: "feare"; K: "fierce." 125 *climatures* regions (Q²; DYCE, K:

As harbingers preceding still the fates
And prologue to the omen coming on,
Have heaven and earth together demonstrated
Unto our climatures and countrymen.   125

Enter Ghost *again.*

But soft! behold! Lo, where it comes again!
I'll cross it, though it blast me. — Stay, illusion!

[Ghost] *spreads his arms.*

If thou hast any sound, or use of voice,
Speak to me.
If there be any good thing to be done,   130
. That may to thee do ease, and grace to me,
Speak to me.
If thou art privy to thy country's fate,
Which happily foreknowing may avoid,
O, speak!   135
Or if thou hast uphoarded in thy life
Extorted treasure in the womb of earth
(For which, they say, you spirits oft walk in death),

The cock crows.

Speak of it! Stay, and speak! — Stop it, Marcellus!

"climature").   127 *I'll cross . . . blast me* Horatio crosses the Ghost's path so as to
pass directly before its face, calling upon it to stay. The apparition then stands still
and he adjures it to speak. The Ghost is about to obey when the cock crows. Horatio's
courage comes out strongly here, for to cross a spirit, or to let it cross you, was
even more dangerous than to speak to it [K].   128–39 *If thou hast . . . Speak of it*
Horatio shows a scholar's knowledge in his enumeration of the causes that send
ghosts back to earth. He mentions (1) some good action which remains undone;
(2) some disclosure for the benefit or protection of surviving friends; (3) the revelation of buried treasure. Abundant illustration of all three points occurs in European folklore [K].   131 *do ease* relieve thy conscience and let thee rest in peace
[K]. *grace to me* be set to my credit as a virtuous action. Only on this condition
does Horatio promise to carry out the apparition's wishes, for he cannot be sure
that it is not a malignant ghost or even a demon [K].   134 *happily* haply, perhaps.   139 *Stay* The Ghost starts as if to go. Then the cock crows, and it stalks
away. Horatio forgets his learning in his excitement and calls upon Marcellus,
whom the spirit must pass in its course, to "stop it," though that is impossible [K].

MAR.   Shall I strike at it with my partisan?   140

HOR.   Do, if it will not stand.

BER.   'Tis here!

HOR.   'Tis here!

MAR.   'Tis gone!   *Exit* Ghost.
        We do it wrong, being so majestical,
        To offer it the show of violence;
        For it is as the air, invulnerable,   145
        And our vain blows malicious mockery.

BER.   It was about to speak, when the cock crew.

HOR.   And then it started, like a guilty thing
        Upon a fearful summons. I have heard
        The cock, that is the trumpet to the morn,
        Doth with his lofty and shrill-sounding throat   150
        Awake the god of day; and at his warning,
        Whether in sea or fire, in earth or air,
        Th' extravagant and erring spirit hies
        To his confine; and of the truth herein   155
        This present object made probation.

MAR.   It faded on the crowing of the cock.
        Some say that ever, 'gainst that season comes
        Wherein our Saviour's birth is celebrated,
        This bird of dawning singeth all night long;   160
        And then, they say, no spirit dare stir abroad,
        The nights are wholesome, then no planets strike,
        No fairy takes, nor witch hath power to charm,
        So hallow'd and so gracious is that time.

HOR.   So have I heard and do in part believe it.   165

---

140 *partisan* halberd, pike.   146 *malicious mockery* a hollow mockery of doing harm; mere imitation of injury [K].   151 *lofty* high-pitched.   152 *at his warning* when the cock's crow warns them of sunrise. Ghosts, trolls, devils, and the like, according to a very old belief, cannot endure the sunlight [K].   154 *extravagant* out of bounds.   *erring* wandering.   156 *object* sight.   158 *'gainst* just before. 160 *This bird* Q²; Q¹, F¹, K: "The bird."   162 *wholesome* free not only from witchcraft and demonic influences, but from contagion, which was commonly ascribed to the night air [K].   *strike* Regularly used for the sudden malignant action ascribed to an evil planet [K].   163 *takes* bewitches, enchants.   164 *gracious* blessed. *that time* Q¹, Q²; F¹, K: "the time."   165 *in part* Horatio speaks with his

But look, the morn, in russet mantle clad,
Walks o'er the dew of yon high eastward hill.
Break we our watch up; and by my advice
Let us impart what we have seen to-night
Unto young Hamlet; for, upon my life,   170
This spirit, dumb to us, will speak to him.
Do you consent we shall acquaint him with it,
As needful in our loves, fitting our duty?

MAR.   Let's do 't, I pray; and I this morning know
Where we shall find him most convenient.   *Exeunt.* 175

◇◇◇◇◇◇◇◇◇◇◇◇◇◇◇

SCENE II.
[*Elsinore. A room of state in the Castle.*]

Flourish. Enter Claudius, King of Denmark, Gertrude
the Queen, Hamlet, Polonius, Laertes *and his sister*
Ophelia, [Voltemand, Cornelius,] Lords Attendant.

KING.   Though yet of Hamlet our dear brother's death
The memory be green, and that it us befitted
To bear our hearts in grief, and our whole kingdom
To be contracted in one brow of woe,
Yet so far hath discretion fought with nature   5
That we with wisest sorrow think on him
Together with remembrance of ourselves.
Therefore our sometimes sister, now our queen,
Th' imperial jointress to this warlike state,
Have we, as 'twere with a defeated joy,   10

---

habitual caution [K].   166 *in russet mantle clad* The dawn is cloudy or misty.
"Russet" was a kind of coarse homespun, either brown or grey in colour [K].
175 *convenient* Q²; Q¹, F¹, K: "conueniently."
    I.II. 2 *befitted* would befit.   5 *discretion* wise moderation (which teaches us to
restrain our natural grief) [K].   7 *ourselves* myself and all of you. A suggestion
that the marriage was not merely a personal affair, but an advantage to the
whole state. If Claudius had meant "myself" only, he would have said "ourself" [K].
8 *sometime* former.   9 *jointress* a widow who has "jointure," an estate which falls
to her on the death of her husband [K].   The implication is that Gertrude has
inherited the crown through the death of her first husband and Claudius attained
it by marriage to her.   10 *defeated* destroyed, nullified.

With an auspicious, and a dropping eye,
With mirth in funeral, and with dirge in marriage,
In equal scale weighing delight and dole,
Taken to wife; nor have we herein barr'd
Your better wisdoms, which have freely gone   15
With this affair along. For all, our thanks.
Now follows, that you know, young Fortinbras,
Holding a weak supposal of our worth,
Or thinking by our late dear brother's death
Our state to be disjoint and out of frame,   20
Colleagued with this dream of his advantage,
He hath not fail'd to pester us with message
Importing the surrender of those lands
Lost by his father, with all bands of law,
To our most valiant brother. So much for him.   25
Now for ourself and for this time of meeting.
Thus much the business is: we have here writ
To Norway, uncle of young Fortinbras,
Who, impotent and bedrid, scarcely hears
Of this his nephew's purpose, to suppress   30
His further gait herein, in that the levies,
The lists, and full proportions are all made
Out of his subject; and we here dispatch
You, good Cornelius, and you, Voltemand,
For bearers of this greeting to old Norway,   35
Giving to you no further personal power

---

11 *auspicious* of happy aspect or expression [ĸ].   14 *barr'd* shut out; left uncon-
sulted.   15 *Your better wisdoms* Not "your judgment, which is better than mine,"
but "your wise counsel as to what it was better for me to do," "your wise pref-
erence" [ĸ].   15–16 *freely . . . along* heartily agreed with me throughout this
affair [ĸ].   17 *that you know* what you already know. The Councillors are ac-
quainted with the demands of young Fortinbras, but not with the King's pur-
posed reply (lines 26–33) [ĸ].   18 *our worth* my ability to govern.   20 *disjoint . . .
frame* Synonymous: "disjointed," "broken in its structure." Such fullness of phrase
is still characteristic of the official style [ĸ].   21 *Colleagued . . . advantage* with
no ally except his false notion that this is a favourable moment for him.
"Dream" is emphatic [ĸ].   24 *bands* bonds; binding covenants and decisions
[ĸ].   28 *Norway* the King of Norway.   29 *impotent* feeble.   31 *gait* procedure.   31-2 *levies . . . proportions* Three synonyms [ĸ].   33 *subject* subjects.
37 *business* negotiate.   38 *dilated* expressed in full.   39 *and let . . . duty* and

> To business with the King, more than the scope
> Of these dilated articles allow.   [*Gives a paper.*]
> Farewell, and let your haste commend your duty.

COR., VOLT.   In that, and all things, will we show our duty.   40

KING.   We doubt it nothing. Heartily farewell.

> *Exeunt* Voltemand *and* Cornelius.

> And now, Laertes, what's the news with you?
> You told us of some suit. What is't, Laertes?
> You cannot speak of reason to the Dane
> And lose your voice. What wouldst thou beg, Laertes,   45
> That shall not be my offer, not thy asking?
> The head is not more native to the heart,
> The hand more instrumental to the mouth,
> Than is the throne of Denmark to thy father.
> What wouldst thou have, Laertes?

LAER.   My dread lord,   50
> Your leave and favour to return to France;
> From whence though willingly I came to Denmark
> To show my duty in your coronation,
> Yet now I must confess, that duty done,
> My thoughts and wishes bend again toward France   55
> And bow them to your gracious leave and pardon.

KING.   Have you your father's leave? What says Polonius?

---

let your promptness express, in action, the usual formula of farewell. This would
be "We commend our duty to your Highness" [K].   41 *nothing* not at all.
42 *And now, Laertes* Ceremony over, and the state business dispatched, Claudius
falls gracefully into a familiar strain, which becomes still more intimate as he
proceeds. At line 45 he abandons the royal "we" and the formal "you" for the
personal and affectionate "I" ("my") and "thou." He is affable as well as kingly,
and Shakespeare clearly meant to depict him as endowed with distinct charm in
speech and bearing [K].   46 *my offer, not thy asking* something granted before
it is asked [K].   47 *native to* naturally associated with; bound by ties of nature
to [K].   48 *instrumental* serviceable.   49 *thy father* Polonius is a noble of the
highest rank. Claudius is obviously indebted to him for assistance in procuring
his election as King. Both Claudius and the Queen are genuinely fond of the
old Councillor, slightly bored though they may sometimes be by his occasional
prosing. Cf. IV. I.12 [K].   56 *pardon* permission to depart.

POL.	He hath, my lord, wrung from me my slow leave
	By laboursome petition, and at last
	Upon his will I seal'd my hard consent. 60
	I do beseech you give him leave to go.
KING.	Take thy fair hour, Laertes. Time be thine,
	And thy best graces spend it at thy will!
	But now, my cousin Hamlet, and my son —
HAM.	[*aside*] A little more than kin, and less than kind! 65
KING.	How is it that the clouds still hang on you?
HAM.	Not so, my lord. I am too much i' th' sun.
QUEEN.	Good Hamlet, cast thy nighted colour off,
	And let thine eye look like a friend on Denmark.
	Do not for ever with thy vailed lids 70
	Seek for thy noble father in the dust.
	Thou know'st 'tis common. All that lives must die,
	Passing through nature to eternity.
HAM.	Ay, madam, it is common.
QUEEN.	If it be,
	Why seems it so particular with thee? 75
HAM.	Seems, madam? Nay, it is. I know not "seems."
	'Tis not alone my inky cloak, good mother,
	Nor customary suits of solemn black,
	Nor windy suspiration of forc'd breath,
	No, nor the fruitful river in the eye, 80

58–60 *wrung . . . consent* Q²; not in F¹.   62 *Take thy fair hour* A graceful adaptation of the familiar "Carpe diem": "Thy life is now at its most delightful season. Be it thine to enjoy" [K].   63 *graces* good qualities (of every kind). The verses combine permission for Laertes to enjoy his youth while it lasts ("Time be thine") with the wish that such enjoyment may be guided by the best qualities of his nature [K].   64 *cousin* kinsman, outside of the immediate family.   65 *more than kin* Being a son, he is more than a mere kinsman (cousin). *less than kind* Being a kinsman, he is less than a son (kind) — with a pun on "kind" in the sense of "kindly in my feelings." Hamlet's speech is intentionally riddling.   67 *too much i' th' sun* (a) too much your son, as you have just named me (b) too fully disinherited — out in the sun, rather than in the house where I belong; the expression was proverbial (F¹; Q²: "in the sonne," which makes clear the quibble).   69 *Denmark* Claudius.   70 *vailed* downcast.   72 *common* universal.   73 *nature* natural life.   74 *it is common* Hamlet puns on the sense of "common" as usually applied to a whore: "open to all."   75 *particular* personal, as if it were an individual ex-

Nor the dejected haviour of the visage,
Together with all forms, moods, shapes of grief,
That can denote me truly. These indeed seem,
For they are actions that a man might play;
But I have that within which passes show —   85
These but the trappings and the suits of woe.

KING.   'Tis sweet and commendable in your nature, Hamlet,
To give these mourning duties to your father;
But you must know, your father lost a father;
That father lost, lost his, and the survivor bound   90
In filial obligation for some term
To do obsequious sorrow. But to persever
In obstinate condolement is a course
Of impious stubbornness. 'Tis unmanly grief;
It shows a will most incorrect to heaven,   95
A heart unfortified, a mind impatient,
An understanding simple and unschool'd;
For what we know must be, and is as common
As any the most vulgar thing to sense,
Why should we in our peevish opposition   100
Take it to heart? Fie! 'tis a fault to heaven,
A fault against the dead, a fault to nature,
To reason most absurd, whose common theme
Is death of fathers, and who still hath cried,
From the first corse till he that died to-day,   105
"This must be so." We pray you throw to earth

---

perience [K].   79 *windy . . . breath* A scornfully elaborate phrase for "heavy
sighs" [K].   80 *fruitful* teeming, abundant.   81 *haviour* appearance.   82 *moods*
moody appearances.   83 *denote* F¹; Q²: "deuote."   85 *passes* surpasses (Q²; F¹, K:
"passeth").   *show* mere outward signs.   92 *obsequious sorrow* sorrow befitting obsequies (funeral rites) [K].   93 *obstinate condolement* mourning that refuses to be
comforted.   95 *incorrect to heaven* uncorrected — not brought into submission to
God's will [K].   99 *As any . . . sense* as anything that is the commonest object
of sight or hearing [K].   100 *peevish* childish, foolish.   101–2 *a fault . . . nature*
a triple fault, involving (1) rebellion against God's will; (2) unfilial feelings — as
if one blamed one's father for dying; (3) revolt against the established order of
nature — for death is as natural as life [K].   103 *common theme* for the natural
order of things proclaims that death must be the universal lot of mankind [K].
104 *still* always.   106 *We* The royal "we" appropriately introduces the sentence
relating to succession to the throne [K].

This unprevailing woe, and think of us
As of a father; for let the world take note
You are the most immediate to our throne,
And with no less nobility of love   110
Than that which dearest father bears his son
Do I impart toward you. For your intent
In going back to school in Wittenberg,
It is most retrograde to our desire;
And we beseech you, bend you to remain   115
Here in the cheer and comfort of our eye,
Our chiefest courtier, cousin, and our son.

QUEEN.   Let not thy mother lose her prayers, Hamlet.
I pray thee stay with us, go not to Wittenberg.

HAM.   I shall in all my best obey you, madam.   120

KING.   Why, 'tis a loving and a fair reply.
Be as ourself in Denmark. Madam, come.
This gentle and unforc'd accord of Hamlet
Sits smiling to my heart; in grace whereof,
No jocund health that Denmark drinks to-day   125
But the great cannon to the clouds shall tell,
And the King's rouse the heaven shall bruit again,
Respeaking earthly thunder. Come away.

Flourish. Exeunt all but Hamlet.

HAM.   O that this too too solid flesh would melt,

---

107 *unprevailing* unavailing.   109 *most immediate* next in line. Thus Claudius
names Hamlet heir to the throne. See Supplementary Notes.   110 *nobility of love*
distinguished affection [K].   112 *impart* express myself [K].   113 *school* your
university studies. The University of Wittenberg (founded in 1502, united with
that of Halle in 1817) was at the height of its reputation in Shakespeare's day
and was much esteemed in England because of its connection with Luther and
the Reformation [K].   114 *retrograde* contrary.   115 *bend you* bow your will;
submit your inclination [K].   116 *our eye* my royal presence; at court [K].   122
Be as ourself regard yourself as King to all intents and purposes [K].   124 *Sits
. . . heart* gives me heartfelt satisfaction [K].   127 *rouse* drink.   *bruit* echo.
129 *solid* F¹; Q¹, Q²: "sallied"; WILSON: "sullied," of which "sallied" is a common variant spelling. This has been a much debated reading. Critics who favour
"sullied" or "sallied" argue that it is to the impurity of his flesh rather than

Thaw, and resolve itself into a dew!   130
Or that the Everlasting had not fix'd
His canon 'gainst self-slaughter! O God! God!
How weary, stale, flat, and unprofitable
Seem to me all the uses of this world!
Fie on't! ah, fie! 'Tis an unweeded garden   135
That grows to seed; things rank and gross in nature
Possess it merely. That it should come to this!
But two months dead! Nay, not so much, not two.
So excellent a king, that was to this
Hyperion to a satyr; so loving to my mother   140
That he might not beteem the winds of heaven
Visit her face too roughly. Heaven and earth!
Must I remember? Why, she would hang on him
As if increase of appetite had grown
By what it fed on; and yet, within a month —   145
Let me not think on't! Frailty, thy name is woman! —
A little month, or ere those shoes were old
With which she followed my poor father's body
Like Niobe, all tears — why she, even she
(O God! a beast that wants discourse of reason   150
Would have mourn'd longer) married with my uncle;
My father's brother, but no more like my father
Than I to Hercules. Within a month,
Ere yet the salt of most unrighteous tears
Had left the flushing in her galled eyes,   155
She married. O, most wicked speed, to post

---

its solidity that Hamlet is referring.   132 *canon* divine law.   137 *merely* entirely.
to this F¹; Q²: "thus."   140 *Hyperion* the sun god, the most beautiful of the
divinities. The manly beauty of the elder Hamlet is several times emphasized [K].
satyr the half-man, half-goat of Greek mythology, symbolic of sexual promiscuity.
141 *beteem* allow.   149 *Niobe* a mother who boasted that her children were more
beautiful than Apollo and Diana. When her children were slain by these deities,
Zeus turned her to stone which wept tears forever.   150 *discourse of reason* the
process or faculty of reasoning [K].   153 *Than I to Hercules* A suggestion as to
Hamlet's personal appearance. He is strong and active — a good fencer — but not
stalwart [K]. But certainly no mortal could seriously compare himself to Hercules.
154 *unrighteous* because they were insincere [K].   155 *left the flushing* allowed
the redness to disappear [K]. *galled* irritated, inflamed.

With such dexterity to incestuous sheets!
It is not, nor it cannot come to good.
But break my heart, for I must hold my tongue!

                        Enter Horatio, Marcellus, *and* Bernardo.

HOR.   Hail to your lordship!

HAM.   I am glad to see you well.   160
Horatio! — or I do forget myself.

HOR.   The same, my lord, and your poor servant ever.

HAM.   Sir, my good friend — I'll change that name with you.
And what make you from Wittenberg, Horatio?
Marcellus?   165

MAR.   My good lord!

HAM.   I am very glad to see you. — [*To* Bernardo] Good even,
sir. —
But what, in faith, make you from Wittenberg?

HOR.   A truant disposition, good my lord.

HAM.   I would not hear your enemy say so,   170
Nor shall you do my ear that violence
To make it truster of your own report
Against yourself. I know you are no truant.
But what is your affair in Elsinore?
We'll teach you to drink deep ere you depart.   175

HOR.   My lord, I came to see your father's funeral.

HAM.   I prithee do not mock me, fellow student.
I think it was to see my mother's wedding.

---

157 *dexterity* speed, eager haste. *incestuous* The marriage of a woman to the brother of her dead husband was regarded as incestuous by both the Anglican and the Catholic churches. King Henry VIII had been permitted to marry Catherine of Aragon, wife of his deceased brother Arthur, by a papal dispensation which Elizabethan Protestants regarded as invalid. 160 *I am glad . . . well* A courteous greeting, mechanically uttered before Hamlet sees who it is. The next line is spoken in enthusiastic recognition of his friend [K]. 163 *change* exchange. 164 *make you from* are you doing away from. 169 *A truant disposition* a feeling that I should like to run away from school. 174 *affair* real business. 175 *to drink*

HOR.   Indeed, my lord, it followed hard upon.

HAM.   Thrift, thrift, Horatio! The funeral bak'd meats   180
        Did coldly furnish forth the marriage tables.
        Would I had met my dearest foe in heaven
        Or ever I had seen that day, Horatio!
        My father — methinks I see my father.

HOR.   Where, my lord?

HAM.   In my mind's eye, Horatio.   185

HOR.   I saw him once, 'a was a goodly king.

HAM.   'A was a man, take him for all in all.
        I shall not look upon his like again.

HOR.   My lord, I think I saw him yesternight.

HAM.   Saw? who?   190

HOR.   My lord, the King your father.

HAM.   The King my father?

HOR.   Season your admiration for a while
        With an attent ear, till I may deliver,
        Upon the witness of these gentlemen,
        This marvel to you.

HAM.   For God's love let me hear!   195

HOR.   Two nights together had these gentlemen
        (Marcellus and Bernardo) on their watch
        In the dead waste and middle of the night
        Been thus encount'red. A figure like your father,
        Armed at point exactly, cap-a-pe,   200
        Appears before them and with solemn march
        Goes slow and stately by them. Thrice he walk'd

---

deep Q¹, F¹; Q²: "for to drinke."   180 *Thrift* mere economy. A bitter jest. The
only reason for such haste was, he says, to save the remnants of the funeral
feast [K].   181 *coldly* when cold.   182 *dearest* most bitter.   183 *Or ever* before
ever.   185 *Where* Q²; F¹, K: "O, where."   186 *'a* Q²; F¹: "he"; K: "He." *goodly*
handsome.   187 *'A* Q²; F¹, K: "He."   192 *Season your admiration* moderate or
control your astonishment [K].   193 *deliver* report, relate.   198 *waste* Q², F¹; Q¹,
K: "vast." The two words are actually variant forms.   200 *at point* completely.
cap-a-pe from head to foot.

By their oppress'd and fear-surprised eyes,
Within his truncheon's length; whilst they distill'd
Almost to jelly with the act of fear,   205
Stand dumb and speak not to him. This to me
In dreadful secrecy impart they did,
And I with them the third night kept the watch;
Where, as they had deliver'd, both in time,
Form of the thing, each word made true and good,   210
The apparition comes. I knew your father.
These hands are not more like.

HAM.   But where was this?

MAR.   My lord, upon the platform where we watch.

HAM.   Did you not speak to it?

HOR.   My lord, I did;
But answer made it none. Yet once methought   215
It lifted up it head and did address
Itself to motion, like as it would speak;
But even then the morning cock crew loud,
And at the sound it shrunk in haste away
And vanish'd from our sight.

HAM.   'Tis very strange.   220

HOR.   As I do live, my honour'd lord, 'tis true;
And we did think it writ down in our duty
To let you know of it.

HAM.   Indeed, indeed, sirs. But this troubles me.
Hold you the watch to-night?

BOTH. [MAR. AND BER.]   We do, my lord.   225

HAM.   Arm'd, say you?

---

203 *oppress'd* overwhelmed by the horror of the sight [K]. *fear-surprised* seized
upon by fear [K].   204 *truncheon's length* The truncheon was a short staff or
baton, carried as a sign of military command [K]. *distill'd* dissolved, disinte-
grated.   205 *with the act of fear* by the action of fear.   207 *In dreadful secrecy* as
a dread secret; under a solemn pledge of silence [K].   209 *deliver'd* reported.
213 *watch* Q²; F¹, K: "watcht."   216 *it head* its head (an old form of the genitive).
216–17 *did address . . . speak* began to make such movements as indicated that
it meant to speak [K]. *address* apply.   224 *Indeed, indeed* Q¹, F¹; Q²: "Indeede."

BOTH.	Arm'd, my lord.
HAM.	From top to toe?
BOTH.	My lord, from head to foot.
HAM.	Then saw you not his face?
HOR.	O, yes, my lord! He wore his beaver up. 230
HAM.	What, look'd he frowningly?
HOR.	A countenance more in sorrow than in anger.
HAM.	Pale or red?
HOR.	Nay, very pale.
HAM.	And fix'd his eyes upon you?
HOR.	Most constantly.
HAM.	I would I had been there. 235
HOR.	It would have much amaz'd you.
HAM.	Very like, very like. Stay'd it long?
HOR.	While one with moderate haste might tell a hundred.
BOTH.	Longer, longer.
HOR.	Not when I saw't.
HAM.	His beard was grizzled — no? 240
HOR.	It was, as I have seen it in his life, A sable silver'd.
HAM.	I will watch to-night. Perchance 'twill walk again.
HOR.	I warr'nt it will.

---

230 *beaver* visor, movable face-guard of his helmet.   232 *countenance* expression
(of the face).   235 *constantly* unswervingly.   236 *amaz'd you* confused your
thoughts. Horatio does not mean merely that Hamlet would have been astonished,
but that he would have been unable to think at all — would not have known what
to think of the nature and purpose of the apparition [K].   237 *Very like, very like*
F¹; Q²: "Very like." Hamlet's repetitive habit of speech has been noted.   238 *tell*
count.   240 *grizzled* grey. "A sable silver'd" means exactly the same thing: "black
with white hairs intermixed" [K].

HAM.   If it assume my noble father's person,
I'll speak to it, though hell itself should gape   245
And bid me hold my peace. I pray you all,
If you have hitherto conceal'd this sight,
Let it be tenable in your silence still;
And whatsoever else shall hap to-night,
Give it an understanding but no tongue.   250
I will requite your loves. So, fare you well.
Upon the platform, 'twixt eleven and twelve,
I'll visit you.

ALL.   Our duty to your honour.

HAM.   Your loves, as mine to you. Farewell.

Exeunt [*all but* Hamlet].

My father's spirit — in arms? All is not well.   255
I doubt some foul play. Would the night were come!
Till then sit still, my soul. Foul deeds will rise,
Though all the earth o'erwhelm them, to men's eyes.

Exit.

---

244 *assume* Hamlet does not know whether the apparition was his father's ghost or a demon that had taken the shape of his father [K].   245 *gape* open wide. 246 *hold my peace* Hamlet is thinking of the danger of speaking to a demon [K]. 248 *Let it be tenable* regard it as something that must be held [K].   256 *I doubt some foul play* I suspect that something is wrong. "Foul play" did not to the Elizabethans, as to us, suggest exclusively murder. Hamlet has no definite suspicion of the truth until the Ghost reveals it (I.v.25–6) [K].   257 *Foul* Q¹, F¹; Q²: "fonde."

    I.III. 3 *convoy* means of conveyance.   6 *fashion* a habit of young men or

◇◇◇◇◇◇◇◇◇◇◇◇◇◇◇◇

SCENE III.
[*Elsinore. A room in the house of* Polonius.]

Enter Laertes *and* Ophelia.

LAER.   My necessaries are embark'd. Farewell.
And, sister, as the winds give benefit
And convoy is assistant, do not sleep,
But let me hear from you.

OPH.   Do you doubt that?

LAER.   For Hamlet, and the trifling of his favour,   5
Hold it a fashion, and a toy in blood;
A violet in the youth of primy nature,
Forward, not permanent — sweet, not lasting;
The perfume and suppliance of a minute;
No more.

OPH.   No more but so?

LAER.   Think it no more.   10
For nature crescent does not grow alone
In thews and bulk; but as this temple waxes,
The inward service of the mind and soul
Grows wide withal. Perhaps he loves you now,
And now no soil nor cautel doth besmirch   15
The virtue of his will; but you must fear,

---

young princes [K].   *toy in blood* caprice of youthful passion [K].   7 *in . . .
nature* in the early prime (the springtime of life) [K].   8 *Forward* early.   9 *The
perfume . . . minute* something that makes a passing minute sweet and fills it
up; the pleasant pastime of a minute [K].   10 *No more but so* only that and no
more? See Supplementary Notes.   11 *nature crescent* a man's nature (or being)
as it grows [K].   12 *thews* sinews.   *this temple* the body.   *waxes* grows.   14 *Grows
wide withal* grows more extensive and elaborate along with it (the body's growth).
15 *soil* evil thought.   *cautel* deceit.   16 *will* desire.

His greatness weigh'd, his will is not his own;
For he himself is subject to his birth.
He may not, as unvalued persons do,
Carve for himself, for on his choice depends   20
The safety and health of this whole state,
And therefore must his choice be circumscrib'd
Unto the voice and yielding of that body
Whereof he is the head. Then if he says he loves you,
It fits your wisdom so far to believe it   25
As he in his particular act and place
May give his saying deed; which is no further
Than the main voice of Denmark goes withal.
Then weigh what loss your honour may sustain
If with too credent ear you list his songs,   30
Or lose your heart, or your chaste treasure open
To his unmast'red importunity.
Fear it, Ophelia, fear it, my dear sister,
And keep you in the rear of your affection,
Out of the shot and danger of desire.   35
The chariest maid is prodigal enough
If she unmask her beauty to the moon.
Virtue itself scapes not calumnious strokes.
The canker galls the infants of the spring
Too oft before their buttons be disclos'd,   40
And in the morn and liquid dew of youth

---

17 *His greatness weigh'd* when his high rank is taken into consideration.   18 *For
. . . birth* F¹; not in Q². 20 *Carve for himself* indulge his own fancy; choose for
himself. The figure (which had become a mere idiom) alludes to the carver's opportunity to select some special tidbit [K]. 21 *health* welfare. 23 *voice and
yielding* authority and assent. 26 *in . . . place* acting as he must in his special
circumstances and under the restrictions of his rank [K]. 28 *main* mighty,
powerful; not "chief" [K]. *goes withal* agrees with. 30 *credent* credulous. *list*
listen to. 34 *affection* feelings. Do not let yourself go so far forward as your
natural feelings, if unrestrained, might lead you. The military metaphor is
carried out in the next line. Laertes, like his father, is fond of elaborate figures
of speech and rather plumes himself upon his elegant language [K]. 36 *chariest*
most sparing; most cautious and circumspect [K]. 39 *canker* rose caterpillar.
Laertes is reciting a series of "sentences" or "proverbs." 40 *buttons* buds. 42
blastments blights. 44 *Youth . . . near* youth, in its natural ardor, often rebels
against itself (acts contrary to its better nature), even if no tempter is at hand.
The impulses and passions that rise against reason and self-control are often

Contagious blastments are most imminent.
Be wary then; best safety lies in fear.
Youth to itself rebels, though none else near.

OPH.   I shall th' effect of this good lesson keep   45
As watchman to my heart. But, good my brother,
Do not as some ungracious pastors do,
Show me the steep and thorny way to heaven,
Whiles, like a puff'd and reckless libertine,
Himself the primrose path of dalliance treads   50
And recks not his own rede.

LAER.   O, fear me not!

Enter Polonius.

I stay too long. But here my father comes.
A double blessing is a double grace;
Occasion smiles upon a second leave.

POL.   Yet here, Laertes? Aboard, aboard, for shame!   55
The wind sits in the shoulder of your sail,
And you are stay'd for. There — my blessing with thee!
And these few precepts in thy memory
Look thou character. Give thy thoughts no tongue,
Nor any unproportion'd thought his act.   60
Be thou familiar, but by no means vulgar:

---

described as rebels or insurgents [K]. To "rebel" often means "to lust."   45–51
I shall . . . rede Ophelia is quietly amused at the wise airs of her brother, who
resembles her father in his fondness for holding forth. She receives the sermon
demurely; and then, when he is least expecting a retort, she bids him take a leaf
out of his own book. The effect is diverting; Laertes suddenly remembers that
he is in a hurry [K].   45 *effect* purport, substance.   50 *dalliance* pleasure, self-
indulgence.   51 *recks not his own rede* heeds not his own counsel [K]. *fear me
not* don't worry about me.   54 *Occasion smiles . . . leave* opportunity treats me
kindly in granting me this second good-bye [K].   58 *these few precepts* Polonius's
advice is sound and sensible — not more "worldly wise" than the occasion war-
rants; and it concludes with a precept which raises the whole speech to a high
ethical standard [K]. Though trite-sounding today, the speech is not to be taken
as comic. It has often been compared to the advice of Euphues to Philautus in
John Lyly's novel, EUPHUES.   59 *character* engrave, inscribe.   60 *unproportion'd*
out of harmony with reason and good conduct [K].   61 *vulgar* indiscriminate in
friendship [K].

Those friends thou hast, and their adoption tried,
Grapple them unto thy soul with hoops of steel;
But do not dull thy palm with entertainment
Of each new-hatch'd, unfledg'd courage. Beware   65
Of entrance to a quarrel; but being in,
Bear't that th' opposed may beware of thee.
Give every man thine ear, but few thy voice;
Take each man's censure, but reserve thy judgment.
Costly thy habit as thy purse can buy,   70
But not express'd in fancy; rich, not gaudy;
For the apparel oft proclaims the man,
And they in France of the best rank and station
Are most select and generous, chief in that.
Neither a borrower nor a lender be;   75
For loan oft loses both itself and friend,
And borrowing dulls the edge of husbandry.
This above all — to thine own self be true,
And it must follow, as the night the day,
Thou canst not then be false to any man.   80
Farewell. My blessing season this in thee!

LAER.   Most humbly do I take my leave, my lord.

POL.   The time invites you. Go, your servants tend.

LAER.   Farewell, Ophelia, and remember well
What I have said to you.

OPH.   'Tis in my memory lock'd,   85
And you yourself shall keep the key of it.

LAER.   Farewell.   *Exit.*

---

64 *dull thy palm* make your hand callous (with handshaking, so that it can no longer feel the difference between true friends and false ones). *entertainment* welcoming.   65 *courage* man of spirit, young blood (Q²; F¹, K: "Comrade"). 67 *Bear't* conduct the affair. *opposed* opponent.   68 *voice* approval.   69 *censure* judgment, opinion.   71 *express'd in fancy* showing its costliness by anything fantastic about it. The next phrase repeats the idea [K].   74 *Are most . . . in that* show their fine taste and their gentlemanly instincts more in that than in any other point of manners [K].   76 *loan* F¹: "lone"; Q²: "loue."   77 *borrowing . . . husbandry* a habit of borrowing makes one less keen about economy [K].   78–80 *This above all . . . man* Thus Polonius rises from his salutary precepts of worldly

POL.   What is't, Ophelia, he hath said to you?

OPH.   So please you, something touching the Lord Hamlet.

POL.   Marry, well bethought!   90
       'Tis told me he hath very oft of late
       Given private time to you, and you yourself
       Have of your audience been most free and bounteous.
       If it be so — as so 'tis put on me,
       And that in way of caution — I must tell you   95
       You do not understand yourself so clearly
       As it behooves my daughter and your honour.
       What is between you? Give me up the truth.

OPH.   He hath, my lord, of late made many tenders
       Of his affection to me.   100

POL.   Affection? Pooh! You speak like a green girl,
       Unsifted in such perilous circumstance.
       Do you believe his tenders, as you call them?

OPH.   I do not know, my lord, what I should think.

POL.   Marry, I will teach you! Think yourself a baby   105
       That you have ta'en these tenders for true pay,
       Which are not sterling. Tender yourself more dearly,
       Or (not to crack the wind of the poor phrase,
       Running it thus) you'll tender me a fool.

OPH.   My lord, he hath importun'd me with love   110
       In honourable fashion.

POL.   Ay, fashion you may call it. Go to, go to!

---

wisdom to one great general truth which includes and ennobles them all [K].
81 *season this* ripen this advice; bring it to fruition in good conduct [K].   83 *tend*
are waiting.   94 *put on me* brought to my attention.   99 *tenders* offers.   102
Unsifted untried, inexperienced.   106 *tenders* (a) offers (b) coins — legal tender.
107 *not sterling* (a) insincere (b) counterfeit. *Tender yourself* hold or regard yourself.   109 *Running* COLLIER; Q²: "Wrong"; F¹: "Roaming." *tender me a fool* (a)
give me a fool for a daughter, by making a fool of yourself (b) show me to the
world as a fool (c) present me with a baby, born to you out of wedlock. "Fool"
was a common term of endearment, virtually synonymous with "child."   112
fashion in precisely the same sense in which Laertes uses the word in line 6 [K].

OPH.   And hath given countenance to his speech, my lord,
        With almost all the holy vows of heaven.

POL.   Ay, springes to catch woodcocks! I do know,   115
        When the blood burns, how prodigal the soul
        Lends the tongue vows. These blazes, daughter,
        Giving more light than heat, extinct in both
        Even in their promise, as it is a-making,
        You must not take for fire. From this time   120
        Be something scanter of your maiden presence.
        Set your entreatments at a higher rate
        Than a command to parley. For Lord Hamlet,
        Believe so much in him, that he is young,
        And with a larger tether may he walk   125
        Than may be given you. In few, Ophelia,
        Do not believe his vows; for they are brokers,
        Not of that dye which their investments show,
        But mere implorators of unholy suits,
        Breathing like sanctified and pious bawds,   130
        The better to beguile. This is for all:
        I would not, in plain terms, from this time forth
        Have you so slander any moment leisure
        As to give words or talk with the Lord Hamlet.
        Look to't, I charge you. Come your ways.   135

OPH.   I shall obey, my lord.   *Exeunt.*

---

113 *countenance* authority, confirmation.   115 *springes* snares. The woodcock
(though in fact an intelligent bird) served as a proverbial synonym for credulous
foolishness. It was even supposed to have actually no brains [K] (Q⁴; Q², F¹:
"springs").   116 *prodigal* superabundantly.   117–19 *These blazes . . . is a-
making* such flashes of youthful fancy, which have more show than substance,
and whose appearance and reality both die out suddenly, even while the promise
is being uttered. Polonius is embroidering the proverb: "Hot love soon cold"
[K].   122 *entreatments* negotiations before surrender. Polonius is using the con-
ventional metaphor in which the lady is compared to a castle beseiged by her
lover.   123 *command to parley* request by the castle's beseiger for a conference.
126 *In few* in brief.   127 *brokers* panders, procurers.   128 *Not . . . show*
Ophelia has described Hamlet's vows as "holy." Polonius retorts that their holi-

◇◇◇◇◇◇◇◇◇◇◇◇◇◇◇◇

[SCENE IV.
Elsinore. The platform before the Castle.]

Enter Hamlet, Horatio, *and* Marcellus.

HAM.   The air bites shrewdly; it is very cold.

HOR.   It is a nipping and an eager air.

HAM.   What hour now?

HOR.   I think it lacks of twelve.

MAR.   No, it is struck.

HOR.   Indeed? I heard it not. It then draws near the season   5
        Wherein the spirit held his wont to walk.

                    *A flourish of trumpets, and two pieces
                    go off.*

        What does this mean, my lord?

HAM.   The King doth wake to-night and takes his rouse,
        Keeps wassail, and the swagg'ring upspring reels,
        And, as he drains his draughts of Rhenish down,   10
        The kettledrum and trumpet thus bray out
        The triumph of his pledge.

HOR.   Is it a custom?

---

ness is mere disguise; they wear the garb of innocence, but that, he says, is not
their true colour [K]. *investments* attire.   129 *mere* out-and-out.   130 *Breathing . . . bawds* speaking in soft and persuasive accents, like hypocritical tempters
[K]. *bawds* THEOBALD; Q², F¹: "bonds."   133 *slander* disgrace. *moment* momen-
tary.
    I.IV. 1 *shrewdly* wickedly (literally, "cursedly").   2 *eager* sharp.   6 *the spirit*
Hamlet does not commit himself on the question whether or not the apparition
is his father's ghost. Cf. I.II.199, 211, 244 [K].   8 *doth wake . . . rouse* sits up
late and drinks deep [K].   9 *upspring* Either (a) a vigorous dance of German
origin, or (b) upstart — the King.   12 *triumph of his pledge* splendid feat of
health-drinking in which he drains the cup at a draught [K].

HAM.   Ay, marry, is't;
        But to my mind, though I am native here
        And to the manner born, it is a custom   15
        More honour'd in the breach than the observance.
        This heavy-headed revel east and west
        Makes us traduc'd and tax'd of other nations;
        They clip us drunkards and with swinish phrase
        Soil our addition; and indeed it takes   20
        From our achievements, though perform'd at height,
        The pith and marrow of our attribute.
        So oft it chances in particular men
        That, for some vicious mole of nature in them,
        As in their birth, — wherein they are not guilty,   25
        Since nature cannot choose his origin, —
        By the o'ergrowth of some complexion,
        Oft breaking down the pales and forts of reason,
        Or by some habit that too much o'erleavens
        The form of plausive manners, that these men   30
        Carrying, I say, the stamp of one defect,
        Being nature's livery, or fortune's star,
        His virtues else — be they as pure as grace,
        As infinite as man may undergo —
        Shall in the general censure take corruption   35
        From that particular fault. The dram of e'il
        Doth all the noble substance often dout

16 *More honour'd . . . observance* more honourable to break than to observe.
17–38 *This heavy-headed . . . scandal* Q²; not in F¹, probably because disparagement
of the Danes might have been politically dangerous after 1603, since Anne of
Denmark (wife of James I) was Queen of England.   19 *clip* clepe, call. *swinish
phrase* calling us pigs.   20 *Soil our addition* sully our reputation.   21 *at
height* at the full height (the acme) of possible achievement [K].   22 *attribute*
honour, reputation.   23 *in particular men* in the case of individuals (precisely
as in the case of whole nations, which so far Hamlet has been considering [K].
24 *some vicious . . . in them* some natural fault which is a blemish. In what
follows three ways are mentioned in which this blemish may originate: (1) their
birth, i.e. by inheritance; (2) by the over-development of some natural tendency;
(3) by some habit accidentally or thoughtlessly contracted [K].   27 *the o'ergrowth
of some complexion* the over-development of some part of their constitution [K].
See Supplementary Notes.   28 *pales* barriers, fences.   29 *o'erleavens* pervasively
modifies (as leaven changes dough) [K].   30 *plausive* pleasing.   32 *nature's livery*
something by which the man is marked by nature. This covers both (1) any inherited peculiarity of temperament and (2) any such peculiarity as results from

To his own scandal.

Enter Ghost.

HOR.   Look, my lord, it comes!

HAM.   Angels and ministers of grace defend us!
Be thou a spirit of health or goblin damn'd,   40
Bring with thee airs from heaven or blasts from hell,
Be thy intents wicked or charitable,
Thou com'st in such a questionable shape
That I will speak to thee. I'll call thee Hamlet,
King, father, royal Dane. O, answer me!   45
Let me not burst in ignorance, but tell
Why thy canoniz'd bones, hearsed in death,
Have burst their cerements; why the sepulchre
Wherein we saw thee quietly interr'd,
Hath op'd his ponderous and marble jaws   50
To cast thee up again. What may this mean
That thou, dead corse, again in complete steel,
Revisits thus the glimpses of the moon,
Making night hideous, and we fools of nature
So horridly to shake our disposition   55
With thoughts beyond the reaches of our souls?
Say, why is this? wherefore? What should we do?

Ghost *beckons* Hamlet.

HOR.   It beckons you to go away with it,

"the o'ergrowth of some complexion" [K]. *fortune's star* something determined by mere luck. This refers to the accidental forming of "some habit" [K].   33 *His* Q²; THEOBALD, K: "Their." The transition to the singular is quite natural since Hamlet is thinking of himself. *virtues else* other qualities.   34 *may undergo* can sustain or support [K].   35 *take corruption* be infected (in the world's opinion). The world will see only this one fault and overlook their many virtues [K].   36 *dram* small amount. *e'il* evil (Q²: "eale").   37 *often dout* often banish, nullify (STEEVENS; Q²: "of a doubt").   38 *scandal* disgrace.   40 *of health* good (as opposed to a demon).   42 *charitable* benevolent.   43 *questionable* which prompts me to question.   47 *canoniz'd* buried with all sacred rites. *hearsed* entombed.   48 *cerements* the waxed cloth in which the body was wrapped [K].   49 *interr'd* Q²; F¹: "enurn'd"; F², K: "inurn'd."   54–6 *fools of nature . . . souls* causing us (who are, in such a case, reduced to the condition of fools by our weak human nature) to agitate our frame of mind with thoughts which grasp at more than our souls can comprehend [K].   57 *do* Emphatic. Hamlet (like Horatio in I.I.130) thinks that the Ghost has come back to impose some duty on those who survive [K].

As if it some impartment did desire
To you alone.

MAR.   Look with what courteous action   60
It waves you to a more removed ground.
But do not go with it!

HOR.   No, by no means!

HAM.   It will not speak. Then I will follow it.

HOR.   Do not, my lord!

HAM.   Why, what should be the fear?
I do not set my life at a pin's fee;   65
And for my soul, what can it do to that,
Being a thing immortal as itself?
It waves me forth again. I'll follow it.

HOR.   What if it tempt you toward the flood, my lord,
Or to the dreadful summit of the cliff   70
That beetles o'er his base into the sea,
And there assume some other, horrible form
Which might deprive your sovereignty of reason
And draw you into madness? Think of it.
The very place puts toys of desperation,   75
Without more motive, into every brain
That looks so many fathoms to the sea
And hears it roar beneath.

HAM.   It waves me still.
Go on. I'll follow thee.

MAR.   You shall not go, my lord.

HAM.   Hold off your hands!   80

HOR.   Be rul'd. You shall not go.

---

59 *impartment* communication.   61 *removed* distant.   62 *No, by no means*
Hamlet's friends still fear that the apparition is a demon. This comes out clearly
in lines 69–78. Hamlet knows the danger, but is determined to take the risk; he
cares nothing for his life, and no demon can hurt his soul [K].   63 *I will* Q²; F¹,
K: "will I."   65 *fee* value.   72 *assume . . . form* change its shape from that
of your father to a form that shall be horrible [K].   73 *deprive . . . reason* take
away the control by which reason governs you.   75–8 *The very . . . beneath* Q²;
not in F¹.   75 *toys of desperation* desperate fancies or impulses [K].   81 *My fate*

HAM.   My fate cries out
And makes each petty artire in this body
As hardy as the Nemean lion's nerve.   [Ghost *beckons*.]
Still am I call'd. Unhand me, gentlemen.
By heaven, I'll make a ghost of him that lets me! —   85
I say, away! — Go on. I'll follow thee.

                                Exeunt Ghost *and* Hamlet.

HOR.   He waxes desperate with imagination.

MAR.   Let's follow. 'Tis not fit thus to obey him.

HOR.   Have after. To what issue will this come?

MAR.   Something is rotten in the state of Denmark.   90

HOR.   Heaven will direct it.

MAR.   Nay, let's follow him.   *Exeunt.*

◇◇◇◇◇◇◇◇◇◇◇◇◇◇◇◇

[SCENE V.
*Elsinore. The Castle. Another part of the forti-
fications.*]

Enter Ghost *and* Hamlet.

HAM.   Whither wilt thou lead me? Speak! I'll go no further.

GHOST.   Mark me.

HAM.   I will.

GHOST.   My hour is almost come,
When I to sulph'rous and tormenting flames

---

cries out Hamlet feels instinctively that this is the supreme moment of his life.
The Ghost speaks to him, as it were, with the tongue of destiny [K].   82 *artire*
artery, in the sense of "sinew."   83 *Nemean* To kill the lion of Nemea (a valley in
Argolis) and fetch his skin was one of the Twelve Labours of Hercules [K].   *nerve*
sinew.   85 *lets* hinders.   89 *Have after* let us follow.   90 *state* government,
administration.

    I.v. 1 *no further* Hamlet is still uncertain whether the apparition is a ghost
or a demon [K].   3 *flames* of purgatory, not hell.

    Must render up myself.

HAM.   Alas, poor ghost!

GHOST.   Pity me not, but lend thy serious hearing   5
        To what I shall unfold.

HAM.   Speak. I am bound to hear.

GHOST.   So art thou to revenge, when thou shalt hear.

HAM.   What?

GHOST.   I am thy father's spirit,
        Doom'd for a certain term to walk the night,   10
        And for the day confin'd to fast in fires,
        Till the foul crimes done in my days of nature
        Are burnt and purg'd away. But that I am forbid
        To tell the secrets of my prison house,
        I could a tale unfold whose lightest word   15
        Would harrow up thy soul, freeze thy young blood,
        Make thy two eyes, like stars, start from their spheres,
        Thy knotted and combined locks to part,
        And each particular hair to stand an end
        Like quills upon the fretful porpentine.   20
        But this eternal blazon must not be
        To ears of flesh and blood. List, list, O, list!
        If thou didst ever thy dear father love —

HAM.   O God!

GHOST.   Revenge his foul and most unnatural murder.   25

HAM.   Murder?

---

6 *bound* in duty bound; obliged (in reason and charity) [K].   11 *fast* do penance.   12 *foul crimes . . . nature* sins committed while I was alive. These are the ordinary sins of mortal life.   16 *young* strong, full of life.   17 *like stars . . . spheres* Each planet (according to the Ptolemaic astronomy) was fixed in a hollow sphere concentric with the earth and revolving about it as a centre [K].   19 *an end* on end.   20 *fretful* Q¹, F¹; Q²: "fearefull."   *porpentine* porcupine.   21 *eternal blazon* proclamation or disclosure of the secrets of eternity, i.e. of the world beyond the grave [K].   23 *If thou didst . . . love* This adjuration, with Hamlet's reply, suggests the tender affection which existed between father and son [K].   26 *Murder* Hamlet's horrified exclamation shows that up to this time he had no definite suspicion of the truth [K].   30 *meditation* thought.   31 *apt* ready.   32 *duller* more insensible.   *fat weed* the Asphodel, which grows on the bank of the river Lethe in the Greek Hades. One draught of Lethe's water causes the

GHOST.	Murder most foul, as in the best it is;
	But this most foul, strange, and unnatural.

HAM.	Haste me to know't, that I, with wings as swift	
	As meditation or the thoughts of love,	30
	May sweep to my revenge.	

GHOST.	I find thee apt;	
	And duller shouldst thou be than the fat weed	
	That rots itself in ease on Lethe wharf,	
	Wouldst thou not stir in this. Now, Hamlet, hear.	
	'Tis given out that, sleeping in my orchard,	35
	A serpent stung me. So the whole ear of Denmark	
	Is by a forged process of my death	
	Rankly abus'd. But know, thou noble youth,	
	The serpent that did sting thy father's life	
	Now wears his crown.	

HAM.	O my prophetic soul!	40
	My uncle?	

GHOST.	Ay, that incestuous, that adulterate beast,	
	With witchcraft of his wit, with traitorous gifts —	
	O wicked wit and gifts, that have the power	
	So to seduce! — won to his shameful lust	45
	The will of my most seeming-virtuous queen.	
	O Hamlet, what a falling-off was there,	
	From me, whose love was of that dignity	
	That it went hand in hand even with the vow	
	I made to her in marriage, and to decline	50

departed spirit to forget his former life in the world.　　33 *rots* F¹; Q²: "rootes." This reading has been much debated. *wharf* bank.　　35 *orchard* garden.　　37 *process* account.　　38 *abus'd* deceived.　　40 *O my prophetic soul* my soul, by its abhorrence of my uncle, foreshadowed this revelation. To suppose that Hamlet had definitely suspected the murder destroys the dramatic force of the Ghost's message [K].　　42 *adulterate* adulterous. Hamlet had not suspected adultery. He had been shocked and grieved by the "o'erhasty marriage" (which the Church regarded as incestuous), but what he now learns comes with all the horror of an unsuspected enormity. Note especially line 105 [K].　　43 *Witchcraft of his wit* Claudius, then, had a keen intellect (wit) and seductive gifts of mind and manner [K].　　45 *won . . . lust* The implication is that Gertrude had been false to her first husband while he still lived, but this is not made entirely clear, and it has been the subject of much argument.　　50 *decline* fall back.

Upon a wretch whose natural gifts were poor
To those of mine!
But virtue, as it never will be mov'd,
Though lewdness court it in a shape of heaven,
So lust, though to a radiant angel link'd,   55
Will sate itself in a celestial bed
And prey on garbage.
But soft! methinks I scent the morning air.
Brief let me be. Sleeping within my orchard,
My custom always of the afternoon,   60
Upon my secure hour thy uncle stole,
With juice of cursed hebona in a vial,
And in the porches of my ears did pour
The leperous distilment; whose effect
Holds such an enmity with blood of man   65
That swift as quicksilver it courses through
The natural gates and alleys of the body,
And with a sudden vigour it doth posset
And curd, like eager droppings into milk,
The thin and wholesome blood. So did it mine;   70
And a most instant tetter bark'd about,
Most lazar-like, with vile and loathsome crust
All my smooth body.
Thus was I, sleeping, by a brother's hand
Of life, of crown, of queen, at once dispatch'd;   75
Cut off even in the blossoms of my sin,
Unhous'led, disappointed, unanel'd,
No reck'ning made, but sent to my account

---

54 *shape of heaven* angelic disguise.   61 *secure* unheeding, free from suspicion.
62 *hebona* ebony, the sap of which was thought to be rank poison [K]. Others
have suggested that Shakespeare meant the poisonous herb, henbane.   68 *posset*
curdle, coagulate. A posset was a curdled drink made of spiced wine or ale, hot
milk, grated biscuit, pulp of apples, etc. The compound was something like a
custard, and was often said to be "eaten" [K] (F¹; Q²: "possesse").   71 *bark'd*
covered (as with the bark of a tree) [K].   72 *lazar-like* like a leper.   75 *at once
dispatched* deprived all at the same time and in an instant.   77 *Unhous'led* not
having received the sacrament of the Eucharist. *disappointed* unprepared for
death by confession and absolution. *unanel'd* without extreme unction.   80
O, horrible . . . horrible Q², F¹; K gives the line to Hamlet.   81 *nature* natural
feeling — such as a son would normally have for a father.   83 *luxury* lechery.

With all my imperfections on my head.
O, horrible! O, horrible! most horrible!   80
If thou hast nature in thee, bear it not.
Let not the royal bed of Denmark be
A couch for luxury and damned incest.
But, howsoever thou pursues this act,
Taint not thy mind, nor let thy soul contrive   85
Against thy mother aught. Leave her to heaven,
And to those thorns that in her bosom lodge
To prick and sting her. Fare thee well at once.
The glowworm shows the matin to be near
And gins to pale his uneffectual fire.   90
Adieu, adieu, adieu! Remember me.   *Exit.*

HAM. O all you host of heaven! O earth! What else?
And shall I couple hell? O, fie! Hold, hold, my heart!
And you, my sinews, grow not instant old,
But bear me stiffly up. Remember thee?   95
Ay, thou poor ghost, whiles memory holds a seat
In this distracted globe. Remember thee?
Yea, from the table of my memory
I'll wipe away all trivial fond records,
All saws of books, all forms, all pressures past   100
That youth and observation copied there,
And thy commandment all alone shall live
Within the book and volume of my brain,
Unmix'd with baser matter. Yes, by heaven!
O most pernicious woman!   105
O villain, villain, smiling, damned villain!

---

84 *pursues* Normal Elizabethan usage (Q², F¹; K: "pursuest.")   85 *Taint not thy
mind* do not let your mind be so affected by passion as to lead you into an act
contrary to nature (such as killing your own mother).   89 *matin* dawn.   90
his uneffectual fire its fire which gives no heat and which dies out entirely and
becomes of no effect as soon as day dawns [K].   93 *couple hell* call also on the
spirits of hell to aid me in my vengeance.   *O, fie* Q², F¹; not in CAPELL, K, but
important as indicating Hamlet's rejection of the help of demons in his task.   95
stiffly F¹; Q²: "swiftly."   96 *whiles* Q²; F¹, K: "while."   97 *this distracted globe*
He grasps his head with both hands, as if it were bursting [K].   98 *table* tablet.
Small ivory tablets were used for memoranda. Cf. line 107 [K].   99 *fond* foolish.
100 *saws of books* wise sayings extracted from books [K].   *forms* ideas.   *pressures*
impressions.

My tables! Meet it is I set it down
That one may smile, and smile, and be a villain;
At least I am sure it may be so in Denmark.   [*Writes.*]
So, uncle, there you are. Now to my word: 110
It is "Adieu, adieu! Remember me."
I have sworn't.

HOR.   (*within*) My lord, my lord!

Enter Horatio *and* Marcellus.

MAR.   Lord Hamlet!

HOR.   Heaven secure him!

HAM.   So be it!

MAR.   Illo, ho, ho, my lord!   115

HAM.   Hillo, ho, ho, boy! Come, bird, come.

MAR.   How is't my noble lord?

HOR.   What news, my lord?

HAM.   O, wonderful!

HOR.   Good my lord, tell it.

HAM.   No, you will reveal it.

HOR.   Not I, my lord, by heaven!

MAR.   Nor I, my lord.   120

HAM.   How say you then? Would heart of man once think it?
But you'll be secret?

BOTH.   Ay, by heaven, my lord.

HAM.   There's ne'er a villain dwelling in all Denmark
But he's an arrant knave.

HOR.   There needs no ghost, my lord, come from the grave   125

---

107 *My tables* In his excitement, Hamlet instinctively follows habit and jots down
the "happy thought" that has occurred to him [ĸ]. *Meet* proper.   110 *my word*
my motto; that which expresses the guiding principle of my life henceforth [ĸ].
113 *Heaven secure him* Thus Horatio once more expresses his fear that the
apparition may be a demon [ĸ].   116 *Hillo . . . bird, come* Hamlet converts
Marcellus' call to the cry of a falconer. See Supplementary Notes. *bird* F¹; Q²: "And."
127 *circumstance* ceremony, polite conversation.   132 *Look you* F¹; not in Q².
136 *by Saint Patrick* Hamlet still speaks rather wildly, swearing by a saint whom

To tell us this.

HAM.   Why, right! You are in the right!
And so, without more circumstance at all,
I hold it fit that we shake hands and part;
You, as your business and desire shall point you,
For every man hath business and desire,   130
Such as it is; and for my own poor part,
Look you, I'll go pray.

HOR.   These are but wild and whirling words, my lord.

HAM.   I am sorry they offend you, heartily;
Yes, faith, heartily.

HOR.   There's no offence, my lord.   135

HAM.   Yes, by Saint Patrick, but there is, Horatio,
And much offence too. Touching this vision here,
It is an honest ghost, that let me tell you.
For your desire to know what is between us,
O'ermaster't as you may. And now, good friends,   140
As you are friends, scholars, and soldiers,
Give me one poor request.

HOR.   What is't, my lord? We will.

HAM.   Never make known what you have seen to-night.

BOTH.   My lord, we will not.

HAM.   Nay, but swear't.

HOR.   In faith,   145
My lord, not I.

MAR.   Nor I, my lord — in faith.

HAM.   Upon my sword.

MAR.   We have sworn, my lord, already.

---

a Dane would not be expected to adjure. There is no allusion (as some have
thought) to "blunders and confusion"; nor is it likely that Hamlet is thinking
of St. Patrick's Purgatory — a cave in Ireland, supposed to afford an entrance to
the world beyond the grave [K].   138 *honest* straightforward and honourable
— not a demon.   140 *as you may* as well as you can.   147 *Upon my sword* The
hilt of his sword forms a cross, upon which each is to lay his right hand when
he swears [K].   *sworn . . . already* since "in faith" is an oath [K].

HAM.   Indeed, upon my sword, indeed.

                        Ghost *cries under the stage.*

GHOST. Swear.

HAM.   Aha boy, say'st thou so? Art thou there, truepenny?   150
        Come on! You hear this fellow in the cellarage.
        Consent to swear.

HOR.   Propose the oath, my lord.

HAM.   Never to speak of this that you have seen.
        Swear by my sword.

GHOST. [*beneath*] Swear.   155

HAM.   Hic et ubique? Then we'll shift our ground.
        Come hither, gentlemen,
        And lay your hands again upon my sword.
        Never to speak of this that you have heard:
        Swear by my sword.   160

GHOST. [*beneath*] Swear by his sword.

HAM.   Well said, old mole! Canst work i' th' earth so fast?
        A worthy pioner! Once more remove, good friends.

HOR.   O day and night, but this is wondrous strange!

HAM.   And therefore as a stranger give it welcome.   165
        There are more things in heaven and earth, Horatio,
        Than are dreamt of in your philosophy.
        But come!
        Here, as before, never, so help you mercy,
        How strange or odd soe'er I bear myself   170

---

150 *truepenny* honest old boy.   156 *Hic et ubique* here and everywhere — a
wanderer's motto [K]. It has been called also a magician's formula, used in con-
juring.   159-60 *Never to . . . my sword* F¹; Q² reverses the order of the lines.
163 *pioner* miner, digger. Pioners or pioneers were footsoldiers who dug trenches
and mines [K].   165 *as a stranger give it welcome* It was a point of good manners,
when receiving strangers into one's house, not to question them about themselves
[K].   167 *your philosophy* this philosophy that people make so much of [K]. He
means "natural philosophy" or "science" which denies the existence of ghosts.
172 *put . . . on* A clear allusion to his purpose of counterfeiting madness [K].
antic fantastic.   174 *encumb'red* folded, with an air of solemn importance, as of
one who knows more than he cares to tell and hugs a secret to his breast [K].

(As I perchance hereafter shall think meet
To put an antic disposition on),
That you, at such times seeing me, never shall,
With arms encumb'red thus, or this headshake,
Or by pronouncing of some doubtful phrase,   175
As "Well, well, we know," or "We could, an if we
          would,"
Or "If we list to speak," or "There be, an if they might,"
Or such ambiguous giving out, to note
That you know aught of me — this not to do,
So grace and mercy at your most need help you,   180
Swear.

GHOST.   [*beneath*] Swear.

                                                    [*They swear.*]

HAM.   Rest, rest, perturbed spirit! So, gentlemen,
With all my love I do commend me to you;
And what so poor a man as Hamlet is   185
May do t' express his love and friending to you,
God willing, shall not lack. Let us go in together;
And still your fingers on your lips, I pray.
The time is out of joint. O cursed spite
That ever I was born to set it right!   190
Nay, come, let's go together.   *Exeunt.*

---

178 *giving out* utterance. *note* indicate.   179 *this not to do* F¹; Q²: "this doe
sweare."   181 *Swear* F¹, Q¹; not in Q².   184 *commend me to you* protest my
devotion to you. The phrase means literally "hand myself over to you" [K].   185
so poor Hamlet alludes to his uncle's having obtained the election to the kingship
which would naturally have fallen to him. Cf. III.ii.324-8 [K].   188 *still* always.
189 *O cursed spite* This phrase, in Elizabethan usage, was equivalent to the
modern "What an infernal nuisance!" though more dignified than our idiom.
Hamlet is resolved to avenge his father, but he is too highly civilized to welcome
the duty that the savage code of his nation and time imposes. Thus he differs
from the stock "revenger" in the old plays, who (in Senecan fashion) revels in
bloodthirstiness [K].   191 *together* as friends and equals.

Act Two

[SCENE I.
Elsinore. A room in the house of Polonius.]

Enter Polonius *and* Reynaldo.

POL. Give him this money and these notes, Reynaldo.

REY. I will, my lord.

POL. You shall do marvellous wisely, good Reynaldo,
Before you visit him, to make inquire
Of his behaviour.

REY. My lord, I did intend it.   5

POL. Marry, well said, very well said. Look you, sir,
Inquire me first what Danskers are in Paris;
And how, and who, what means, and where they keep,
What company, at what expense; and finding
By this encompassment and drift of question   10
That they do know my son, come you more nearer
Than your particular demands will touch it.
Take you, as 'twere, some distant knowledge of him;

II.I. 1 *Give him . . . notes* The dialogue serves to establish that about six
or eight weeks have passed, enough time for Laertes to get to Paris, spend his
money, and send home for more. *notes* memoranda.   3 *marvellous* wonderfully
(Q², K: "marvell's," a spelling variant).   7 *Danskers* Danes.   9 *finding* if you
find.   10 *By this . . . question* by this roundabout means and by giving your
conversation this turn. "Question" may mean either "conversation" or "inquiry"
[K].   11–12 *come you . . . touch it* then you come nearer (to the information
you are seeking) than you can do by any personal questions. Polonius proceeds
to show how this may be done — namely by making remarks that shall tempt
the hearer to tell what he may have observed [K].   19 *put on him* attribute to

40

As thus, "I know his father and his friends,
And in part him." Do you mark this, Reynaldo?   15

REY.   Ay, very well, my lord.

POL.   "And in part him, but," you may say, "not well.
But if't be he I mean, he's very wild
Addicted so and so"; and there put on him
What forgeries you please; marry, none so rank   20
As may dishonour him — take heed of that;
But, sir, such wanton, wild, and usual slips
As are companions noted and most known
To youth and liberty.

REY.   As gaming, my lord.

POL.   Ay, or drinking, fencing, swearing, quarrelling,   25
Drabbing. You may go so far.

REY.   My lord, that would dishonour him.

POL.   Faith, no, as you may season it in the charge.
You must not put another scandal on him,
That he is open to incontinency.   30
That's not my meaning. But breathe his faults so
     quaintly
That they may seem the taints of liberty,
The flash and outbreak of a fiery mind,
A savageness in unreclaimed blood,
Of general assault.

REY.   But, my good lord —   35

POL.   Wherefore should you do this?

REY.   Ay, my lord,

---

him.   20 *forgeries* inventions, lies. *rank* flagrant.   22 *wanton* gay.   25 *fencing*
Not discreditable in itself, but a valued accomplishment (see IV.vii.70–102). The
fencing schools, however, were frequented by wild young bloods, and to spend
much time in such places might be a sign of dissipation [K].   26 *Drabbing*
whoring.   28 *season it in the charge* modify or soften the accusation in the very
act of bringing it [K].   30 *incontinency* sexual overindulgence.   31 *breathe . . .
quaintly* suggest his faults so delicately — with such delicate reticence [K].   32
taints of liberty faults incident to lack of restraint [K].   34 *unreclaimed* not re-
called from a state of wild nature; untamed by age and experience [K].   35 *Of
general assault* attacking everybody; to which all young men are exposed [K].

I would know that.

POL.   Marry, sir, here's my drift,
And I believe it is a fetch of warrant.
You laying these slight sullies on my son
As 'twere a thing a little soil'd i' th' working,   40
Mark you,
Your party in converse, him you would sound,
Having ever seen in the prenominate crimes
The youth you breathe of guilty, be assur'd
He closes with you in this consequence: 45
"Good sir," or so, or "friend," or "gentleman" —
According to the phrase or the addition
Of man and country —

REY.   Very good, my lord.

POL.   And then, sir, does 'a this — 'a does — What was I about
to say? By the mass, I was about to say something! Where   50
did I leave?

REY.   At "closes in the consequence," at "friend or so," and
"gentleman."

POL.   At "closes in the consequence" — Ay, marry!
He closes thus: "I know the gentleman.   55
I saw him yesterday, or t'other day,
Or then, or then, with such or such; and, as you say,
There was 'a gaming; there o'ertook in's rouse;
There falling out at tennis"; or perchance,
"I saw him enter such a house of sale,"   60
Videlicet, a brothel, or so forth.

---

37 *drift* meaning.   38 *fetch* device, trick.   *of warrant* allowable (F¹; Q²: "of wit").
39 *sullies* F¹; Q²: "sallies."   40 *soil'd i' th' working* soiled by the experiences that
accompany growth from youth to manhood. The figure comes from the marks
that one's hands leave on a delicate material [K].   *i' th'* F¹; Q²: "with."   43
Having ever seen if he has ever seen.   *crimes* faults. Very common in the general
sense [K].   44 *breathe of* make these suggestions about.   45 *He closes . . . con-*
sequence he will be sure to agree with you, following up your remark as follows
[K].   47 *addition* title.   52–3 *at "friend" . . . "gentleman"* F¹; not in Q².   58
o'ertook in's rouse surprised or overcome (by intoxication) in his drinking [K].
59 *falling out* quarrelling.   61 *Videlicet* namely.   63 *carp* Merely used to carry
out the figure with Polonian thoroughness. Any other fish would do as well [K].
But there may be a quibble on "carp" in the sense of "talk."   65 *windlasses*

See you now —
Your bait of falsehood takes this carp of truth;
And thus do we of wisdom and of reach,
With windlasses and with assays of bias,   65
By indirections find directions out.
So, by my former lecture and advice,
Shall you my son. You have me, have you not?

REY.   My lord, I have.

POL.   God b' wi' ye, fare ye well!

REY.   Good my lord!   [*Going.*] 70

POL.   Observe his inclination in yourself.

REY.   I shall, my lord.

POL.   And let him ply his music.

REY.   Well, my lord.

POL.   Farewell!   *Exit* Reynaldo.

Enter Ophelia.

How now, Ophelia? What's the matter?

OPH.   O my lord, my lord, I have been so affrighted!   75

POL.   With what, i' th' name of God?

OPH.   My lord, as I was sewing in my closet,
Lord Hamlet, with his doublet all unbrac'd,
No hat upon his head, his stockings foul'd,
Ungart'red, and down-gyved to his ankle;   80
Pale as his shirt, his knees knocking each other,

---

roundabout ways. *assays of bias* indirect attempts. The "bias" is the curve which
the bowl makes in reaching its goal — like a "curve" in baseball [K]. 66 *By
indirections . . . out* by indirect means discover truths [K]. 68 *have* understand.
71 *in yourself* by personal observation — as well as by the method Polonius has
explained. 73 *ply his music* Merely a parting direction to Reynaldo to see that
Laertes does not neglect his practice of music — an art in which every gentleman
was expected to have some skill [K]. But it may also be the equivalent of "Give
him enough rope" or "Let him sow his wild oats." 77 *closet* private room. 78
doublet jacket. *unbrac'd* unlaced. 79 *No hat* Hats were often worn in-doors.
Ophelia would have expected Hamlet at the door with his hat on, but he would
remove it as he crossed the threshold [K]. *foul'd* soiled. 80 *down-gyved* dan-
gling like gyves or fetters round his ankles [K].

And with a look so piteous in purport
As if he had been loosed out of hell
To speak of horrors — he comes before me.

POL.   Mad for thy love?

OPH.   My lord, I do not know,   85
But truly I do fear it.

POL.   What said he?

OPH.   He took me by the wrist and held me hard;
Then goes he to the length of all his arm,
And, with his other hand thus o'er his brow,
He falls to such perusal of my face   90
As he would draw it. Long stay'd he so.
At last, a little shaking of mine arm,
And thrice his head thus waving up and down,
He rais'd a sigh so piteous and profound
As it did seem to shatter all his bulk   95
And end his being. That done, he lets me go,
And with his head over his shoulder turn'd
He seem'd to find his way without his eyes,
For out o' doors he went without their help
And to the last bended their light on me.   100

POL.   Come, go with me. I will go seek the King.
This is the very ecstasy of love,
Whose violent property fordoes itself
And leads the will to desperate undertakings
As oft as any passion under heaven   105
That does afflict our natures. I am sorry.
What, have you given him any hard words of late?

OPH.   No, my good lord; but, as you did command,

---

85 *Mad* Hamlet had already begun to "put an antic disposition on" (I.v.172),
and Polonius, like the King and Queen, was concerned to discover the cause
(cf. II.ii.48–50). Now he thinks he has it [K].   95 *bulk* body — literally, the trunk.
102 *ecstasy* madness.   103 *Whose . . . itself* which has this property when it is
violent — that it destroys itself (i.e. the person who suffers from it) [K].   112
quoted noted, observed.   113 *wrack* literally, "shipwreck."   *beshrew* curse.   114
proper to characteristic of.   115 *cast beyond ourselves* overshoot ourselves; err
by going too far. It is characteristic of the young not to see all there is in a

I did repel his letters and denied
His access to me.

POL.   That hath made him mad.   110
I am sorry that with better heed and judgment
I had not quoted him. I fear'd he did but trifle
And meant to wrack thee; but beshrew my jealousy!
By heaven, it is as proper to our age
To cast beyond ourselves in our opinions   115
As it is common for the younger sort
To lack discretion. Come, go we to the King.
This must be known; which, being kept close, might
    move
More grief to hide than hate to utter love.
Come.   *Exeunt.* 120

❖❖❖❖❖❖❖❖❖❖❖❖❖

SCENE II. [*Elsinore. A room in the Castle.*]

Flourish. Enter King *and* Queen, Rosencrantz, *and*
    Guildenstern, *cum aliis.*

KING.   Welcome, dear Rosencrantz and Guildenstern.
Moreover that we much did long to see you,
The need we have to use you did provoke
Our hasty sending. Something have you heard
Of Hamlet's transformation. So call it,   5
Sith nor th' exterior nor the inward man
Resembles that it was. What it should be,
More than his father's death, that thus hath put him
So much from th' understanding of himself,

---

matter; of the old to see more than there is in it [K].   118–19 *which, being . . .
utter love* for us to conceal it might cause the King (and us) more sorrow than he
will feel displeasure at learning that Hamlet loves you. Polonius, though of very
high rank, does not believe that the King and Queen will approve Hamlet's
marrying Ophelia. He is mistaken, as the Queen's words prove in V.I.230 [K].
close secret.
    II.II. 2 *Moreover that* besides the fact that.   5 *So call* Q²; F¹, K: "So I call."
6 *Sith* since.   7 *that* what.

I cannot dream of. I entreat you both   10
That, being of so young days brought up with him,
And since so neighbour'd to his youth and haviour,
That you vouchsafe your rest here in our court
Some little time; so by your companies
To draw him on to pleasures, and to gather   15
So much as from occasion you may glean,
Whether aught to us unknown afflicts him thus
That, open'd, lies within our remedy.

QUEEN. Good gentlemen, he hath much talk'd of you,
And sure I am two men there are not living   20
To whom he more adheres. If it will please you
To show us so much gentry and good will
As to expend your time with us awhile
For the supply and profit of our hope,
Your visitation shall receive such thanks   25
As fits a king's remembrance.

ROS.   Both your Majesties
Might, by the sovereign power you have of us,
Put your dread pleasures more into command
Than to entreaty.

GUIL.   But we both obey,
And here give up ourselves, in the full bent,   30
To lay our service freely at your feet,
To be commanded.

KING.   Thanks, Rosencrantz and gentle Guildenstern.

QUEEN. Thanks, Guildenstern and gentle Rosencrantz.

---

11 *of* from. Rosencrantz and Guildenstern are two young noblemen who had
been selected, as the custom was, to be Hamlet's playfellows when he was a
small boy, and to share his studies and sports until he went to the university [K].
12 *so . . . haviour* so closely associated with his life and ways throughout his
youth [K].   13 *vouchsafe your rest* consent to remain.   16 *occasion* opportunity.
17 *Whether . . . thus* Q²; not in F¹.   18 *open'd* if it is disclosed. The metaphor
is from the opening of an infection by surgery. See Supplementary Notes.   21
more adheres is more attached. Both the King and the Queen overestimate
Hamlet's intimacy with these two noblemen. Hamlet treats them familiarly, to
be sure, but he knows better than to trust them [K].   22 *gentry* courtesy.   24
supply fulfillment. *profit* furtherance.   28 *dread pleasures* wishes as our sover-
eigns. *into* in the form of.   30 *in the full bent* with full intention. The figure

	And I beseech you instantly to visit	35

And I beseech you instantly to visit   35
My too much changed son. — Go, some of you,
And bring these gentlemen where Hamlet is.

GUIL.   Heavens make our presence and our practices
Pleasant and helpful to him!

QUEEN.   Ay, amen!

Exeunt Rosencrantz *and* Guildenstern, [*with some* Attendants].

Enter Polonius.

POL.   Th' ambassadors from Norway, my good lord,   40
Are joyfully return'd.

KING.   Thou still hast been the father of good news.

POL.   Have I, my lord? Assure you, my good liege,
I hold my duty as I hold my soul,
Both to my God and to my gracious king;   45
And I do think — or else this brain of mine
Hunts not the trail of policy so sure
As it hath us'd to do — that I have found
The very cause of Hamlet's lunacy.

KING.   O, speak of that! That do I long to hear.   50

POL.   Give first admittance to th' ambassadors.
My news shall be the fruit to that great feast.

KING.   Thyself do grace to them, and bring them in.

[*Exit* Polonius.]

He tells me, my dear Gertrude, he hath found

---

is from the bending of a bow when one takes aim [ĸ].   38 *practices* actions. The
word in Shakespeare's day had a pejorative connotation, meaning "plots" or
"machinations," although this sense is not here intended by Guildenstern.   42
still always.   43 *Assure you* F¹; Q²: "I assure."   44–5 *I hold . . . king* I regard
my duty both to God and to my king as highly as I value my soul [ĸ].   47
policy statecraft.   48 *hath us'd to do* formerly did. His pursuit of "policy" is
compared to the pursuit of a scent by a hunting dog.   52 *fruit* dessert.   53
grace honour.   54 *He tells me* The King, throughout the first part of the play,
confides immediately to his wife anything that he learns about Hamlet. This
is not without importance in determining the feeling of Claudius toward his
stepson [ĸ].

The head and source of all your son's distemper.   55

QUEEN.   I doubt it is no other but the main,
His father's death and our o'erhasty marriage.

KING.   Well, we shall sift him.

Enter Polonius, Voltemand, *and* Cornelius.

Welcome, my good friends.
Say, Voltemand, what from our brother Norway?

VOLT.   Most fair return of greetings and desires.   60
Upon our first, he sent out to suppress
His nephew's levies; which to him appear'd
To be a preparation 'gainst the Polack,
But better look'd into, he truly found
It was against your Highness; whereat griev'd,   65
That so his sickness, age, and impotence
Was falsely borne in hand, sends out arrests
On Fortinbras; which he, in brief, obeys,
Receives rebuke from Norway, and, in fine,
Makes vow before his uncle never more   70
To give th' assay of arms against your Majesty.
Whereon old Norway, overcome with joy,
Gives him threescore thousand crowns in annual fee
And his commission to employ those soldiers,
So levied as before, against the Polack;   75
With an entreaty, herein further shown,

[*Gives a paper.*]

That it might please you to give quiet pass

---

55 *head* fountainhead, origin.   56 *doubt* suspect.   *the main* the main thing, i.e.
the general subject that has occupied his thoughts of late [K].   57 *o'erhasty* F¹;
Q²: "hastie."   61 *Upon our first* as soon as we made known our business [K].
63 *preparation* military expedition.   65 *griev'd* aggrieved, offended, indignant.
66 *impotence* feeble health.   67 *borne in hand* deceived. The phrase implies not
merely a single act, but a systematic course of deception [K].   *arrests* writs of
arrest, summoning him to the King's presence [K].   69 *in fine* in conclusion.
71 *To . . . arms* to bring the question to the test of warfare [K].   73 *threescore*
Q²; F¹, K: "three."   *fee* income.   77 *quiet pass* unmolested passage.   79–80 *On
such . . . set down* on such conditions with regard to the public safety as are (in

Through your dominions for this enterprise,
On such regards of safety and allowance
As therein are set down.

KING.   It likes us well;   80
And at our more consider'd time we'll read,
Answer, and think upon this business.
Meantime we thank you for your well-took labour.
Go to your rest; at night we'll feast together.
Most welcome home!   *Exeunt* Ambassadors.

POL.   This business is well ended.   85
My liege, and madam, to expostulate
What majesty should be, what duty is,
Why day is day, night night, and time is time,
Were nothing but to waste night, day, and time.
Therefore, since brevity is the soul of wit,   90
And tediousness the limbs and outward flourishes,
I will be brief. Your noble son is mad.
Mad call I it; for, to define true madness,
What is't but to be nothing else but mad?
But let that go.

QUEEN.   More matter, with less art.   95

POL.   Madam, I swear I use no art at all.
That he is mad, 'tis true: 'tis true 'tis pity;
And pity 'tis 'tis true. A foolish figure!
But farewell it, for I will use no art.
Mad let us grant him then. And now remains   100
That we find out the cause of this effect —
Or rather say, the cause of this defect,

---

this document) submitted for your approval. "Allowance" is common in this
sense [K].   80 *likes* pleases.   81 *our more consider'd time* time when I have
more leisure for consideration.   86 *My liege* Polonius begins a set speech, which
has an exordium (lines 86–105), a narrative part (lines 106–46), and a peroration
(lines 147–51) [K]. *expostulate* discuss.   90 *brevity is the soul of wit* This,
like many other lines of Shakespeare, has become a proverb in a sense different
from that which it bears in its own context. "Wit" here signifies "wisdom." The
whole remark means: "The wise or instructive part of every speech may be put
in a few words; and what often makes wisdom tedious is the ornaments or
flourishes with which it is decked out" [K].   98 *figure* figure of speech.

For this effect defective comes by cause.
Thus it remains, and the remainder thus.
Perpend.   105
I have a daughter (have while she is mine),
Who in her duty and obedience, mark,
Hath given me this. Now gather, and surmise.

[*Reads*] *the letter.*

"To the celestial, and my soul's idol, the most beautified
Ophelia," —   110

That's an ill phrase, a vile phrase; "beautified" is a vile
phrase. But you shall hear. Thus: [*Reads.*]

"In her excellent white bosom, these, &c."

QUEEN.   Came this from Hamlet to her?

POL.   Good madam, stay awhile. I will be faithful.   [*Reads.*] 115

    "Doubt thou the stars are fire;
       Doubt that the sun doth move;
       Doubt truth to be a liar;
       But never doubt I love.

    "O dear Ophelia, I am ill at these numbers; I have 120
not art to reckon my groans; but that I love thee best,
O most best, believe it. Adieu.
      "Thine evermore, most dear lady, whilst this ma-
                 chine is to him, HAMLET."
This, in obedience, hath my daughter shown me;   125
And more above, hath his solicitings,

---

105 *Perpend* listen and consider carefully.   106 *have while she is mine* The fondness for distinctions which characterizes the style of Polonius will not allow him
to use even so simple a word as "have" without splitting hairs [K].   111 *a vile
phrase* Polonius takes the word to mean "made beautiful by artificial means,"
whereas Hamlet had meant it as "endowed with beauty."   116 *Doubt . . . fire*
Hamlet's poetry is poor, as he himself confesses; but it was expected that every
lover should show his devotion in verse [K].   117 *doth move* about the earth, as
it was believed to do in the Ptolemaic astronomy.   120 *ill at these numbers* a
poor hand at this verse-making [K].   121 *reckon my groans* express my love sorrows in the set forms of verse [K].   123–4 *whilst . . . him* as long as this body remains his; as long as he lives. Hamlet thinks of his body as a complicated piece
of mechanism to which his soul supplies the motive power [K].   126 *above* be-

As they fell out by time, by means, and place,
All given to mine ear.

KING.   But how hath she
Receiv'd his love?

POL.   What do you think of me?

KING.   As of a man faithful and honourable.   130

POL.   I would fain prove so. But what might you think,
When I had seen this hot love on the wing
(As I perceiv'd it, I must tell you that,
Before my daughter told me), what might you,
Or my dear Majesty your queen here, think,   135
If I had play'd the desk or table book,
Or given my heart a winking, mute and dumb,
Or look'd upon this love with idle sight?
What might you think? No, I went round to work
And my young mistress thus I did bespeak: 140
"Lord Hamlet is a prince, out of thy star.
This must not be." And then I prescripts gave her,
That she should lock herself from his resort,
Admit no messengers, receive no tokens.
Which done, she took the fruits of my advice,   145
And he, repelled, a short tale to make,
Fell into a sadness, then into a fast,
Thence to a watch, thence into a weakness,
Thence to a lightness, and, by this declension,
Into the madness wherein now he raves,   150
And all we mourn for.

---

sides (F¹; Q²: "about").   136 *play'd . . . table book* stored the matter away in
my own mind, as one locks up letters in a desk or makes private memoranda
in one's tablets or note-book [K].   137 *given . . . winking* forced my heart to
shut its eyes to what was going on [K]. *winking* F¹; Q²: "working," preferred by
some editors as meaning "mental operation."   138 *idle sight* foolish (unseeing)
eyes.   139 *What might you think* Polonius implies that they could then have supposed him capable of intriguing to obtain a royal alliance for his daughter [K].
round directly.   140 *bespeak* speak to.   141 *out of thy star* beyond what destiny
prescribes for you.   142 *prescripts* definite orders.   145 *she . . . advice* she
carried out my advice. Good advice "bears fruit" when it is carried out in action
[K].   146 *repelled* Q²; F¹, K: "repulsed."   148 *watch* sleeplessness.   149 *lightness*
lightheadedness. *declension* steady decline, downward course.

KING.   Do you think 'tis this?

QUEEN.   It may be, very like.

POL.   Hath there been such a time — I would fain know that —
         That I have positively said " 'Tis so,"
         When it prov'd otherwise?

KING.   Not that I know.   155

POL.   [*points to his head and shoulder*] Take this from this, if
              this be otherwise.
         If circumstances lead me, I will find
         Where truth is hid, though it were hid indeed
         Within the centre.

KING.   How may we try it further?

POL.   You know sometimes he walks four hours together   160
         Here in the lobby.

QUEEN.   So he does indeed.

POL.   At such a time I'll loose my daughter to him.
         Be you and I behind an arras then.
         Mark the encounter. If he love her not,
         And be not from his reason fall'n thereon,   165
         Let me be no assistant for a state,
         But keep a farm and carters.

KING.   We will try it.

                  Enter Hamlet, *reading on a book.*

QUEEN.   But look where sadly the poor wretch comes reading.

POL.   Away, I do beseech you, both away!
         I'll board him presently. O, give me leave.   170

---

159 *centre* the earth's centre, which was also the centre of the universe according
to the Ptolemaic astronomy [K].   160 *four* Commonly used in the sense of "several," or as we might say "three or four."   162 *loose* let loose (as one would
release a dog from a leash or let loose a bull to a cow). The animalistic implica-
tions of the term may be a carry-over from the old play.   163 *arras* hanging
tapestry.   165 *thereon* on that account.   167 s.d. *reading on a book* A stage convention indicating a serious mode. Some editors would have Hamlet enter following line 159 and remain hidden to the others while he overhears Polonius' plan.
This might explain much of what follows.   168 *sadly* soberly — with no necessary implication of sorrow.   170 *board* accost. *presently* at once.   174 *fishmonger* Merely a bit of Hamlet's pretended insanity. For him to call the

                        Exeunt King *and* Queen, [*with* At-
                        tendants].

       How does my good Lord Hamlet?

HAM.   Well, God-a-mercy.

POL.   Do you know me, my lord?

HAM.   Excellent well. You are a fishmonger.

POL.   Not I, my lord.   175

HAM.   Then I would you were so honest a man.

POL.   Honest, my lord?

HAM.   Ay, sir. To be honest, as this world goes, is to be one
        man pick'd out of ten thousand.

POL.   That's very true, my lord.   180

HAM.   For if the sun breed maggots in a dead dog, being a god
        kissing carrion — Have you a daughter?

POL.   I have, my lord.

HAM.   Let her not walk i' th' sun. Conception is a blessing, but
        as your daughter may conceive — friend, look to't.   185

POL.   [*aside*] How say you by that? Still harping on my daugh-
        ter. Yet he knew me not at first. 'A said I was a fish-
        monger. 'A is far gone, far gone! And truly in my youth
        I suff'red much extremity for love — very near this. I'll
        speak to him again. — What do you read, my lord?   190

HAM.   Words, words, words.

POL.   What is the matter, my lord?

---

elegantly dressed, dignified, and overrefined courtier — the pattern of all that is
elaborate in manners — a fish-seller was the very maddest thing he could say [K].
But the word was also common slang for "procurer" or "bawd" just as "fish" was
common for "whore."   176 *honest* chaste.   181 *a god* the sun god, Apollo. That
the sun had the power to create new life by shining upon dead matter is an
ancient belief (WARBURTON; Q², F¹: "a good").   184 *Let . . . sun* (a) keep her at
home, away from the temptation of public resorts [K] (b) protect her from the
danger of conception (c) keep her away from me — the son.   184-5 *but as* Q²;
F¹, K: "but not as."   187-8 *'A . . . 'A* Q²; F¹, K: "He . . . He."   188 *far gone,
far gone* F¹; Q²: "far gone."

HAM.   Between who?

POL.   I mean, the matter that you read, my lord.

HAM.   Slanders, sir; for the satirical rogue says here that old 195
        men have grey beards; that their faces are wrinkled;
        their eyes purging thick amber and plum-tree gum; and
        that they have a plentiful lack of wit, together with
        most weak hams. All which, sir, though I most power-
        fully and potently believe, yet I hold it not honesty to 200
        have it thus set down; for you yourself, sir, shall grow
        old as I am if, like a crab, you could go backward.

POL.   [*aside*] Though this be madness, yet there is method
        in't. — Will you walk out of the air, my lord?

HAM.   Into my grave?   205

POL.   Indeed, that is out o' th' air. [*Aside*] How pregnant
        sometimes his replies are! a happiness that often mad-
        ness hits on, which reason and sanity could not so pros-
        perously be delivered of. I will leave him and suddenly
        contrive the means of meeting between him and my 210
        daughter. — My honourable lord, I will most humbly
        take my leave of you.

HAM.   You cannot take from me anything that I will more
        willingly part withal — except my life, except my life,
        except my life.   215

                    Enter Rosencrantz *and* Guildenstern.

POL.   Fare you well, my lord.

HAM.   These tedious old fools!

193 *Between who* He takes "matter" to mean "cause for a quarrel."   200 *honesty*
honourable conduct. Hamlet means that, although all these things are facts, yet
it is not fair to mention them in satirizing old men, since the old are not to
blame for their age. If they could "walk backward," they would quickly return
to a time of life when none of these gibes would be true [K].   201 *shall grow*
Q²; F¹, K: "should be."   206 *pregnant* meaningful.   207 *happiness* cleverness
(of word or idea).   208 *sanity* F¹; Q²: "sanctity."   209–10 *and suddenly . . . him*
F¹; not in Q².   213 *cannot take* Q²; F¹, K: "cannot sir take."   *will more* F¹; Q²; "will
not more."   217 *These . . . fools* This fling may or may not be heard by
Polonius, who is on his way out. Anyhow, Hamlet, whose normal manners are

POL.   You go to seek the Lord Hamlet. There he is.

ROS.   [to Polonius] God save you, sir!   *Exit* [Polonius].

GUIL.   My honour'd lord!   220

ROS.   My most dear lord!

HAM.   My excellent good friends! How dost thou, Guildenstern? Ah, Rosencrantz! Good lads, how do ye both?

ROS.   As the indifferent children of the earth.

GUIL.   Happy in that we are not over-happy. On Fortune's   225
cap we are not the very button.

HAM.   Nor the soles of her shoe?

ROS.   Neither, my lord.

HAM.   Then you live about her waist, or in the middle of her
favours?   230

GUIL.   Faith, her privates we.

HAM.   In the secret parts of Fortune? O, most true! she is a
strumpet. What news?

ROS.   None, my lord, but that the world 's grown honest.

HAM.   Then is doomsday near! But your news is not true. Let   235
me question more in particular. What have you, my
good friends, deserved at the hands of Fortune that she
sends you to prison hither?

GUIL.   Prison, my lord?

HAM.   Denmark 's a prison.   240

ROS.   Then is the world one.

---

very courteous, feigns madness by being as rude as he can. Nobody takes offence
at his rudeness, for all accept it as a symptom of insanity [K].   **222** *excellent* F¹;
Q²: "extent."   **224** *As . . . earth* like the general run of mortals [K].   **225** *over-
happy* F¹; Q²: "euer happy."   **226** *cap* F¹; Q²: "lap."   **231** *privates* intimate
friends (with an obscene quibble).   **233** *strumpet* Fortune is so called proverbially
because she grants favours to all men and is constant to none [K].   **235–65** *Let
me question . . . dreadfully attended* F¹; not in Q². The derogative references
to Denmark probably caused the passage to be censored since Anne of Denmark
was Queen of England when Q² was printed in 1604.

HAM.   A goodly one; in which there are many confines, wards, and dungeons, Denmark being one o' th' worst.

ROS.   We think not so, my lord.

HAM.   Why, then 'tis none to you; for there is nothing either 245 good or bad but thinking makes it so. To me it is a prison.

ROS.   Why, then your ambition makes it one. 'Tis too narrow for your mind.

HAM.   O God, I could be bounded in a nutshell and count 250 myself a king of infinite space, were it not that I have bad dreams.

GUIL.   Which dreams indeed are ambition; for the very substance of the ambitious is merely the shadow of a dream.   255

HAM.   A dream itself is but a shadow.

ROS.   Truly, and I hold ambition of so airy and light a quality that it is but a shadow's shadow.

HAM.   Then are our beggars bodies, and our monarchs and outstretch'd heroes the beggars' shadows. Shall we to 260 th' court? for, by my fay, I cannot reason.

BOTH.   We'll wait upon you.

HAM.   No such matter! I will not sort you with the rest of my servants; for, to speak to you like an honest man, I am most dreadfully attended. But in the beaten way of 265

---

242 *goodly* spacious. *confines* cells.   248 *your ambition* They suspect that Hamlet's secret trouble is disappointment at not having succeeded to the throne, and on this matter they insist on sounding him throughout the interview. Hamlet soon discovers their theory, and he teases them by giving them ground for thinking they are right, but no clear evidence [K].   253 *Which dreams* Hamlet has intentionally wandered from the point which Rosencrantz is trying to investigate, and Guildenstern rather skillfully brings him back to it. The result, however, is simply a quibbling dialogue on the general subject of ambition. Thus Hamlet outwits his cross-examiners [K].   259-60 *Then are . . . shadows* This is simply an instance of the paradoxical reasoning in which the wits of Shakespeare's time delighted. Guildenstern has said, in effect, that ambition is merely a shadow; Hamlet argues as follows: "If ambition is a shadow, our monarchs and heroes, who are entirely composed of ambition, must be shadows, and our beggars, the only persons in the world who have no ambition, must alone be composed of

friendship, what make you at Elsinore?

ROS.   To visit you, my lord; no other occasion.

HAM.   Beggar that I am, I am even poor in thanks; but I
thank you; and sure, dear friends, my thanks are too
dear a halfpenny. Were you not sent for? Is it your own   270
inclining? Is it a free visitation? Come, deal justly with
me. Come, come! Nay, speak.

GUIL.   What should we say, my lord?

HAM.   Why, anything — but to th' purpose. You were sent for;
and there is a kind of confession in your looks, which   275
your modesties have not craft enough to colour. I know
the good King and Queen have sent for you.

ROS.   To what end, my lord?

HAM.   That you must teach me. But let me conjure you by the
rights of our fellowship, by the consonancy of our   280
youth, by the obligation of our ever-preserved love, and
by what more dear a better proposer can charge you
withal, be even and direct with me, whether you were
sent for or no.

ROS.   [*aside to* Guildenstern] What say you?   285

HAM.   [*aside*] Nay then, I have an eye of you. — If you love me,
hold not off.

GUIL.   My lord, we were sent for.

HAM.   I will tell you why. So shall my anticipation prevent

---

real substance. If, now, the beggars are the only real bodies, and the monarchs and
heroes are shadows, then the monarchs and heroes must be the shadows of the
beggars, since there cannot be a shadow without a real body to cast it." "Outstretch'd" suggests the fantastic length of a man's shadow. The hero seems very
tall, but he is in fact only the ludicrously elongated shadow of some quite ordinary beggar [K].   262 *wait upon* escort.   263 *sort* associate.   265 *dreadfully
attended* have poor servants.   268 *Beggar that I am* This is intended to foster
their belief that Hamlet is suffering from disappointed ambition [K].   269–70
too dear a halfpenny too dear at the price of a halfpenny. His thanks are worth-
less, he implies, since he has no power in the state [K].   271 *justly* honestly.   280
consonancy harmony, accord.   282–3 *by what . . . withal* by anything more
sacred still that a better talker might urge in appealing to you [K]. *can charge*
Q²; F¹, K: "could charge."   283 *even* frank.   289 *prevent* forestall.

your discovery, and your secrecy to the King and Queen 290
moult no feather. I have of late — but wherefore I know
not — lost all my mirth, forgone all custom of exercises;
and indeed, it goes so heavily with my disposition that
this goodly frame, the earth, seems to me a sterile promontory; this most excellent canopy, the air, look you, 295
this brave o'erhanging firmament, this majestical roof
fretted with golden fire — why, it appeareth nothing to
me but a foul and pestilent congregation of vapours.
What a piece of work is a man! how noble in reason!
how infinite in faculties! in form and moving how ex- 300
press and admirable! in action how like an angel! in apprehension how like a god! the beauty of the world, the
paragon of animals! And yet to me what is this quintessence of dust? Man delights not me — nor woman neither, though by your smiling you seem to say so.   305

ROS.   My lord, there was no such stuff in my thoughts.

HAM.   Why did you laugh then, when I said "Man delights
        not me"?

ROS.   To think, my lord, if you delight not in man, what
        lenten entertainment the players shall receive from you. 310
        We coted them on the way, and hither are they coming
        to offer you service.

HAM.   He that plays the king shall be welcome — his Majesty

---

290 *discovery* confession, disclosure.   291 *moult no feather* i.e. be left unim-
paired. A hawk when it cast or shed (moulted) its feathers was useless and could
not be flown.   294 *frame* fabric, structure.   294–5 *sterile promontory* barren
rocky point jutting out into a sea of eternity [ᴋ].   296 *brave* splendid.   297
fretted adorned with fretwork — like the ceiling of a magnificent hall [ᴋ].   297–8
nothing to me but Q²; F¹, ᴋ: "no other thing than."   300 *faculties* mental powers.
express precisely adapted to its purpose — like a delicately adjusted piece of
mechanism [ᴋ].   303 *quintessence* finest extract or sublimation (a term from
alchemy).   304 *nor woman* Q²; F¹, ᴋ: "no, nor woman."   310 *lenten entertainment* poor reception.   311 *coted* passed.   314 *adventurous knight* knight errant,
wandering in search of adventures.   315 *foil and target* sword and small shield.
316 *humourous man* eccentric man, suffering from a particular whimsical trait,
often a stock character in Elizabethan plays.   316–18 *the clown . . . o' th' sere*
F¹; not in Q². *tickle o' th' sere* like a "hair trigger," ever ready to go off.   318–19
the lady . . . for't the lady shall speak her mind freely (as ladies like to do) even
if that should spoil the regularity of the metre [ᴋ].   *halt* limp.   322 *residence*

shall have tribute of me; the adventurous knight shall
use his foil and target; the lover shall not sigh gratis; 315
the humorous man shall end his part in peace; the
clown shall make those laugh whose lungs are tickle o'
th' sere; and the lady shall say her mind freely, or the
blank verse shall halt for't. What players are they?

ROS.   Even those you were wont to take such delight in, the 320
tragedians of the city.

HAM.   How chances it they travel? Their residence, both in
reputation and profit, was better both ways.

ROS.   I think their inhibition comes by the means of the late
innovation.   325

HAM.   Do they hold the same estimation they did when I was
in the city? Are they so follow'd?

ROS.   No indeed are they not.

HAM.   How comes it? Do they grow rusty?

ROS.   Nay, their endeavour keeps in the wonted pace; but 330
there is, sir, an eyrie of children, little eyases, that cry
out on the top of question and are most tyrannically
clapp'd for't. These are now the fashion, and so berattle
the common stages (so they call them) that many wearing rapiers are afraid of goose-quills and dare scarce 335
come thither.

HAM.   What, are they children? Who maintains 'em? How are

---

remaining at home (rather than travelling). **324–5** *their inhibition . . . late
innovation* what hinders them from remaining at home is the new fashion. This
fashion is the emergence of companies of child actors as rivals to the adult companies, rather than any specific government decree restricting players, as has
sometimes been supposed. **329–52** *How comes it . . . load too* F¹; not in Q², perhaps because Queen Anne of Denmark had taken the Children of the Chapel
Royal under her protection. **331** *eyrie* nest or brood — used only of birds of
prey [K]. *eyases* young hawks. **331–2** *cry . . . question* shriek out their speeches
in a key above that of natural talk — referring to the "childish treble" of the
youngsters' voices. "Question" often means "talk" or "conversation" [K]. **333–4**
berattle . . . stages In their plays these children berate the adult theatres, which
they style contemptuously "the common stages" [K]. **334–6** *many wearing . . .
thither* many gentlemen are so afraid of satirical pens that they hardly dare visit
an ordinary theatre lest the world think them behind the times. The "goosequills"
are the pens of the poets who, in writing plays for the child actors, insert speeches
berating "common stages" as unfit to be patronized by any person of taste [K].

they escoted? Will they pursue the quality no longer
than they can sing? Will they not say afterwards, if
they should grow themselves to common players (as it 340
is most like, if their means are no better), their writers
do them wrong to make them exclaim against their own
succession.

ROS.   Faith, there has been much to do on both sides; and the
nation holds it no sin to tarre them to controversy. 345
There was, for a while, no money bid for argument unless the poet and the player went to cuffs in the question.

HAM.   Is't possible?

GUIL.   O, there has been much throwing about of brains.   350

HAM.   Do the boys carry it away?

ROS.   Ay, that they do, my lord — Hercules and his load too.

HAM.   It is not very strange; for my uncle is King of Denmark,
and those that would make mouths at him while my
father lived give twenty, forty, fifty, a hundred ducats 355
apiece for his picture in little. 'Sblood, there is something in this more than natural, if philosophy could
find it out.

Flourish for the Players.

GUIL.   There are the players.

HAM.   Gentlemen, you are welcome to Elsinore. Your hands. 360

338 *escoted* supported (financially).   339–43 *Will they . . . own succession* will
they give up the stage when their voices change? If not, they must become "common players" in the course of time, and then they may well blame their authors
for having put into their mouths satirical attacks on their own "succession," i.e.
on what they themselves are going to be by-and-by [K].   *most like* POPE; F¹: "like
most."   344 *to do* ado.   *on both sides* The grown-up players had retorted by
satirizing the child actors [K].   345 *tarre* egg on, incite.   346 *bid for argument*
paid for a plot.   347–8 *question* dialogue. For a time no play was saleable unless
it embodied a quarrelsome dialogue between a Poet and a Player (on the subject
of the grown-up actors and the children's companies) [K].   352 *Hercules and his
load* A possible allusion to the Globe theatre, which is said to have had Hercules
holding up the world (his load) on its signboard.   354 *mouths* grimaces (Q²; F¹,
K: "mowes").   356 *picture in little* miniature.   *'Sblood* by God's blood.   357
philosophy science.   361 *Come then* Q²; F¹, K: "Come."   362 *comply . . . garb*

Come then, th' appurtenance of welcome is fashion
and ceremony. Let me comply with you in this garb,
lest my extent to the players (which I tell you must
show fairly outwards) should more appear like entertainment than yours. You are welcome. But my uncle- 365
father and aunt-mother are deceiv'd.

GUIL.   In what, my dear lord?

HAM.   I am but mad north-north-west. When the wind is
southerly I know a hawk from a handsaw.

Enter Polonius.

POL.   Well be with you, gentlemen!   370

HAM.   Hark you, Guildenstern — and you too — at each ear a
hearer! That great baby you see there is not yet out of
his swaddling clouts.

ROS.   Happily he's the second time come to them; for they
say an old man is twice a child.   375

HAM.   I will prophesy he comes to tell me of the players. Mark
it. — You say right, sir; a Monday morning; 'twas then
indeed.

POL.   My lord, I have news to tell you.

HAM.   My lord, I have news to tell you. When Roscius was 380
an actor in Rome —

POL.   The actors are come hither, my lord.

HAM.   Buzz, buzz!

---

use compliments (of cordiality) [ᴋ].   363 *extent* display of cordiality.   364 *show*
appear.   364–5 *entertainment* welcome.   369 *I know a hawk from a handsaw* A
proverb: "I can distinguish between things that do not resemble each other at
all"; "I have some little common sense and discrimination." Some think the
proverb was taken from the sport of falconry and was originally "to know a
hawk from a hernshaw (a heron)" but it has not been found in that form, and
the corruption, if there be one, is probably older than Shakespeare's time [ᴋ].
377–8 *then indeed* Q²; F¹, ᴋ: "so indeed."   380–1 *When Roscius . . . Rome* Since
Roscius lived in Cicero's time, the remark might well inform Polonius that his
news is stale news; but the old man takes it as mere madness and goes on with
the speech which Hamlet has interrupted [ᴋ].   383 *Buzz* chatter. A rude exclamation signifying that Hamlet takes no interest in what Polonius says, and
perhaps also that his news is old news [ᴋ].

POL.   Upon my honour —

HAM.   Then came each actor on his ass —   385

POL.   The best actors in the world, either for tragedy, com-
        edy, history, pastoral, pastoral-comical, historical-pas-
        toral, tragical-historical, tragical-comical-historical-pas-
        toral; scene individable, or poem unlimited. Seneca
        cannot be too heavy, nor Plautus too light. For the law 390
        of writ and the liberty, these are the only men.

HAM.   O Jephthah, judge of Israel, what a treasure hadst
        thou!

POL.   What treasure had he, my lord?

HAM.   Why,   395

                "One fair daughter, and no more,
                The which he loved passing well."

POL.   [aside] Still on my daughter.

HAM.   Am I not i' th' right, old Jephthah?

POL.   If you call me Jephthah, my lord, I have a daughter   400
        that I love passing well.

HAM.   Nay, that follows not.

POL.   What follows then, my lord?

HAM.   Why,

                "As by lot, God wot,"   405

        and then, you know,

388-9 *tragical-historical, tragical-comical-historical-pastoral* F¹; not in Q². 389
scene individable, or poem unlimited dramas that observe the unities of place
and time, and also those which give no heed to such limitations [K]. *Seneca* the
most influential of Roman writers of tragedy in Shakespeare's day. 390 *Plautus*
one of the most influential of comic writers, the other being Terrence. *light* (a)
frivolous, inconsequential (b) wanton, licentious. 390-1 *law of writ and the liberty*
plays written according to the orthodox critical rules, and those not written by
these rules. 392 *Jephthah* He killed his only daughter after vowing, in return
for victory, that he would kill the first person he saw after defeating the Am-
monites. See JUDGES, XI. The ballad was a popular one, extant in various forms.
401 *passing* surpassingly. 408 *row* stanza. *chanson* ballad. 409 *my abridgment*
that which cuts short my speech — the players. 411-12 *old friend* Q²; F¹, K: "my
old friend." 412 *valanc'd* fringed (with a beard). 414 *lady* the boy who played

"It came to pass, as most like it was."

The first row of the pious chanson will show you more; for look where my abridgment comes

Enter four or five Players.

You are welcome, masters; welcome, all. — I am glad 410
to see thee well. — Welcome, good friends. — O, old
friend! Why, thy face is valanc'd since I saw thee last.
Com'st thou to beard me in Denmark? — What, my
young lady and mistress? By'r Lady, your ladyship is
nearer to heaven than when I saw you last by the alti- 415
tude of a chopine. Pray God your voice, like a piece of
uncurrent gold, be not crack'd within the ring. — Masters, you are all welcome. We'll e'en to't like French-
falconers, fly at anything we see. We'll have a speech
straight. Come, give us a taste of your quality. Come, a 420
passionate speech.

1. PLAY. What speech, my good lord?

HAM.   I heard thee speak me a speech once, but it was never
acted; or if it was, not above once; for the play, I remember, pleas'd not the million, 'twas caviary to the 425
general; but it was (as I receiv'd it, and others, whose
judgments in such matters cried in the top of mine) an
excellent play, well digested in the scenes, set down with
as much modesty as cunning. I remember one said there
were no sallets in the lines to make the matter savoury, 430

---

female roles.   416 *chopine* lady's thick-soled shoe, worn to make her appear
taller.   417 *crack'd* A coin would not pass if it had a crack extending from
the edge to a point inside the circle that surrounded the monarch's head or other
device. Hamlet's pun is clear enough. He hopes that the boy's voice is not so
cracked as to spoil its "ring" — that it is still "as clear as a bell" [K].   418 *French*
Q¹, F¹; Q²: "friendly."   419 *fly . . . see* let the hawk fly in quest of any bird in sight;
undertake anything, no matter how difficult [K].   420 *quality* professional skill.
421 *passionate* emotional.   425–6 *caviary to the general* a delicacy not appreciated
by the general run of playgoers [K]. "Caviary" (the original form of the word)
was a novelty in Shakespeare's England, fondness for which was a taste which
had to be acquired.   427 *cried in the top of* were of more authority than.   429
modesty, moderation. *cunning* skill.   430 *sallets* salads; hence, figuratively, highly
seasoned or spicy passages [K].

nor no matter in the phrase that might indict the author
of affectation; but call'd it an honest method, as wholesome as sweet, and by very much more handsome than
fine. One speech in't I chiefly lov'd. 'Twas Æneas' tale
to Dido, and thereabout of it especially where he speaks   435
of Priam's slaughter. If it live in your memory, begin at
this line — let me see, let me see:

"The rugged Pyrrhus, like th' Hyrcanian beast — "

'Tis not so; it begins with Pyrrhus:

"The rugged Pyrrhus, he whose sable arms,   440
Black as his purpose, did the night resemble
When he lay couched in the ominous horse,
Hath now this dread and black complexion smear'd
With heraldry more dismal. Head to foot
Now is he total gules, horridly trick'd   445
With blood of fathers, mothers, daughters, sons,
Bak'd and impasted with the parching streets,
That lend a tyrannous and a damned light
To their lord's murder. Roasted in wrath and fire,
And thus o'ersized with coagulate gore,   450
With eyes like carbuncles, the hellish Pyrrhus
Old grandsire Priam seeks."

So, proceed you.

POL.   Fore God, my lord, well spoken, with good accent and
good discretion.   455

1. PLAY.   "Anon he finds him,
Striking too short at Greeks. His antique sword,

---

432 *affectation* F¹; Q²: "affection." *honest* in good taste.   432-4 *as wholesome
. . . than fine* Q²; not in F¹. *wholesome* sound and clear.   *more handsome than
fine* elegant, but not gaudy or over-decorated [K].   434-5 *Æneas' . . . Dido*
In Marlowe's play, DIDO QUEEN OF CARTHAGE, there is a long speech, which
Shakespeare may have known, in which Æneas tells Dido the story of the
fall of Troy and Priam's death, following closely the second book of Virgil's
ÆNEID.   438 *Pyrrhus* the son of Achilles. *Hyrcanian beast* Hyrcania was a region
in Asia famous for its tigers.   442 *couched* hidden.   444 *dismal* ill-omened.
445 *gules* red (a heraldic term).   *trick'd* adorned.   447 *impasted* turned into a
crust, baked.   *parching* burning. The city was on fire.   450 *o'ersized* glued over.
coagulate clotted.   451 *carbuncles* jewels believed to emit light.   457 *antique
sword* that which he had used in his youth.   459 *Repugnant to command* refus-

Rebellious to his arm, lies where it falls,
Repugnant to command. Unequal match'd,
Pyrrhus at Priam drives, in rage strikes wide;   460
But with the whiff and wind of his fell sword
Th' unnerved father falls. Then senseless Ilium,
Seeming to feel this blow, with flaming top
Stoops to his base, and with a hideous crash
Takes prisoner Pyrrhus' ear. For lo! his sword,   465
Which was declining on the milky head
Of reverend Priam, seem'd i' th' air to stick.
So, as a painted tyrant, Pyrrhus stood,
And, like a neutral to his will and matter,
Did nothing.   470
But, as we often see, against some storm,
A silence in the heavens, the rack stand still,
The bold winds speechless, and the orb below
As hush as death — anon the dreadful thunder
Doth rend the region; so, after Pyrrhus' pause,   475
Aroused vengeance sets him new awork;
And never did the Cyclops' hammers fall
On Mars's armour, forg'd for proof eterne,
With less remorse than Pyrrhus' bleeding sword
Now falls on Priam.   480
Out, out, thou strumpet Fortune! All you gods,
In general synod take away her power;
Break all the spokes and fellies from her wheel,
And bowl the round nave down the hill of heaven,
As low as to the fiends!"   485

POL.   This is too long.

---

ing to be used.   461 *fell* cruel.   462 *unnerved* feeble in sinew [K].   *Then* . . .
Ilium F¹; not in Q². *senseless* having no feeling. *Ilium* Used in the medieval sense
of the "arx" (citadel) of Troy, not of Troy as a whole [K].   464 *his* its.   466 *declining* bending toward.   469 *like . . . matter* "His will" means "his purpose";
"his matter," "the accomplishment of his purpose." As a neutral stands between
two parties, so Pyrrhus paused midway between his purpose and its fulfillment
[K].   471 *against* just before.   472 *rack* clouds.   473 *orb* round earth.   475 *the
region* the sky.   477 *Cyclops'* The Cyclopes were the gigantic workmen of Vulcan
(Hephæstus), the god of smith's work and the manufacture of armour [K].   478
for proof externe to stand the test forever [K].   479 *remorse* pity.   483 *fellies* seg-
ments of the rim of a wooden wheel.   484 *nave* hub.

HAM.   It shall to the barbers, with your beard. — Prithee say
        on. He's for a jig or a tale of bawdry, or he sleeps. Say
        on; come to Hecuba.

1. PLAY.   But who, ah woe! had seen the mobled queen —   490

HAM.   "The mobled queen"?

POL.   That's good! "Mobled queen" is good.

1. PLAY.   "Run barefoot up and down, threat'ning the flames
            With bisson rheum; a clout upon that head
            Where late the diadem stood, and for a robe,   495
            About her lank and all o'erteemed loins,
            A blanket, in the alarm of fear caught up —
            Who this had seen, with tongue in venom steep'd
            'Gainst Fortune's state would treason have pronounc'd.
            But if the gods themselves did see her then,   500
            When she saw Pyrrhus make malicious sport
            In mincing with his sword her husband's limbs,
            The instant burst of clamour that she made
            (Unless things mortal move them not at all)
            Would have made milch the burning eyes of heaven   505
            And passion in the gods."

POL.   Look, whe'r he has not turn'd his colour, and has tears
        in's eyes. Prithee no more!

HAM.   'Tis well. I'll have thee speak out the rest of this soon.
        — Good my lord, will you see the players well bestow'd?   510
        Do you hear? Let them be well us'd; for they are the

488 *a jig* a short comic dialogue in song and with dance, often performed at the
end of Elizabethan plays.   490 *ah woe* Q⁴; Q²: "a woe"; F¹, K: "O who." *mobled*
muffled. The word is unusual and strikes Hamlet as odd. Polonius, however, ad-
mires it just because it is unusual. He also wishes to soothe Hamlet's irritation by
finding something to praise in the Player's speech [K].   492 *Mobled . . . good*
F¹; not in Q².   494 *bisson rheum* blinding tears. *clout* cloth.   496 *o'erteemed*
worn out by childbearing. She had borne fifty-two.   499 *state* government (of
the world).   504 *Unless . . . at all* unless the Epicurean doctrine be true, that
the gods live in unruffled calm and are never disturbed by sympathy for mankind [K].   505 *milch* flowing with tears; literally, yielding milk [K]. *eyes* the
stars.   507 *wh'er* whether.   510 *bestow'd* lodged and taken care of.   511–12
they are . . . the time they summarize and record the events of the time.   516
God's bodykins A common grotesque oath. "Bodykins" means "little body," i.e.

abstract and brief chronicles of the time. After your
death you were better have a bad epitaph than their ill
report while you live.

POL.   My lord, I will use them according to their desert.   515

HAM.   God's bodykins, man, much better! Use every man after
his desert, and who shall scape whipping? Use them
after your own honour and dignity. The less they de-
serve, the more merit is in your bounty. Take them in.

POL.   Come, sirs.   520

HAM.   Follow him, friends. We'll hear a play to-morrow.

    Exeunt Polonius *and* Players [*except
    the First*].

Dost thou hear me, old friend? Can you play "The
Murder of Gonzago"?

1. PLAY.   Ay, my lord.

HAM.   We'll ha't to-morrow night. You could, for a need, study   525
a speech of some dozen or sixteen lines which I would
set down and insert in't, could you not?

1. PLAY.   Ay, my lord.

HAM.   Very well. Follow that lord — and look you mock him
not. [*Exit* First Player.] My good friends, I'll leave you   530
till night. You are welcome to Elsinore.

ROS.   Good my lord!

---

the "host" or "consecrated wafer" [K] (F¹; Q²: "bodkin," a common variant form).
517 *who shall* Q²; F¹, K: "who should."   518 *after* according to.   522–3 *The
Murder of Gonzago* No such drama is known, nor is it likely that it ever existed
apart from the tragedy of HAMLET. Plays within plays, however, were common
[K].   526 *dozen or sixteen lines* Much ingenuity has been wasted in identifying
Hamlet's dozen or sixteen lines, as if we were to suppose that Shakespeare wrote
THE MURDER OF GONZAGO without them and then inserted them somewhere [K].
529–30 *mock him not* Another indication of Hamlet's courtesy. He himself can
poke fun at Polonius, for his mockery will pass as madness and is therefore not an
insult. But it would be quite another thing for the players to make sport of the old
nobleman, and Hamlet is alive to the temptation they might feel to follow his
own example, especially since they may not have heard of his supposed madness
[K].

HAM.   Ay, so, God b' wi' ye!

> *Exeunt* [Rosencrantz *and* Guilden-
> stern].

> Now I am alone.
> O, what a rogue and peasant slave am I!
> Is it not monstrous that this player here,   535
> But in a fiction, in a dream of passion,
> Could force his soul so to his own conceit
> That, from her working, all his visage wann'd,
> Tears in his eyes, distraction in's aspect,
> A broken voice, and his whole function suiting   540
> With forms to his conceit? And all for nothing!
> For Hecuba!
> What's Hecuba to him, or he to Hecuba,
> That he should weep for her? What would he do,
> Had he the motive and the cue for passion   545
> That I have? He would drown the stage with tears
> And cleave the general ear with horrid speech;
> Make mad the guilty and appal the free,
> Confound the ignorant, and amaze indeed
> The very faculties of eyes and ears.   550
> Yet I,
> A dull and muddy-mettled rascal, peak
> Like John-a-dreams, unpregnant of my cause,
> And can say nothing! No, not for a king,
> Upon whose property and most dear life   555

---

537 *Could . . . conceit* could force his soul into such accord with his conception
(of the part he played) that by the operation of his soul (upon his bodily powers),
his whole face grew pale [K].   540 *whole function* all the powers of his body.
541 *forms to his conceit* appearances to match his conception of his role.   543 *to
Hecuba* F¹; Q²: "to her."   548 *Make mad . . . free* By his description of the
crime he would drive those spectators mad who had any such sin on their
conscience, and would horrify even the innocent [K].   549 *the ignorant* those
who had not intelligence enough to comprehend the actor's words [K]. *amaze*
paralyze, stun.   552 *A dull . . . rascal* a stupid and poor-spirited wretch [K].
peak go around moping and pining.   553 *Like John a-dreams* like one in a
dream. *unpregnant* with no real feeling, without plans for executing.   556
defeat destruction. *Am I a coward* See Supplementary Notes.   559-60 *gives
. . . lungs* insults me by calling me the worst kind of liar.   562 *pigeon-
liver'd* The supposed gentleness of the dove was explained in the old physiology on

A damn'd defeat was made. Am I a coward?
Who calls me villain? breaks my pate across?
Plucks off my beard and blows it in my face?
Tweaks me by th' nose? gives me the lie i' th' throat
As deep as to the lungs? Who does me this, ha?   560
'Swounds, I should take it! for it cannot be
But I am pigeon-liver'd and lack gall
To make oppression bitter, or ere this
I should have fatted all the region kites,
With this slave's offal. Bloody, bawdy villain!   565
Remorseless, treacherous, lecherous, kindless villain!
O, vengeance!
Why, what an ass am I! This is most brave,
That I, the son of a dear father murder'd,
Prompted to my revenge by heaven and hell,   570
Must (like a whore) unpack my heart with words
And fall a-cursing like a very drab,
A scullion!
Fie upon't! foh! About, my brains! Hum, I have heard
That guilty creatures, sitting at a play,   575
Have by the very cunning of the scene
Been struck so to the soul that presently
They have proclaim'd their malefactions;
For murder, though it have no tongue, will speak
With most miraculous organ. I'll have these players   580
Play something like the murder of my father
Before mine uncle. I'll observe his looks;
I'll tent him to the quick. If 'a do blench,

---

the theory that it had no gall and hence no bitterness or capacity for resentment
[K].   564 *the region kites* the kites (bird of prey) of the air.   565 *offal* guts.
566 *Remorseless* without pity.   *kindless* unnatural.   567 *O, vengeance* F¹; not in
Q², and possibly an actor's interpolation.   568 *brave* fine, noble.   569 *father* Q³;
not in Q², F¹.   570 *by heaven and hell* Heaven prompts him to revenge because
his uncle deserves death; hell, because he is actuated by anger and hatred [K].
571 *unpack* unload, relieve.   572 *drab* whore.   573 *scullion* kitchen wench (F¹; Q²:
"stallyon," which some editors prefer as meaning "a male whore").   574 *About*
go to work.   *brains* Q²; F¹, K: "brain."   579–80 *For murder . . . organ* That
"murder will out" is an ancient notion. Hamlet may be referring specifically to
the old folk belief that when a corpse was approached by its murderer, the
"tongues" of its wounds (like mouths) would bleed afresh and thus accuse the
murderer.   583 *tent* probe.   *'a do* Q²; F¹, K: "he but."   *blench* flinch.

I know my course. The spirit that I have seen
May be a devil; and the devil hath power   585
T' assume a pleasing shape; yea, and perhaps
Out of my weakness and my melancholy,
As he is very potent with such spirits,
Abuses me to damn me. I'll have grounds
More relative than this. The play's the thing   590
Wherein I'll catch the conscience of the King.   *Exit.*

---

588 *such spirits* such conditions of one's temperament [K].   589 *Abuses* deceives,
deludes (by appearing in the likeness of my father and falsely accusing my uncle
of murder [K].   *damn me* by persuading me to kill an innocent man [K].   590
More relative referring back more surely from the evidence to the fact — hence,
more positive and cogent, more conclusive [K].
III.I. 1 *drift of conference* leading him on in conversation.   *conference* Q²; F¹, K:

[Act Three

SCENE I. *Elsinore. A room in the Castle.*]

Enter King, Queen, Polonius, Ophelia, Rosencrantz, Guildenstern, *and* Lords.

KING.　And can you by no drift of conference
　　　　Get from him why he puts on this confusion,
　　　　Grating so harshly all his days of quiet
　　　　With turbulent and dangerous lunacy?

ROS.　He does confess he feels himself distracted,　　5
　　　　But from what cause 'a will by no means speak.

GUIL.　Nor do we find him forward to be sounded,
　　　　But with a crafty madness keeps aloof
　　　　When we would bring him on to some confession
　　　　Of his true state.

QUEEN.　　　　　　　　Did he receive you well?　　10

ROS.　Most like a gentleman.

GUIL.　But with much forcing of his disposition.

ROS.　Niggard of question, but of our demands
　　　　Most free in his reply.

"circumstance."　2 *puts on this confusion* acts in this distracted manner.　3 *Grating* disturbing, irritating.　6 *'a* Q²; F¹, ᴋ: "he."　7 *forward* eager, ready. *sounded* probed, examined.　12 *disposition* mood; inclination at the time (not, general disposition). Guildenstern is no fool, and he has seen the effort which it costs Hamlet to be cordial [ᴋ].　13 *Niggard of* sparing of, reluctant to engage in. *question* conversation (not "interrogation").　*of our demands* to our questions.

QUEEN.   Did you assay him
          To any pastime?   15

ROS.   Madam, it so fell out that certain players
          We o'erraught on the way. Of these we told him,
          And there did seem in him a kind of joy
          To hear of it. They are here about the court,
          And, as I think, they have already order   20
          This night to play before him.

POL.   'Tis most true;
          And he beseech'd me to entreat your Majesties
          To hear and see the matter.

KING.   With all my heart, and it doth much content me
          To hear him so inclin'd.   25
          Good gentlemen, give him a further edge
          And drive his purpose into these delights.

ROS.   We shall, my lord.

                    Exeunt Rosencrantz *and* Guilden-
                    stern.

KING.   Sweet Gertrude, leave us too;
          For we have closely sent for Hamlet hither,
          That he, as 'twere by accident, may here   30
          Affront Ophelia.
          Her father and myself (lawful espials)
          Will so bestow ourselves that, seeing unseen,
          We may of their encounter frankly judge

14–15 *assay . . . pastime* try to attract him to any sport or amusement, in order
to relieve his mind [K].   17 *o'erraught* overtook and passed.   23 *the matter* the
subject matter — the performance.   24 *content* please. Claudius is genuinely eager
to live at peace with his stepson for two reasons — his own safety, and his love
for the Queen, who is naturally distressed by the present situation. It is only
after he learns that Hamlet knows of the murder, and there can be no peace
between them (that is, after the play within the play), that he takes measures to
destroy Hamlet [K].   26 *edge* encouragement.   27 *into* Q²; F¹, K: "on To."   29
closely privately.   31 *Affront* meet face to face.   32 *lawful espials* being justified
in spying upon him (F¹; not in Q²).   33 *bestow* station.   34 *encounter* meeting,
interview.   35 *as he is behav'd* according to how he acts.   40–2 *So shall . . .
honours* This conveys to Ophelia and her father a suggestion that the marriage
which Polonius had thought impossible (II.II.141–2) would be quite agreeable to

And gather by him, as he is behav'd,   35
If't be th' affliction of his love, or no,
That thus he suffers for.

QUEEN.   I shall obey you;
And for your part, Ophelia, I do wish
That your good beauties be the happy cause
Of Hamlet's wildness. So shall I hope your virtues   40
Will bring him to his wonted way again,
To both your honours.

OPH.   Madam, I wish it may.

                    [*Exit* Queen.]

POL.   Ophelia, walk you here. — Gracious, so please you,
We will bestow ourselves. — [*To* Ophelia] Read on this
    book,
That show of such an exercise may colour   45
Your loneliness. — We are oft to blame in this,
'Tis too much prov'd, that with devotion's visage
And pious action we do sugar o'er
The devil himself.

KING.   [*aside*]   O, 'tis too true!
How smart a lash that speech doth give my conscience! 50
The harlot's cheek, beautied with plast'ring art,
Is not more ugly to the thing that helps it
Than is my deed to my most painted word.
O heavy burden!

---

the King and Queen [K].   41 *wonted* customary, usual.   44 *book* A prayer book
(see line 89) or some book of devotion, as the word "exercise" (for "religious exercise") suggests [K].   45 *colour* give a specious (colourable) pretext to [K].   46
loneliness F¹; Q²: "lowlines."   46 *to blame* blameworthy, culpable. Polonius does
not mean that Ophelia is doing wrong. He simply moralizes the situation in a
general way. A young woman with a prayer book, but not praying, is a good
emblem for the hypocrisy of us mortals [K].   47 *prov'd* found true by experience.
49–54 *O, 'tis . . . burden* The audience is here for the first time clearly informed
of Claudius' guilt and that the Ghost was "honest" and not a demon. It must have
this information in preparation for the "play-within-the-play" scene to follow.
See Supplementary Notes.   52 *to* in comparison with. The haggard cheek under
the paint is ugly in contrast with the paint that beautifies it [K].

POL.   I hear him coming. Let's withdraw, my lord.   55

                        Exeunt [King *and* Polonius].

                  Enter Hamlet.

HAM.   To be, or not to be — that is the question:
       Whether 'tis nobler in the mind to suffer
       The slings and arrows of outrageous fortune
       Or to take arms against a sea of troubles,
       And by opposing end them. To die — to sleep —   60
       No more; and by a sleep to say we end
       The heartache, and the thousand natural shocks
       That flesh is heir to. 'Tis a consummation
       Devoutly to be wish'd. To die — to sleep.
       To sleep — perchance to dream: ay, there's the rub!   65
       For in that sleep of death what dreams may come
       When we have shuffled off this mortal coil,
       Must give us pause. There's the respect
       That makes calamity of so long life.
       For who would bear the whips and scorns of time,   70
       Th' oppressor's wrong, the proud man's contumely,
       The pangs of despis'd love, the law's delay,
       The insolence of office, and the spurns
       That patient merit of th' unworthy takes,
       When he himself might his quietus make   75
       With a bare bodkin? Who would fardels bear,
       To grunt and sweat under a weary life,

---

56 *To be, or not to be* to live or to die. Hamlet is thinking of suicide. But see Supplementary Notes. There has been much diversity of opinion as to the meaning of the soliloquy.   63 *consummation* final settlement of everything [K].   65 *the rub* the impediment, the difficulty. A metaphor from bowls. A "rub" is any obstruction which hinders or deflects the course of the bowl [K].   67 *shuffled off* cast off as an encumbrance.   *mortal coil* (a) the tumult and turmoil of human affairs (b) the human body, the wrapping of flesh which entangles the soul and which may be "shuffled" off by the death.   68 *respect* consideration.   69 *of so long life* so long-lived, so lasting. If it were not for this impediment, Hamlet argues, no one would endure calamity long [K].   71 *contumely* insulting behaviour.   73–4 *the spurns . . . takes* the insults which good, long-suffering men must take from evil men in positions of authority.   75 *his quietus make* settle his own account [K].   76 *a bare bodkin* a mere dagger.   *fardels* burdens (Q²; F¹, K: "these fardels").   77 *grunt* groan. Not an undignified word in Elizabethan times [K].   79 *undiscover'd* unexplored.   *bourn* confines; literally, boundary.   80 *No*

But that the dread of something after death —
The undiscover'd country, from whose bourn
No traveller returns — puzzles the will,   80
And makes us rather bear those ills we have
Than fly to others that we know not of?
Thus conscience does make cowards of us all,
And thus the native hue of resolution
Is sicklied o'er with the pale cast of thought,   85
And enterprises of great pitch and moment
With this regard their currents turn awry
And lose the name of action. — Soft you now!
The fair Ophelia! — Nymph, in thy orisons
Be all my sins rememb'red.

OPH.   Good my lord,   90
How does your honour for this many a day?

HAM.   I humbly thank you; well, well, well.

OPH.   My lord, I have remembrances of yours
That I have longed long to re-deliver.
I pray you, now receive them.

HAM.   No, not I!   95
I never gave you aught.

OPH.   My honour'd lord, you know right well you did,
And with them words of so sweet breath compos'd
As made the things more rich. Their perfume lost,

---

traveller returns Critics have worried over this, since, they remark, the Ghost had
returned. But Hamlet is thinking of human beings, not of ghosts [K]. It may be,
however, as has been suggested, that Hamlet in his dejection has given up all
hope that the Ghost may have actually been his father's spirit.   83 *conscience*
consciousness, reflection, consideration.   84 *native* The natural complexion of
resolution is ruddy or sanguine [K].   85 *cast* shade (of colour).   *thought* melancholy, despondency.   86 *pitch* height — the highest point reached by a soaring
falcon (Q²; F¹, K: "pith").   *moment* importance.   87 *regard* consideration.   89
Nymph A courtly way of addressing a lady, not uncommon in the old language
of compliment. [K]. Whether Hamlet is being serious or ironical in this
greeting has been much debated.   *orisons* prayers.   92 *well, well, well* F¹;
Q²: "well."   95–6 *No . . . aught* Several explanations are possible: (a) the gifts
I gave were too trivial to really be called gifts (b) those things I gave were un-
important since I did not really give my heart (c) I am not the Hamlet who gave
those things; therefore beware of me. See Supplementary Notes.

Take these again; for to the noble mind   100
Rich gifts wax poor when givers prove unkind.
There, my lord.

HAM.   Ha, ha! Are you honest?

OPH.   My lord?

HAM.   Are you fair?   105

OPH.   What means your lordship?

HAM.   That if you be honest and fair, your honesty should admit no discourse to your beauty.

OPH.   Could beauty, my lord, have better commerce than with
honesty?   110

HAM.   Ay, truly; for the power of beauty will sooner transform
honesty from what it is to a bawd than the force of
honesty can translate beauty into his likeness. This was
sometime a paradox, but now the time gives it proof. I
did love you once.   115

OPH.   Indeed, my lord, you made me believe so.

HAM.   You should not have believ'd me; for virtue cannot so
inoculate our old stock but we shall relish of it. I loved
you not.

OPH.   I was the more deceived.   120

HAM.   Get thee to a nunnery! Why wouldst thou be a breeder
of sinners? I am myself indifferent honest, but yet I could

---

103 *honest* chaste. It has been conjectured that the change in Hamlet's tone is
due to his awareness of the plot against him, either because he sees a movement
behind the arras, or because he has heard the conversation at II.ii.160–7.   107–8
admit . . . beauty not permit your beauty to be used for dishonest purposes (as a
decoy to entrap me).   109 *commerce* intercourse, association.   113 *translate*
transform.   114 *sometime* formerly.   *now . . . proof* Hamlet is thinking of
his mother's sin, which well might make him feel that there is no purity left in
the world [K].   117–18 *cannot so . . . stock* cannot, by grafting, so change our
sinful nature (inherited from Adam) that we shall not still have some flavour of
it. The figure is that of a crabtree (a wild apple) in which a bud or shoot of a
better sort has been set as a graft. The fruit, Hamlet says, will still taste of the
old stock [K].   121 *nunnery* Only by complete withdrawal from the world, he
says, can she avoid becoming a breeder of sinners. It is not likely that Hamlet
here is using the word with its common slang meaning of "brothel," as has sometimes been suggested.   122 *indifferent honest* tolerably virtuous.   124–5 *ambitious*

accuse me of such things that it were better my mother
had not borne me. I am very proud, revengeful, ambitious; with more offences at my beck than I have   125
thoughts to put them in, imagination to give them
shape, or time to act them in. What should such fellows
as I do, crawling between earth and heaven? We are
arrant knaves all; believe none of us. Go thy ways to a
nunnery. Where's your father?   130

OPH.   At home, my lord.

HAM.   Let the doors be shut upon him, that he may play the
fool nowhere but in's own house. Farewell.

OPH.   O, help him, you sweet heavens!

HAM.   If thou dost marry, I'll give thee this plague for thy   135
dowry: be thou as chaste as ice, as pure as snow, thou
shalt not escape calumny. Get thee to a nunnery. Go,
farewell. Or if thou wilt needs marry, marry a fool; for
wise men know well enough what monsters you make of
them. To a nunnery, go; and quickly too. Farewell.   140

OPH.   O heavenly powers, restore him!

HAM.   I have heard of your paintings too, well enough. God
hath given you one face, and you make yourselves another. You jig, you amble, and you lisp; you nickname
God's creatures and make your wantonness your igno-   145
rance. Go to, I'll no more on't! it hath made me mad.
I say, we will have no moe marriages. Those that are

Whether or not Hamlet suspects that Ophelia is a decoy, or that there are
listeners, he is prudent enough to encourage the notion that Rosencrantz and
Guildenstern had formed — that thwarted ambition is the cause of his madness
(II.ii.248). Soon, however, he assigns another cause (line 146). The result is
confusion, which is what he designed [K].   130 *Where's your father* See Supplementary Notes.   139 *monsters* Alluding to the favourite Elizabethan jest of the
horns supposed to grow upon a man's head if his wife is unfaithful [K].   142
your paintings i.e. those of you ladies in general. Painting the face appears to
have been an almost universal fashion amongst Elizabethan ladies, and the
dramatists and satirists are never weary of attacking it [K].   144 *jig . . . amble*
two kinds of affected gait.   *lisp* talk in an affected manner.   144–6 *you nickname . . . ignorance* you give new and affected names to ordinary things and
then pretend that this affectation (wantonness) is due to ignorance.   147 *moe*
more.

married already — all but one — shall live; the rest shall
keep as they are. To a nunnery, go.   *Exit.*

OPH.   O, what a noble mind is here o'erthrown!   150
The courtier's, soldier's, scholar's, eye, tongue, sword,
Th' expectancy and rose of the fair state,
The glass of fashion and the mould of form,
Th' observ'd of all observers — quite, quite down!
And I, of ladies most deject and wretched,   155
That suck'd the honey of his musick'd vows,
Now see that noble and most sovereign reason,
Like sweet bells jangled, out of time and harsh;
That unmatch'd form and feature of blown youth
Blasted with ecstasy. O, woe is me   160
T' have seen what I have seen, see what I see!

Enter King *and* Polonius.

KING.   Love? his affections do not that way tend;
Nor what he spake, though it lack'd form a little,
Was not like madness. There's something in his soul
O'er which his melancholy sits on brood;   165
And I do doubt the hatch and the disclose
Will be some danger; which for to prevent,
I have in quick determination
Thus set it down: he shall with speed to England
For the demand of our neglected tribute.   170
Haply the seas, and countries different,
With variable objects, shall expel

---

149 *keep* remain.   151 *soldier's, scholar's* Q², F¹; HANMER, K: "scholar's, soldier's."
152 *expectancy* hope for the future (F¹; Q²: "expectation").   *rose* adornment —
that which makes our "fair state" beautiful.   153 *glass* mirror.   *mould of form*
perfect model for deportment and courtly manners.   154 *Th' observ'd of all
observers* he to whom all courtiers (observers) paid deference.   156 *musick'd*
sweetly spoken (Q²; F¹, K: "Musicke").   157 *most sovereign* since reason should
govern all the faculties [K].   158 *time* Q²; F¹, K: "tune."   159 *feature* F¹; Q²:
"stature."   *blown* full-blown, in full blossom.   160 *ecstasy* madness.   162 *affections* feelings, inclinations.   164 *madness* The King is uncommonly keen. Hamlet
acts the madman well enough to deceive the others, but Claudius is not quite
convinced, and henceforth he is tormented by the fear that Hamlet's insanity is
assumed for some sinister purpose [K].   166 *doubt* fear.   167 *prevent* forestall.
172 *variable objects* the variety of sights incidental to travel [K].   173 *something*

This something-settled matter in his heart,
Whereon his brains still beating puts him thus
From fashion of himself. What think you on't?   175

POL.   It shall do well. But yet do I believe
The origin and commencement of his grief
Sprung from neglected love. — How now, Ophelia?
You need not tell us what Lord Hamlet said.
We heard it all. — My lord, do as you please;   180
But if you hold it fit, after the play
Let his queen mother all alone entreat him
To show his grief. Let her be round with him;
And I'll be plac'd, so please you, in the ear
Of all their conference. If she find him not,   185
To England send him; or confine him where
Your wisdom best shall think.

KING.   It shall be so.
Madness in great ones must not unwatch'd go.

                                            Exeunt.

◇◇◇◇◇◇◇◇◇◇◇◇◇◇◇◇◇◇◇

[SCENE II. *Elsinore. A hall in the Castle.*]

Enter Hamlet *and three of the* Players.

HAM.   Speak the speech, I pray you, as I pronounc'd it to you,
trippingly on the tongue. But if you mouth it, as many
of our players do, I had as lief the town crier spoke my

---

settled somewhat settled.   *matter* subject of thought.   174–5 *Whereon . . . himself* the constant beating of his brains on which subject (whatever it is) makes
him act unnaturally [K].   176 *do well* be sure to help.   178 *neglected* un-
requited.   183 *round* outspoken, direct.   184 *in the ear* within earshot.   185
conference conversation.   *find him not* do not discover his secret trouble.

    III.II. 2 *trippingly* easily — i.e. without exaggerated emphasis or any excessive
deliberation or roundness of utterance; with an approach, therefore, to the
language of real life [K]. Hamlet's advice to the players constitutes the best
expression that we have of Shakespeare's own ideas about acting.   *mouth it*
hold it too long in the mouth, so as to dwell upon the sounds.   3 *lief* soon
(F¹, K: "live," a common variant).   *town crier* Since the town crier wishes to be
heard distinctly at some distance, he must mouth his words, and the result is a
kind of sing-song [K].

lines. Nor do not saw the air too much with your hand, thus, but use all gently; for in the very torrent, tempest, and (as I may say) whirlwind of your passion, you must acquire and beget a temperance that may give it smoothness. O, it offends me to the soul to hear a robustious periwig-pated fellow tear a passion to tatters, to very rags, to split the ears of the groundlings, who (for the most part) are capable of nothing but inexplicable dumb shows and noise. I would have such a fellow whipp'd for o'erdoing Termagant. It out-herods Herod. Pray you avoid it.

PLAYER. I warrant your honour.

HAM. Be not too tame neither; but let your own discretion be your tutor. Suit the action to the word, the word to the action; with this special observance, that you o'erstep not the modesty of nature: for anything so overdone is from the purpose of playing, whose end, both at the first and now, was and is, to hold, as 'twere, the mirror up to nature; to show virtue her own feature, scorn her own image, and the very age and body of the time his form and pressure. Now this overdone, or come tardy off, though it make the unskilful laugh, cannot but make the judicious grieve; the censure of the which one must in your allowance o'erweigh a whole theatre of others. O, there be players that I have seen play, and heard others praise, and that highly (not to speak it profanely), that, neither having the accent of Christians, nor the gait of Christian, pagan, nor man, have so

---

8 *robustious* boisterous.   9 *periwig-pated* Actors of course wore wigs, but these were not the fashion in society [K].   10 *groundlings* spectators who sat or stood in the pit (called "the yard"), which was the cheapest place in the theatre [K]. 11 *capable of* able to appreciate.   11–12 *dumb shows* brief wordless scenes giving the plot of spoken scenes to follow; by Shakespeare's time the device, common in plays of the 1580's, was almost entirely out of fashion.   13 *Termagant* a Saracen deity, proverbial for his ferocity, who appears in medieval romances. *Herod* the ranting tyrant of medieval religious drama.   16 *discretion* normal manner of behaviour.   19 *modesty* moderation.   20 *from* contrary to.   20–1 *at the first* i.e. when the art of acting was first invented [K].   22 *feature* form. 23 *the very age and body of the time* the times exactly as they are. A person's

strutted and bellowed that I have thought some of Nature's journeymen had made men, and not made them
well, they imitated humanity so abominably.

PLAYER.   I hope we have reform'd that indifferently with us, sir.   35

HAM.   O, reform it altogether! And let those that play your
clowns speak no more than is set down for them. For
there be of them that will themselves laugh, to set on
some quantity of barren spectators to laugh too, though
in the mean time some necessary question of the play   40
be then to be considered. That's villainous and shows
a most pitiful ambition in the fool that uses it. Go make
you ready.   *Exeunt* Players.

                    Enter Polonius, Rosencrantz, *and*
                    Guildenstern.

How now, my lord? Will the King hear this piece of
work?   45

POL.   And the Queen too, and that presently.

HAM.   Bid the players make haste. (*Exit* Polonius.) Will you
two help to hasten them?

BOTH.   We will, my lord.   *Exeunt they two.*

HAM.   What, ho, Horatio!   50

                    Enter Horatio.

HOR.   Here, sweet lord, at your service.

HAM.   Horatio, thou art e'en as just a man

---

general appearance is determined by two things — his "age" and his "body" (i.e.
his form or "build") [K].   *his* its.   24 *pressure* shape — literally, impression, as
in wax [K].   24–5 *come tardy off* not executed with sufficient spirit and vigour
[K].   25 *unskilful* the injudicious or undiscriminating among the audience [K].
26 *censure of the which one* opinion of a single one of whom.   27 *in your
allowance* in winning approval of your acting [K].   29–30 *not to speak it profanely* Hamlet apologizes for his apparent flippancy in comparing the Creation
with the work of a master mechanic and his journeymen [K].   33 *journeymen*
workmen who have not yet mastered their trade.   35 *indifferently* fairly well.
39 *quantity of* few.   *barren* stupid.   41 *villainous* vulgar.   42 *uses* practises.
46 *presently* at once.   52 *just* exact, accurate, well-balanced.

As e'er my conversation cop'd withal.

HOR.   O, my dear lord!

HAM.   Nay, do not think I flatter;
For what advancement may I hope from thee,   55
That no revenue hast but thy good spirits
To feed and clothe thee? Why should the poor be flatter'd?
No, let the candied tongue lick absurd pomp,
And crook the pregnant hinges of the knee
Where thrift may follow fawning. Dost thou hear?   60
Since my dear soul was mistress of her choice
And could of men distinguish, her election
Hath seal'd thee for herself. For thou hast been
As one, in suff'ring all, that suffers nothing;
A man that Fortune's buffets and rewards   65
Hast ta'en with equal thanks; and blest are those
Whose blood and judgment are so well comeddled
That they are not a pipe for Fortune's finger
To sound what stop she please. Give me that man
That is not passion's slave, and I will wear him   70
In my heart's core, ay, in my heart of heart,
As I do thee. Something too much of this!
There is a play to-night before the King.
One scene of it comes near the circumstance,
Which I have told thee, of my father's death.   75
I prithee, when thou seest that act afoot,

---

53 *conversation* association, intercourse.   *cop'd withal* dealt with. He is calling
Horatio the most perfect and well-balanced individual he has ever met in his
association with men.   55 *advancement* promotion.   58 *candied* sugared over.
Shakespeare often associates flattery with candy and with dogs.   59 *pregnant
hinges* readily moving (supple) joints [K].   60 *thrift* worldly advantage. *follow*
come as the result of.   61 *was . . . choice* had the power of discriminating [K].
63 *seal'd* set a mark on, chosen.   64–6 *As one . . . equal thanks* Hamlet is describing the Stoic ideal.   67 *blood and judgment* impulse and discretion. Men
who act on mere impulse or who, on the other hand, deliberate until the right
moment is past, are alike exposed to the caprices of Fortune [K].   *comeddled*
mixed together, combined (Q²; F¹, K: "Co-mingled").   69 *To sound . . . please*
to play upon as she likes; to treat as her caprices dictate. Horatio possesses both
impulse and judgment in a well-balanced combination. Thus he neither acts
overhastily, nor delays when action is needed [K].   75 *have told thee* Thus we
learn, for the first time, that Hamlet has told Horatio the Ghost's story [K].
77 *with . . . soul* with observation so keen as to absorb every faculty of thy

Even with the very comment of thy soul
Observe my uncle. If his occulted guilt
Do not itself unkennel in one speech,
It is a damned ghost that we have seen,   80
And my imaginations are as foul
As Vulcan's stithy. Give him heedful note;
For I mine eyes will rivet to his face,
And after we will both our judgments join
In censure of his seeming.

HOR.   Well, my lord.   85
If 'a steal aught the whilst this play is playing,
And scape detecting, I will pay the theft.

> *Sound a flourish. Enter* Trumpets *and*
> Kettledrums. *Danish march. Enter*
> King, Queen, Polonius, Ophelia, Ros-
> encrantz, Guildenstern, *and other*
> Lords *attendant, with the* Guard
> *carrying torches.*

HAM.   They are coming to the play. I must be idle.
Get you a place.

KING.   How fares our cousin Hamlet?   90

HAM.   Excellent, i' faith; of the chameleon's dish. I eat the air,
promise-cramm'd. You cannot feed capons so.

---

soul [K].   78 *occulted* craftily hidden.   79 *unkennel* break loose (like a dog released from its kennel).   *one speech* that which Hamlet has written for insertion in the play.   80 *damned ghost* demon.   82 *stithy* forge, smithy. "Stith" means anvil. Since Vulcan is the god of smiths, his forge must be sooty above all others [K].   85 *In censure of his seeming* in passing judgment on his appearance and behaviour [K].   86 *'a* Q²; F¹, K: "he."   88 *idle* foolish or insane in my words and actions. Hamlet never feigns madness when he is alone with Horatio, who is in his confidence. Here he expressly tells his friend that it is time to act the madman again, since the others are coming [K].   91 *of the chameleon's dish* Hamlet takes the King's "fares" in the sense of "eats." The chameleon was believed to feed upon the air. Hamlet is implying that the promise of succession to the throne is not enough to satisfy him, thus fostering the King's belief that he is mad because of frustrated ambition. There is a further quibble on "heir."   92 *capons* Since the capon was a gelded, overfed rooster, Hamlet may be implying that the King has deprived him of his manhood and is preparing him for the slaughter.

KING.	I have nothing with this answer, Hamlet. These words are not mine.
HAM.	No, nor mine now. [*To* Polonius] My lord, you play'd 95 once i' th' university, you say?
POL.	That did I, my lord, and was accounted a good actor.
HAM.	What did you enact?
POL.	I did enact Julius Cæsar; I was kill'd i' th' Capitol; Brutus kill'd me. 100
HAM.	It was a brute part of him to kill so capital a calf there. Be the players ready?
ROS.	Ay, my lord. They stay upon your patience.
QUEEN.	Come hither, my dear Hamlet, sit by me.
HAM.	No, good mother. Here's metal more attractive. 105
POL.	[*to the* King] O, ho! do you mark that?
HAM.	Lady, shall I lie in your lap?

[*Sits down at* Ophelia's *feet.*]

OPH.	No, my lord.
HAM.	I mean, my head upon your lap?
OPH.	Ay, my lord. 110
HAM.	Do you think I meant country matters?
OPH.	I think nothing, my lord.
HAM	That's a fair thought to lie between maids' legs.
OPH.	What is, my lord?
HAM.	Nothing. 115

---

93 *have nothing with* can make nothing of.   96 *i' th' university* All the great European universities produced plays on festal occasions [K].   103 *stay . . . patience* await your leisure.   105 *here's . . . more attractive* Hamlet sits next to Ophelia so that he can watch the King who is sitting opposite, next to the Queen. He assumes the pose of a melancholy lover. His mad talk takes the form of obscene sexuality.   109 *my head . . . lap* This appears to have been common at private theatrical entertainments [K].   111 *country matters* indecent behaviour. 119 *your only jig-maker* the nonpareil of all writers of comic songs [K].   123-4 *I'll have a suit of sables* I'll throw off my mourning and wear the richest furs that can be found [K].   127-8 *not thinking on* being forgotten.   128 *hobby-*

OPH.   You are merry, my lord.

HAM.   Who, I?

OPH.   Ay, my lord.

HAM.   O God, your only jig-maker! What should a man do
       but be merry? For look you how cheerfully my mother   120
       looks, and my father died within 's two hours.

OPH.   Nay, 'tis twice two months, my lord.

HAM.   So long? Nay then, let the devil wear black, for I'll have
       a suit of sables. O heavens! die two months ago, and not
       forgotten yet? Then there's hope a great man's memory   125
       may outlive his life half a year. But, by'r Lady, he must
       build churches then; or else shall he suffer not thinking
       on, with the hobby-horse, whose epitaph is "For O, for
       O, the hobby-horse is forgot!"

                        Hautboys *play. The* dumb show *enters.*

                        Enter a King *and a* Queen *very lov-*
                        ingly; the Queen *embracing him, and*
                        he her. She kneels, and makes show of
                        protestation unto him. He takes her
                        up, and declines his head upon her
                        neck. He lays him down upon a bank
                        of flowers. She, seeing him asleep,
                        leaves him. Anon comes in a fellow,
                        takes off his crown, kisses it, pours
                        poison in the sleeper's ears, and leaves
                        him. The Queen *returns, finds the*
                        King *dead, and makes passionate ac-*
                        tion. The Poisoner *with some three or*

---

horse a very ancient character in May games and morris dances. In Shakespeare's
time, however, he was frequently omitted, partly because the Puritans regarded
him as a remnant of heathen superstition [K]. It consisted of a man riding a
pasteboard horse, with his legs concealed by a footcloth.   129 s.d. *dumb show*
The reason for the dumb show (when Hamlet has shown his disapproval of such
shows at III.II.11–12) and the failure of Claudius to react to it in any way, are
basic problems which must be resolved for any real understanding of HAMLET
and which accordingly have been the subjects of endless controversy. For one
explanation, see Supplementary Notes.

four Mutes, *come in again, seem to*
condole with her. The dead body is
carried away. The Poisoner *woos the*
Queen *with gifts; she seems harsh and*
unwilling awhile, but in the end ac-
cepts his love.   *Exeunt.*

OPH.   What means this, my lord?   130

HAM.   Marry, this is miching malhecho; it means mischief.

OPH.   Belike this show imports the argument of the play.

Enter Prologue.

HAM.   We shall know by this fellow. The players cannot keep
counsel; they'll tell all.

OPH.   Will 'a tell us what this show meant?   135

HAM.   Ay, or any show that you'll show him. Be not you
asham'd to show, he'll not shame to tell you what it
means.

OPH.   You are naught, you are naught! I'll mark the play.

PRO.   For us, and for our tragedy,   140
Here stooping to your clemency,
We beg your hearing patiently.   [*Exit.*]

HAM.   Is this a prologue, or the posy of a ring?

OPH.   'Tis brief, my lord.

HAM.   As woman's love.   145

Enter [*two* Players *as*] King *and*
Queen.

131 *miching malhecho* sneaking crime. To "mich" (in modern dialect, "meech")
is to "sneak" or "skulk" and "malhecho" is Spanish for "misdeed." Ophelia, who
thinks that Hamlet is raving, tries to soothe him by remarking quietly, "No
doubt this show indicates the plot of the play" [K].   134 *counsel* secrets.   135
'a Q²; F¹: "they"; POPE, K: "he."   139 *naught* obscene. The word had a much
stronger meaning, with a specifically sexual implication, than it has in modern
English.   143 *posy of a ring* Brief mottos in rhyme (poses or poesies) were often
engraved within rings.   146 *Phœbus' cart* the sun god's chariot. The same necessity to make the style of the "play within the play" distinct from the style of
the play itself exists in the case of "The Mousetrap" as in the case of the Pyrrhus
declamation (II.II.438*ff*). Here the difference is marked by the use of rhyme and
by the elaborately sententious manner [K].   147 *Neptune's salt wash* the surging

P. KING. Full thirty times hath Phœbus' cart gone round
          Neptune's salt wash and Tellus' orbed ground,
          And thirty dozen moons with borrowed sheen
          About the world have times twelve thirties been,
          Since love our hearts, and Hymen did our hands,   150
          Unite comutual in most sacred bands.

P. QUEEN. So many journey may the sun and moon
          Make us again count o'er ere love be done!
          But woe is me! you are so sick of late,
          So far from cheer and from your former state,   155
          That I distrust you. Yet, though I distrust,
          Discomfort you, my lord, it nothing must;
          For women's fear and love hold quantity,
          In neither aught, or in extremity.
          Now what my love is, proof hath made you know;   160
          And as my love is siz'd, my fear is so.
          Where love is great, the littlest doubts are fear;
          Where little fears grow great, great love grows there.

P. KING. Faith, I must leave thee, love, and shortly too;
          My operant powers their functions leave to do.   165
          And thou shalt live in this fair world behind,
          Honour'd, belov'd, and haply one as kind
          For husband shalt thou —

P. QUEEN.   O, confound the rest!
          Such love must needs be treason in my breast.
          In second husband let me be accurst!   170

waves of the sea [K]. *Tellus' orbed ground* the earth.   148 *borrowed* from the
moon.   150 *Hymen* god of marriage.   151 *comutual* mutually.   156 *distrust
you* am worried about you.   157–9 *Discomfort . . . extremity* This passage,
which is clearly corrupt in Q², shows signs of revision during the course of writing,
with Shakespeare having failed to delete some of his false starts from his foul
papers. After line 157 appears "For women feare too much, euen as they loue,"
omitted in F¹.   158 *For* F¹; Q²: "And." *hold quantity* agree in proportion.
hold Q²; F¹, K: "holds."   159 *In neither aught* F¹; Q²: "Eyther none, in neither
aught."   160 *love* F¹; Q²: "Lord." *proof* experience.   162–3 *Where love . . . grows
there* Q²; not in F¹.   165 *My operant powers* the physical forces that work in the
functions of life; my vital forces [K].   *leave to do* cease to act.   170 *In . . .
accurst* if I take a second husband, may he prove a curse to me [K].

        None wed the second but who kill'd the first.

HAM.   [*aside*] Wormwood, wormwood!

P.QUEEN.   The instances that second marriage move
        Are base respects of thrift, but none of love.
        A second time I kill my husband dead   175
        When second husband kisses me in bed.

P. KING.   I do believe you think what now you speak;
        But what we do determine oft we break.
        Purpose is but the slave to memory,
        Of violent birth, but poor validity;   180
        Which now, the fruit unripe, sticks on the tree,
        But fall unshaken when they mellow be.
        Most necessary 'tis that we forget
        To pay ourselves what to ourselves is debt.
        What to ourselves in passion we propose,   185
        The passion ending, doth the purpose lose.
        The violence of either grief or joy
        Their own enactures with themselves destroy.
        Where joy most revels, grief doth most lament;
        Grief joys, joy grieves, on slender accident.   190
        This world is not for aye, nor 'tis not strange
        That even our loves should with our fortunes change;
        For 'tis a question left us yet to prove,
        Whether love lead fortune, or else fortune love.
        The great man down, you mark his favourite flies, 195
        The poor advanc'd makes friends of enemies;
        And hitherto doth love on fortune tend,

---

171 *None . . . first* let no woman wed a second husband unless she has murdered
her first husband. Hamlet watches his mother, for he suspects her complicity in
the murder. The Ghost, interrupted by the approach of dawn, has left this point
doubtful (I.v.85–8), and Hamlet's suspicion is not relieved until III.IV.27–30 [K].
172 *Wormwood, wormwood* F¹; Q²: "That's wormwood." 173 *instances* causes.
move prompt. 174 *respects of thrift* considerations of worldly welfare or profit
[K]. 175 *I kill my husband dead* I kill my dead husband a second time, as it
were, by this act of unfaithfulness [K]. 180 *validity* strength. 181 *the fruit*
Q²; F¹, K: "like fruit." 182 *mellow* ripe. A purpose holds until the moment for
action comes, as fruit hangs on the tree so long as it is unripe; but one's purposes fail of their own accord when the moment for action arrives [K]. 184
To pay ourselves A purpose is an obligation laid upon us by ourselves; and we

For who not needs shall never lack a friend,
And who in want a hollow friend doth try,
Directly seasons him his enemy.   200
But, orderly to end where I begun,
Our wills and fates do so contrary run
That our devices still are overthrown;
Our thoughts are ours, their ends none of our own.
So think thou wilt no second husband wed;   205
But die thy thoughts when thy first lord is dead.

P. QUEEN. Nor earth to me give food, nor heaven light,
Sport and repose lock from me day and night,
To desperation turn my trust and hope,
An anchor's cheer in prison be my scope,   210
Each opposite that blanks the face of joy
Meet what I would have well, and it destroy,
Both here and hence pursue me lasting strife,
If, once a widow, ever I be wife!

HAM.   If she should break it now!   215

P. KING. 'Tis deeply sworn. Sweet, leave me here awhile.
My spirits grow dull, and fain I would beguile
The tedious day with sleep.

P. QUEEN.   Sleep rock thy brain,

                                    [*He*] *sleeps.*

And never come mischance between us twain!   *Exit.*

HAM.   Madam, how like you this play?   220

---

readily excuse ourselves for neglecting it, for a man is an indulgent creditor to himself [K].   187-8 *The violence . . . destroy* when either grief or joy is violent, it exhausts itself by its own force, and thus the resolutions formed under its impulse come to naught [K].   *enactures* performances.   190 *on slender accident* as a result of any trifling occurrence [K].   197 *hitherto* so far; up to this point in human history. In other words, "Such has always been the experience of mankind" [K].   199 *hollow* insincere.   200 *seasons him* ripens him into. A false friend, when tested, becomes an enemy.   203 *devices* plans.   *still* always.   209-10 *To desperation . . . scope* Q²; not in F¹.   210 *An anchor's cheer* an anchorite's (hermit's) food.   *scope* limit of my enjoyment.   211 *blanks* blanches, makes pale.   213 *here and hence* in this world and in the next.   217 *My spirits grow dull* I feel weak and tired.

QUEEN.   The lady doth protest too much, methinks.

HAM.   O, but she'll keep her word.

KING.   Have you heard the argument? Is there no offence in't?

HAM.   No, no! They do but jest, poison in jest; no offence i'
th' world.   225

KING.   What do you call the play?

HAM.   "The Mousetrap." Marry, how? Tropically. This play
is the image of a murder done in Vienna. Gonzago is
the duke's name; his wife, Baptista. You shall see anon.
'Tis a knavish piece of work; but what o' that? Your   230
Majesty, and we that have free souls, it touches us not.
Let the gall'd jade winch; our withers are unwrung.

Enter Lucianus.

This is one Lucianus, nephew to the King.

OPH.   You are as good as a chorus, my lord.

HAM.   I could interpret between you and your love, if I could   235
see the puppets dallying.

OPH.   You are keen, my lord, you are keen.

HAM.   It would cost you a groaning to take off mine edge.

OPH.   Still better, and worse.

HAM.   So you mis-take your husbands. — Begin, murderer.   240
Leave thy damnable faces, and begin! Come, the croak-
ing raven doth bellow for revenge.

---

221 *doth protest* Queen Gertrude calmly criticizes the exaggerated style of the
speech. She shows no such disturbance of mind as might indicate a guilty conscience [K].   223 *the argument* an outline of the plot. See Supplementary Notes.
224 *in jest* not in fact, but merely in the play [K].   227 *Tropically* by a trope;
metaphorically [K].   228 *image* exact representation [K].   231 *free* innocent.
232 *gall'd jade* sore-backed, irritated horse of inferior quality.   *winch* wince.
withers the ridge between a horse's shoulders.   *unwrung* not chafed, and therefore not sensitive. Our consciences are clear [K].   233 *nephew to the King* This
would equate the murderer of "The Mousetrap" with Hamlet himself rather than
with Claudius; to the watching court, the play would thus naturally appear as a
threat upon the life of Claudius by his mad nephew, rather than as a depiction
of the murder of the elder Hamlet.   235–6 *I could . . . dallying* if I could look
on at a scene of dalliance between your lover and you, I could tell what it meant.

LUC.　Thoughts black, hands apt, drugs fit, and time agreeing;
　　　Confederate season, else no creature seeing;
　　　Thou mixture rank, of midnight weeds collected,　　245
　　　With Hecate's ban thrice blasted, thrice infected,
　　　Thy natural magic and dire property
　　　On wholesome life usurps immediately.

　　　　　　　　　　Pours the poison in his ears.

HAM.　'A poisons him i' th' garden for's estate. His name 's
　　　Gonzago. The story is extant, and written in very choice　250
　　　Italian. You shall see anon how the murderer gets the
　　　love of Gonzago's wife.

OPH.　The King rises.

HAM.　What, frighted with false fire?

QUEEN.　How fares my lord?　　255

POL.　Give o'er the play.

KING.　Give me some light! Away!

POL.　Lights, lights, lights!

　　　　　　　Exeunt all but Hamlet *and* Horatio.

HAM.　　Why, let the strucken deer go weep,
　　　　　The hart ungalled play;　　260
　　　　For some must watch, while some must sleep:
　　　　　Thus runs the world away.

By the "puppets" Hamlet means Ophelia and her imagined lover. Puppet shows, which were very common, regularly had an interpreter, who sometimes sat on the stage [K].　238 *mine* Q²; F¹, K: "my."　239 *better, and worse* keener as to wit, but worse as to meaning [K].　240 *mis-take* The reference is to the marriage ceremony in which husband and wife "take" one another (Q², F¹: "mistake"; Q¹, K: "must take").　241 *Leave* Q²; F¹, K: "Pox, leaue."　244 *Confederate . . . seeing* the time being in league with me (since this is a favourable moment), and nobody except my confederate, the time, seeing what I am about [K].　245 *mid-night weeds* Poisonous and magic herbs were thought to derive additional power from being collected at some special time, as, for example, at midnight [K].　246 *With Hecate's ban* by the curse (the evil spell) of Hecate, the goddess of witch-craft and black magic [K].　249 *'A* Q²; F¹, K: "He."　254 *false fire* the harmless discharge of a gun loaded with powder only [K].　258 *Pol.* Q²; F¹, K: "All."

Would not this, sir, and a forest of feathers — if the rest
of my fortunes turn Turk with me — with two Provincial
roses on my raz'd shoes, get me a fellowship in a cry of   265
players, sir?

HOR.   Half a share.

HAM.   A whole one I!

   For thou dost know, O Damon dear,
    This realm dismantled was   270
   Of Jove himself; and now reigns here
    A very, very — peacock.

HOR.   You might have rhym'd.

HAM.   O good Horatio, I'll take the ghost's word for a thousand pound! Didst perceive?   275

HOR.   Very well, my lord.

HAM.   Upon the talk of the poisoning?

HOR.   I did very well note him.

HAM.   Aha! Come, some music! Come, the recorders!

   For if the King like not the comedy,   280
   Why then, belike he likes it not, perdy.

Come, some music!

      Enter Rosencrantz *and* Guildenstern.

GUIL.   Good my lord, vouchsafe me a word with you.

HAM.   Sir, a whole history.

GUIL.   The King, sir —   285

---

263 *this* this declamation; the way in which I have spoken these verses. Hamlet
has relieved his excitement by a bit of theatrical spouting [K]. *feathers* plumes,
worn by actors.   264 *turn Turk* turn heathen — i.e. treat me cruelly.   264–5
Provincial roses large rosettes.   265 *raz'd shoes* shoes with slashes, ornamental
designs cut in the leather. He is describing the typical wardrobe of actors. *cry*
pack, troupe.   267 *Half a share* In Shakespeare's time each regular member
of a company of players had his proportion of the receipts instead of a salary.
Some had a full share, some half a share [K].   272 *peacock* WILSON; Q², K:
"pajock," which K suggests as a variant form.   279 *recorders* early wooden
flutes.   281 *belike* probably. *perdy* An old-fashioned oath ("par dieu") used
colloquially for "assuredly" [K].   287 *distemper'd* ill, literally, with the humours

HAM.   Ay, sir, what of him?

GUIL.   Is in his retirement, marvellous distemper'd.

HAM.   With drink, sir?

GUIL.   No, my lord; rather with choler.

HAM.   Your wisdom should show itself more richer to signify 290
this to the doctor; for for me to put him to his purgation
would perhaps plunge him into more choler.

GUIL.   Good my lord, put your discourse into some frame, and
start not so wildly from my affair.

HAM.   I am tame, sir; pronounce.   295

GUIL.   The Queen, your mother, in most great affliction of
spirit hath sent me to you.

HAM.   You are welcome.

GUIL.   Nay, good my lord, this courtesy is not of the right
breed. If it shall please you to make me a wholesome an- 300
swer, I will do your mother's commandment; if not,
your pardon and my return shall be the end of my business.

HAM.   Sir, I cannot.

ROS.   What, my lord?   305

HAM.   Make you a wholesome answer; my wit 's diseas'd. But,
sir, such answer as I can make, you shall command; or
rather, as you say, my mother. Therefore no more, but
to the matter! My mother, you say —

ROS.   Then thus she says: your behaviour hath struck her into 310
amazement and admiration.

of his body out of proper balance.   289 *choler* bile. In the speech that follows
Hamlet puns on the word. The King pretends to be suffering from a sudden
attack of indigestion, causing dizziness — from what we still call a "bilious
attack" [K].   291 *purgation* Hamlet uses the word in three senses (a) purging by
means of a laxative (b) the purification of his soul by confession and penance (c)
bloodletting, the standard medical means of purgation of his day — but with the
implication of killing him.   292 *more* Q²; F¹, K: "farre more." *choler* (a) bile
(b) anger.   293 *frame* coherent form.   300 *wholesome* sane.   302 *pardon* permission to depart.   305 *Ros.* Q²; F¹, K: "Guild."   311 *amazement and admiration*
confusion of mind and wonder [K].

HAM.   O wonderful son, that can so stonish a mother! But is
there no sequel at the heels of this mother's admiration?
Impart.

ROS.   She desires to speak with you in her closet ere you go to   315
bed.

HAM.   We shall obey, were she ten times our mother. Have
you any further trade with us?

ROS.   My lord, you once did love me.

HAM.   And do still, by these pickers and stealers!   320

ROS.   Good my lord, what is your cause of distemper? You do
surely bar the door upon your own liberty, if you deny
your griefs to your friend.

HAM.   Sir, I lack advancement.

ROS.   How can that be, when you have the voice of the King   325
himself for your succession in Denmark?

HAM.   Ay, sir, but "while the grass grows" — the proverb is
something musty.

Enter the Players *with recorders.*

O, the recorders! Let me see one. To withdraw with
you — why do you go about to recover the wind of me,   330
as if you would drive me into a toil?

GUIL.   O my lord, if my duty be too bold, my love is too unmannerly.

HAM.   I do not well understand that. Will you play upon this
pipe?   335

315 *closet* private chamber.   318 *trade* business. The word was common in this
sense and conveys no suggestion that Rosencrantz and Guildenstern are mercenary
agents [K].   320 *pickers and stealers* the ten fingers of his hands.   321 *distemper*
mental illness.   322 *liberty* Rosencrantz hints that Hamlet may be put under
restraint (as a lunatic) if he stubbornly refuses to tell what ails him [K].   324
I lack advancement Again Hamlet suggests frustrated political ambition as the
source of his madness.   327 *the proverb* i.e. while the grass is growing the
horse starves.   328 *musty* and therefore too trite to be quoted in full [K].   329
To withdraw to step aside so as to be out of the hearing of the players. Hamlet
withdraws to one side of the stage with Rosencrantz and Guildenstern, as if he

GUIL.   My lord, I cannot.

HAM.   I pray you.

GUIL.   Believe me, I cannot.

HAM.   I do beseech you.

GUIL.   I know no touch of it, my lord.   340

HAM.   It is as easy as lying. Govern these ventages with your
         fingers and thumbs, give it breath with your mouth, and
         it will discourse most eloquent music. Look you, these
         are the stops.

GUIL.   But these cannot I command to any utt'rance of har-   345
         mony. I have not the skill.

HAM.   Why, look you now, how unworthy a thing you make
         of me! You would play upon me; you would seem to
         know my stops; you would pluck out the heart of my
         mystery; you would sound me from my lowest note to 350
         the top of my compass; and there is much music, ex-
         cellent voice, in this little organ, yet cannot you make it
         speak. 'Sblood, do you think I am easier to be play'd on
         than a pipe? Call me what instrument you will, though
         you can fret me, you cannot play upon me.   355

                      Enter Polonius.

         God bless you, sir!

POL.   My lord, the Queen would speak with you, and pres-
         ently.

HAM.   Do you see yonder cloud that's almost in shape of a
         camel?   360

---

had something of moment to confide to them [K].   330 *go about* undertake.
recover . . . me approach me with the wind away from you. The metaphor is
from hunting.   331 *toil* net.   332-3 *If my duty . . . unmannerly* if, in my devotion to your interests, I am too bold in questioning you, it is my love that
causes this breach of good manners [K].   340 *touch of it* talent for it.   341
ventages stops, wind-holes.   352 *organ* musical instrument.   355 *can fret me*
F¹; Q²: "fret me not."   *fret* Frets are small bars of wire or wood on a guitar or
the like, to guide the fingering. Hamlet puns on the sense of "worry," "agitate"
[K].   357 *presently* at once.

POL.   By th' mass, and 'tis like a camel indeed.

HAM.   Methinks it is like a weasel.

POL.   It is back'd like a weasel.

HAM.   Or like a whale.

POL.   Very like a whale.   365

HAM.   Then I will come to my mother by-and-by. — They fool
        me to the top of my bent. — I will come by-and-by.

POL.   I will say so.   *Exit.*

HAM.   "By-and-by" is easily said. — Leave me, friends.

                              [*Exeunt all but* Hamlet.]

        'Tis now the very witching time of night,   370
        When churchyards yawn, and hell itself breathes out
        Contagion to this world. Now could I drink hot blood
        And do such bitter business as the day
        Would quake to look on. Soft! now to my mother!
        O heart, lose not thy nature; let not ever   375
        The soul of Nero enter this firm bosom.
        Let me be cruel, not unnatural;
        I will speak daggers to her, but use none.
        My tongue and soul in this be hypocrites —

---

361 *By th' mass . . . indeed* Polonius is merely humouring the supposed mad-man. There is nothing absurd in his conduct [K].   366 *I will* Q²; F¹, K: "will I."
367 *to the top of my bent* to the extreme; literally, as fully as a bow may be bent.   370 *witching time* time when witches perform their evil rites.   371 *breathes* F¹; Q²: "breaks."   372 *Contagion* Two ideas combine in this poetic figure. In the night, evil spirits and malign influences were supposed to have more power than by day; and at the same time the night air was regarded as charged with actual contagion [K].   373 *bitter . . . day* F¹; Q²: "business as the bitter day."   375 *nature* natural feeling, such as a son should have for his mother.   376 *soul of Nero* spirit of matricide. The Roman Emperor Nero had

How in my words somever she be shent,   380
To give them seals never, my soul, consent!   *Exit.*

◇◇◇◇◇◇◇◇◇◇◇◇◇◇◇◇◇◇

[SCENE III. *A room in the Castle.*]

Enter King, Rosencrantz, *and* Guildenstern.

KING.   I like him not, nor stands it safe with us
To let his madness range. Therefore prepare you;
I your commission will forthwith dispatch,
And he to England shall along with you.
The terms of our estate may not endure   5
Hazard so near us as doth hourly grow
Out of his brows.

GUIL.   We will ourselves provide.
Most holy and religious fear it is
To keep those many many bodies safe
That live and feed upon your Majesty.   10

ROS.   The single and peculiar life is bound
With all the strength and armour of the mind
To keep itself from noyance; but much more

---

murdered his own mother.   379 *be* Subjunctive: "Let my tongue and soul be hypocrites." His soul is to pretend a savage purpose which it does not feel, and his words are to express it [K].   380 *shent* berated, violently reproved.   381 *give them seals* confirm or fulfill them by action [K].

III.III. 2 *range* roam about freely.   3 *commission* official orders, giving them custody of Hamlet and a sealed letter for the English king. *dispatch* cause to be drawn up.   5 *terms of our estate* my kingly office.   7 *brows* effronteries (Q², F¹, K: "Lunacies." Some editors read "brawls" or "braves").   11 *peculiar* individual. 13 *noyance* harm.

That spirit upon whose weal depends and rests
The lives of many. The cesse of majesty   15
Dies not alone, but like a gulf doth draw
What's near it with it. It is a massy wheel,
Fix'd on the summit of the highest mount,
To whose huge spokes ten thousand lesser things
Are mortis'd and adjoin'd; which when it falls,   20
Each small annexment, petty consequence,
Attends the boist'rous ruin. Never alone
Did the king sigh, but with a general groan.

KING.   Arm you, I pray you, to this speedy voyage;
For we will fetters put about this fear,   25
Which now goes too free-footed.

ROS.   We will haste us.

Exeunt Gentlemen.

Enter Polonius.

POL.   My lord, he's going to his mother's closet.
Behind the arras I'll convey myself
To hear the process. I'll warrant she'll tax him home;
And, as you said, and wisely was it said,   30
'Tis meet that some more audience than a mother,
Since nature makes them partial, should o'erhear
The speech, of vantage. Fare you well, my liege.
I'll call upon you ere you go to bed
And tell you what I know.

KING.   Thanks, dear my lord.   35

Exit [Polonius].

O, my offence is rank, it smells to heaven;

---

14 *weal* welfare.   15 *cesse* cessation, decease.   16 *gulf* whirlpool.   17 *massy*
massive.   22 *ruin* downfall.   24 *Arm you* make yourselves ready.   25 *about*
Q²; F¹, ᴋ: "vpon." *fear* (a) fear itself (b) the object of fear — Hamlet.   26 *Ros.*
Q²; F¹, ᴋ: "Both."   29 *process* conversation.   *tax him home* take him to task
severely.   33 *of vantage* from a favourable position [ᴋ].   36 *rank* foul.   37
primal eldest curse the curse visited upon Cain. See GENESIS, IV.10–12.   39 *Though
inclination . . . will* though I not only wish to pray, but feel a strong impulse
toward prayer [ᴋ]. He need not force himself to pray.   41 *bound* in duty bound.
43 *neglect* leave undone.   46–7 *Whereto . . . offence* for what purpose does
God's mercy exist, if not to confront a man's guilt when that appears as accuser

It hath the primal eldest curse upon't,
A brother's murder! Pray can I not,
Though inclination be as sharp as will.
My stronger guilt defeats my strong intent,   40
And, like a man to double business bound,
I stand in pause where I shall first begin,
And both neglect. What if this cursed hand
Were thicker than itself with brother's blood,
Is there not rain enough in the sweet heavens   45
To wash it white as snow? Whereto serves mercy
But to confront the visage of offence?
And what's in prayer but this twofold force,
To be forestalled ere we come to fall,
Or pardon'd being down? Then I'll look up;   50
My fault is past. But, O, what form of prayer
Can serve my turn? "Forgive me my foul murder"?
That cannot be; since I am still possess'd
Of those effects for which I did the murder —
My crown, mine own ambition, and my queen.   55
May one be pardon'd and retain th' offence?
In the corrupted currents of this world
Offence's gilded hand may shove by justice,
And oft 'tis seen the wicked prize itself
Buys out the law; but 'tis not so above.   60
There is no shuffling; there the action lies
In his true nature, and we ourselves compell'd,
Even to the teeth and forehead of our faults,
To give in evidence. What then? What rests?
Try what repentance can. What can it not?   65
Yet what can it when one cannot repent?
O wretched state! O bosom black as death!

before the Great Judge, and thus to procure his pardon [κ]?   48 *twofold force:*
"Lead us not into temptation," and "Forgive us our trespasses" [κ].   49 *fore-*
stalled prevented (from sinning).   54 *effects* gains, things acquired.   56 *th'*
offence that which has been gained by the crime; the booty [κ].   57 *corrupted*
currents evil courses.   58 *Offence's gilded hand* the gold-laden hand of the
offender.   59–60 *the wicked . . . law* a part of the booty may be used to bribe
the judge [κ].   61–2 *there . . . nature* there (in heaven) the lawsuit (action)
must be brought (lies) according to the true facts of the case.   63 *Even . . .*
faults meeting our offences face to face.

O limed soul, that, struggling to be free,
Art more engag'd! Help, angels! Make assay.
Bow, stubborn knees; and heart with strings of steel,   70
Be soft as sinews of the new-born babe!
All may be well.   *He kneels.*

Enter Hamlet.

HAM.   Now might I do it pat, now he is praying;
And now I'll do't. And so 'a goes to heaven,
And so am I reveng'd. That would be scann'd.   75
A villain kills my father; and for that,
I, his sole son, do this same villain send
To heaven.
Why, this is hire and salary, not revenge!
'A took my father grossly, full of bread,   80
With all his crimes broad blown, as flush as May;
And how his audit stands, who knows save heaven?
But in our circumstance and course of thought,
'Tis heavy with him; and am I then reveng'd,
To take him in the purging of his soul,   85
When he is fit and season'd for his passage?
No.
Up, sword, and know thou a more horrid hent.
When he is drunk asleep; or in his rage;
Or in th' incestuous pleasure of his bed;   90
At game, a-swearing, or about some act
That has no relish of salvation in't —
Then trip him, that his heels may kick at heaven,
And that his soul may be as damn'd and black
As hell, whereto it goes. My mother stays.   95

---

68 *limed* caught as with bird-lime. See Supplementary Notes.   69 *engag'd* stuck
fast, entrapped.   69 *assay* the attempt (addressed to himself).   73 *pat* conveniently.   74 *'a* Q²; F¹, к: "he."   75 *scann'd* considered closely.   79 *hire and
salary* as if I had hired him to murder my father and am now paying him his
wages [к] (F¹; Q²: "base and silly").   80 *'A* Q²; F¹, к: "He." *grossly* in a gross
condition; not purified by repentance, confession, and absolution [к]. *full of
bread* in the full flush of worldly pleasures (as opposed to prayer and fasting)
[к].   81 *crimes* sins. *broad blown* in full bloom. *flush* full of life and vigour.
82 *audit* final account (in the book of judgment) [к].   83 *our . . . thought*
judging as well as our circumstances allow, and letting our thoughts take their

	This physic but prolongs thy sickly days.	*Exit.*
KING.	[*rises*] My words fly up, my thoughts remain below.	
	Words without thoughts never to heaven go.	*Exit.*

◇◇◇◇◇◇◇◇◇◇◇◇◇◇◇◇

[SCENE IV. *The Queen's closet.*]

Enter Queen *and* Polonius.

POL.   'A will come straight. Look you lay home to him.
        Tell him his pranks have been too broad to bear with,
        And that your Grace hath screen'd and stood between
        Much heat and him. I'll silence me even here.
        Pray you be round with him.

HAM.   (*within*)   Mother, mother, mother!   5

QUEEN. I'll warrant you; fear me not. Withdraw; I hear him
        coming.   [Polonius *hides behind the arras.*]

                       Enter Hamlet.

HAM.   Now, mother, what's the matter?

QUEEN. Hamlet, thou hast thy father much offended.

HAM.   Mother, you have my father much offended.   10

QUEEN. Come, come, you answer with an idle tongue.

HAM.   Go, go, you question with a wicked tongue.

QUEEN. Why, how now, Hamlet?

HAM.   What's the matter now?

QUEEN. Have you forgot me?

HAM.   No, by the rood, not so!

---

natural course [K].   86 *season'd* ripened, matured; i.e. thoroughly prepared [K].
passage to the other world.   88 *horrid hent* horrible opportunity.   91 *game,*
a-swearing Q²; F¹, K: "gaming, swearing."   95 *stays* waits.   96 *This physic* the
considerations which lead me to postpone revenge [K].

    III.IV. 1 *'A* Q²; F¹, K: "He." *straight* immediately. *lay home to him* tax him
home, berate him severely.   2 *broad* lawless.   4 *heat* anger (of the King). *silence*
me stop talking and hide myself [K].   5 *round* direct, outspoken (F¹; not in Q²).
6 *warrant* F¹; Q²: "wait." *fear me not* don't worry about me — my ability to
handle the situation.   11 *idle* foolish.   14 *forgot me* forgotten who I am —
your mother. *rood* cross.

You are the Queen, your husband's brother's wife,   15
And (would it were not so!) you are my mother.

QUEEN.   Nay, then I'll set those to you that can speak.

HAM.   Come, come, and sit you down. You shall not budge!
You go not till I set you up a glass
Where you may see the inmost part of you.   20

QUEEN.   What wilt thou do? Thou wilt not murder me?
Help, help, ho!

POL.   [*behind*] What, ho! help, help, help!

HAM.   [*draws*] How now? a rat? Dead for a ducat, dead!
[*Makes a pass through the arras and*]
kills Polonius.

POL.   [*behind*] O, I am slain!

QUEEN.   O me, what hast thou done?   25

HAM.   Nay, I know not. Is it the King?

QUEEN.   O, what a rash and bloody deed is this!

HAM.   A bloody deed — almost as bad, good mother,
As kill a king, and marry with his brother.

QUEEN.   As kill a king?

HAM.   Ay, lady, it was my word.   30

[*Lifts up the arras and sees* Polonius.]

Thou wretched, rash, intruding fool, farewell!
I took thee for thy better. Take thy fortune.

---

17 *those* A threat is implied. The Queen turns to leave the room, as if to summon Claudius, but Hamlet detains her [K].   19 *glass* mirror.   26 *Is it the King* So Hamlet supposed when he made the thrust. In the interval between scenes III and IV, then, there has been enough time for the King to reach the Queen's apartment and conceal himself [K].   29 *As kill . . . brother* A plain accusation that the Queen was an accomplice in the murder of her husband. Her astonishment convinces Hamlet of her innocence; and he makes no further allusion to such complicity, even when she asks "What have I done?" in line 39 [K].   32 *thy better* the King.   33 *busy* meddlesome.   37 *damned custom* habitual evil.   *braz'd* hardened like brass, made impenetrable to shame.   38 *it be* Q²; F¹, K: "it is."   *proof* armour.   *sense* feeling.   40 *Such an act* Hamlet upbraids his mother for her adultery. He no longer accuses her of murder [K].   41 *grace* beauty.   42 *rose* a traditional symbol of purity.   44 *blister* the sign of the

Thou find'st to be too busy is some danger.
Leave wringing of your hands. Peace! sit you down
And let me wring your heart; for so I shall   35
If it be made of penetrable stuff;
If damned custom have not braz'd it so
That it be proof and bulwark against sense.

QUEEN.   What have I done that thou dar'st wag thy tongue
In noise so rude against me?

HAM.   Such an act   40
That blurs the grace and blush of modesty;
Calls virtue hypocrite; takes off the rose
From the fair forehead of an innocent love,
And sets a blister there; makes marriage vows
As false as dicers' oaths. O, such a deed   45
As from the body of contraction plucks
The very soul, and sweet religion makes
A rhapsody of words! Heaven's face does glow
O'er this solidity and compound mass,
With heated visage, as against the doom —   50
Is thought-sick at the act.

QUEEN.   Ay me, what act,
That roars so loud and thunders in the index?

HAM.   Look here upon this picture, and on this,
The counterfeit presentment of two brothers.
See what a grace was seated on this brow;   55
Hyperion's curls; the front of Jove himself;
An eye like Mars, to threaten and command;

harlot. Women convicted of adultery were branded on the forehead.   46 *contraction* the obligation of the marriage contract [K].   48 *A rhapsody of words*
mere senseless verbiage [K].   48–50 *Heaven's face . . . doom* the sun shines
upon this solid earth (compounded of four elements) with burning (shameful)
face, as though in preparation for the day of judgment. The passage, obviously
corrupt in F[1], is obscure and has been variously interpreted. *does* Q[2]; F[1], K:
"doth." *O'er* Q[2]; F[1], K: "Yea." *heated* Q[2]; F[1], K: "tristfull."   51 *thought-sick*
sick at heart.   52 *index* table of contents (which precedes the main body of a
book).   53 *this picture . . . this* Probably full-length portraits are indicated,
although miniatures are usually used on the modern stage.   54 *counterfeit
presentment* representation in portraiture [K].   56 *Hyperion's* the sun god's.
front forehead.

A station like the herald Mercury
New lighted on a heaven-kissing hill:
A combination and a form indeed   60
Where every god did seem to set his seal
To give the world assurance of a man.
This was your husband. Look you now what follows.
Here is your husband, like a mildew'd ear
Blasting his wholesome brother. Have you eyes?   65
Could you on this fair mountain leave to feed,
And batten on this moor? Ha! have you eyes?
You cannot call it love; for at your age
The heyday in the blood is tame, it's humble,
And waits upon the judgment; and what judgment   70
Would step from this to this? Sense sure you have,
Else could you not have motion; but sure that sense
Is apoplex'd; for madness would not err,
Nor sense to ecstasy was ne'er so thrall'd
But it reserv'd some quantity of choice   75
To serve in such a difference. What devil was't
That thus hath cozen'd you at hoodman-blind?
Eyes without feeling, feeling without sight,
Ears without hands or eyes, smelling sans all,
Or but a sickly part of one true sense   80
Could not so mope.

---

58 *station* standing figure.   59 *New lighted* newly alighted.   61 *set his seal*
give his mark of approval.   64 *mildew'd ear* of wheat.   66 *leave* cease.   67
batten gorge yourself.   68 *at your age* To Hamlet, a very young man, his
mother seems too old to feel passionate love. We should not be misled into
exaggerating the Queen's age. She is in what we should call the prime of life [K].
69 *heyday in the blood* liveliness of youthful passion [K].   *tame* under control.
70 *waits upon* defers to.   71–6 *Sense . . . difference* Q²; not in F¹.   *Sense* feeling.
72 *motion* desire.   74 *ecstasy* madness.   *thrall'd* enslaved.   75 *quantity* small
quantity.   76 *serve . . . difference* enable you to choose where the difference
is so great.   77 *cozen'd* cheated, tricked.   *hoodman-blind* blindman's buff. The
Queen, Hamlet implies, had made her choice with as little discrimination as
that shown by the "hoodman" (or blinded person) in a blindman's buff, who
seizes upon anybody within reach and cannot tell one from another [K].   78–81
Eyes . . . mope Q²; not in F¹.   81 *so mope* be so dull and stupid.   82 *Rebellious
hell* The baser elements in our nature are conceived as rising in mutiny against our
nobler selves [K].   86 *gives the charge* makes the attack.   88 *reason panders will*
reason, which should control desire, becomes basely subservient to it [K].   90
grained dyed in grain — cochineal, supposedly the most permanent of dyes (F¹;

O shame! where is thy blush? Rebellious hell,
If thou canst mutine in a matron's bones,
To flaming youth let virtue be as wax
And melt in her own fire. Proclaim no shame   85
When the compulsive ardour gives the charge,
Since frost itself as actively doth burn,
And reason panders will.

QUEEN.   O Hamlet, speak no more!
Thou turn'st mine eyes into my very soul,
And there I see such black and grained spots   90
As will not leave their tinct.

HAM.   Nay, but to live
In the rank sweat of an enseamed bed,
Stew'd in corruption, honeying and making love
Over the nasty sty!

QUEEN.   O, speak to me no more!
These words like daggers enter in mine ears.   95
No more, sweet Hamlet!

HAM.   A murderer and a villain!
A slave that is not twentieth part the tithe
Of your precedent lord; a vice of kings;
A cutpurse of the empire and the rule,
That from a shelf the precious diadem stole   100
And put it in his pocket!

Q²: "greeued"). 91 *leave their tinct* give up their colour. 92 *enseamed* soaked
in grease. Perspiration was believed to be melting body fat. 97 *tithe* tenth part.
98 *precedent* former. *vice of kings* rascally buffoon among kings. The "vice" in
the old morality plays was a comic character [K]. 99 *cutpurse* pickpocket. 101
s.d. *Enter the Ghost* There is no room for discussion whether this is a "sub-
jective" or an "objective" ghost — whether it is a figment of Hamlet's brain or
an actual apparition. Ghosts had the power, it was believed, of appearing and
speaking to one person while remaining invisible and inaudible to all others
present. The fact that a speech is given to the Ghost settles the question. If he
were a delusion, Hamlet would merely imagine that he heard his words, and,
if the audience needed to know what Hamlet imagined he heard, he would
himself repeat them. There is a similar situation in Chapman's tragedy, THE
REVENGE OF BUSSY D'AMBOIS, V.I. [K]. *nightgown* These words are in Q¹ only. The
Ghost appears, not (as in Act I) in armour, but "in his habit as he lived"; in his
dressing gown, attire suitable for the privacy of his own apartment [K]. As a
memorial reconstruction based upon stage performance, Q¹'s stage directions have
much reliability.

QUEEN.   No more!

            Enter the Ghost *in his nightgown.*

HAM.   A king of shreds and patches! —
          Save me and hover o'er me with your wings,
          You heavenly guards! What would your gracious figure?

QUEEN.   Alas, he's mad!   105

HAM.   Do you not come your tardy son to chide,
          That, laps'd in time and passion, lets go by
          Th' important acting of your dread command?
          O, say!

GHOST.   Do not forget. This visitation   110
          Is but to whet thy almost blunted purpose.
          But look, amazement on thy mother sits.
          O, step between her and her fighting soul!
          Conceit in weakest bodies strongest works.
          Speak to her, Hamlet.

HAM.   How is it with you, lady?   115

QUEEN.   Alas, how is't with you,
          That you do bend your eye on vacancy,
          And with th' incorporal air do hold discourse?
          Forth at your eyes your spirits wildly peep;
          And, as the sleeping soldiers in th' alarm,   120
          Your bedded hairs, like life in excrements,
          Start up and stand an end. O gentle son,
          Upon the heat and flame of thy distemper
          Sprinkle cool patience! Whereon do you look?

HAM.   On him, on him! Look you how pale he glares!   125

---

102 *of shreds and patches* threadbare and patched up (in his claims to royalty).
107 *laps'd . . . passion* having permitted the moment to slip and passion to cool.
108 *important* urgent.   112 *amazement* utter confusion of mind [K].   114 *Conceit* imagination.   118 *incorporal* bodiless.   119 *spirits* In moments of excitement the "spirits" or "vital forces" were thought to come, as it were, to the surface, and to cause various symptoms of agitation, such as a wild glare in the eyes [K].   120 *th' alarm* the call to arms.   121 *hairs* ROWE; Q², F¹: "haire." *excrements* in the literal sense of "outgrowths." The hair and nails, being not

His form and cause conjoin'd, preaching to stones,
Would make them capable. — Do not look upon me,
Lest with this piteous action you convert
My stern effects. Then what I have to do
Will want true colour — tears perchance for blood.   130

QUEEN.   To whom do you speak this?

HAM.   Do you see nothing there?

QUEEN.   Nothing at all; yet all that is I see.

HAM.   Nor did you nothing hear?

QUEEN.   No, nothing but ourselves.

HAM.   Why, look you there! Look how it steals away!
My father, in his habit as he liv'd!   135
Look where he goes even now out at the portal!

                                   Exit Ghost.

QUEEN.   This is the very coinage of your brain.
This bodiless creation ecstasy
Is very cunning in.

HAM.   Ecstasy?
My pulse as yours doth temperately keep time   140
And makes as healthful music. It is not madness
That I have utt'red. Bring me to the test,
And I the matter will reword; which madness
Would gambol from. Mother, for love of grace,
Lay not that flattering unction to your soul,   145
That not your trespass but my madness speaks.
It will but skin and film the ulcerous place,

---

exactly a part of the body but rather something growing out of it, were often so
called [K].   123 *distemper* distraction.   124 *patience* self-control.   127 *capable*
of feeling and emotion.   128 *convert* change utterly.   129 *effects* deeds.   135 *as he
liv'd* as he was dressed when alive; not "as if he lived" [K].   138 *ecstasy* madness.
139 *Ecstasy* F¹; not in Q².   144 *gambol from* not merely "wander from," but
"wander away from in a fantastic way" [K].   145 *flattering unction* soothing
ointment. Hamlet urges his mother to take his reproofs and exhortations seriously
and not as the ravings of a maniac [K].

Whiles rank corruption, mining all within,
Infects unseen. Confess yourself to heaven;
Repent what's past; avoid what is to come;   150
And do not spread the compost on the weeds
To make them ranker. Forgive me this my virtue;
For in the fatness of these pursy times
Virtue itself of vice must pardon beg —
Yea, curb and woo for leave to do him good.   155

QUEEN.   O Hamlet, thou hast cleft my heart in twain.

HAM.   O, throw away the worser part of it,
And live the purer with the other half.
Good night — but go not to my uncle's bed.
Assume a virtue, if you have it not.   160
That monster, custom, who all sense doth eat
Of habits evil, is angel yet in this,
That to the use of actions fair and good
He likewise gives a frock or livery,
That aptly is put on. Refrain to-night,   165
And that shall lend a kind of easiness
To the next abstinence; the next more easy;
For use almost can change the stamp of nature,
And either [master] the devil, or throw him out
With wondrous potency. Once more, good night;   170
And when you are desirous to be blest,

---

148 *mining* undermining.   152-5 *Forgive me . . . good* I must ask you to forgive my action in thus upbraiding you, though it is a good action (a virtue) on
my part; for, in these corrupt times, the virtuous cannot chide the vicious without
asking pardon for the liberty — indeed, they must bend the knee (curb) and beg
for leave to benefit them by such needed reproof. Hamlet feels some compunction
at his own harsh language, but he justifies it in the very act of apologizing [K].
153 *fatness . . . times* Hamlet compares the corrupt times to a body that is un-
healthily corpulent [K].   158 *live* F¹; Q²: "leaue."   161-5 *That monster . . . put
on* Custom, who is a monster because he takes away our feeling of the badness of
evil habits, is yet an angel in this point, namely that he likewise makes good
actions easy [K] (Q²; not in F¹).   162 *evil* THEOBALD; Q²: "deuill."   167-70 *the
next . . . potency* Q²; not in F¹.   168 *use* habit.   169 *master* THEOBALD; not in
Q², which obviously has a word missing. Some have suggested "curb."   171-2
And when . . . you and when you show some sign of wishing for the blessing of
heaven, I will be once more your dutiful son and ask your blessing at parting, as

　　　　I'll blessing beg of you. — For this same lord,
　　　　I do repent; but heaven hath pleas'd it so,
　　　　To punish me with this, and this with me,
　　　　That I must be their scourge and minister.　　　　　175
　　　　I will bestow him, and will answer well
　　　　The death I gave him. So again, good night.
　　　　I must be cruel, only to be kind;
　　　　Thus bad begins, and worse remains behind.
　　　　One word more, good lady.

QUEEN.　　　　　　　　　　　　What shall I do?　　　　180

HAM.　　Not this, by no means, that I bid you do:
　　　　Let the bloat King tempt you again to bed;
　　　　Pinch wanton on your cheek; call you his mouse;
　　　　And let him, for a pair of reechy kisses,
　　　　Or paddling in your neck with his damn'd fingers,　175　185
　　　　Make you to ravel all this matter out,
　　　　That I essentially am not in madness,
　　　　But mad in craft. 'Twere good you let him know;
　　　　For who that's but a queen, fair, sober, wise,
　　　　Would from a paddock, from a bat, a gib,　　　　190
　　　　Such dear concernings hide? Who would do so?
　　　　No, in despite of sense and secrecy,
　　　　Unpeg the basket on the house's top,
　　　　Let the birds fly, and like the famous ape,

I used to do [K].　175 *their scourge and minister* heaven's scourge (of punish-ment) and heaven's agent — minister of divine retribution [K].　176 *bestow* dis-pose of.　179 *Thus bad . . . behind* by this act (the killing of Polonius) a bad beginning has been made, but worse things are to come (alluding probably to the killing of the King). *Thus bad* F¹; Q²: "This bad."　180 *One . . . lady* Q²; not in F¹.　182 *bloat* bloated with drinking [K].　183 *wanton* lewdly. *mouse* A common term of endearment.　184 *reechy* nauseous — literally, smoky [K].　186 *ravel . . . out* unravel, explain this matter.　187 *essentially* really, in essence.　190 *paddock . . . gib* toad, bat and cat, all supposedly unclean animals, associated with witches and used in their incantations.　191 *Such dear concernings* matters of such importance to one's self [K].　193 *Unpeg the basket* The fable cited, though it has not been found elsewhere, is easy to reconstruct. An ape finds a basket full of birds on the housetop and opens it. The birds fly away. The ape gets into the basket and jumps out in an attempt to fly, but falls from the roof and breaks his neck [K].

       To try conclusions, in the basket creep   195
       And break your own neck down.

QUEEN.   Be thou assur'd, if words be made of breath,
       And breath of life, I have no life to breathe
       What thou hast said to me.

HAM.   I must to England; you know that?

QUEEN.   Alack,   200
       I had forgot! 'Tis so concluded on.

HAM.   There's letters seal'd; and my two schoolfellows,
       Whom I will trust as I will adders fang'd,
       They bear the mandate; they must sweep my way
       And marshal me to knavery. Let it work;   205
       For 'tis the sport to have the enginer
       Hoist with his own petar; and 't shall go hard
       But I will delve one yard below their mines
       And blow them at the moon. O, 'tis most sweet
       When in one line two crafts directly meet.   210
       This man shall set me packing.
       I'll lug the guts into the neighbour room. —
       Mother, good night. — Indeed, this counsellor
       Is now most still, most secret, and most grave,
       Who was in life a foolish prating knave.   215
       Come, sir, to draw toward an end with you.
       Good night, mother.

                    [Exit the Queen. *Then] exit* Hamlet,
                    tugging in Polonius.

---

195 *try conclusions* experiment.   202–10 *There's . . . meet* Q²; not in F¹.   203 *fang'd* with fangs — whose fangs have not been extracted.   204 *mandate* command.   204 *sweep my way* clear the path before me.   205 *knavery* some crime against myself. The precise nature of the plan Hamlet does not discover until they are at sea, when he opens the commission (see V.II.17–25) [K].   206 *enginer* engineer. The Elizabethan accent was on the first syllable [K].   207 *Hoist* hoisted, blown up. *petar* petard — a kind of bomb used especially for blowing gates

open [κ].   210 *When . . . meet* Another figure from warfare. Hamlet imagines two plotters (the King and himself) as digging a mine and a countermine and suddenly coming face to face in their excavations [κ].   211 *packing* (a) lugging, carrying a load on my back (b) leaving the country in haste — on account of his death [κ].   214 *most grave* An obvious pun [κ].   215 *a foolish* F¹; Q²: "a most foolish."   216 *to draw . . . with you* to come to the end of my business with you. A regular phrase when one is approaching the end of a long speech [κ].

[Act Four

<figure>◇◇</figure>

SCENE I. *Elsinore. A room in the Castle.*]

Enter King *and* Queen, *with* Rosencrantz *and* Guildenstern.

KING. There's matter in these sighs. These profound heaves
You must translate; 'tis fit we understand them.
Where is your son?

QUEEN. Bestow this place on us a little while.

> [*Exeunt* Rosencrantz *and* Guilden-
> stern.]

Ah, mine own lord, what have I seen to-night! 5

KING. What, Gertrude? How does Hamlet?

QUEEN. Mad as the sea and wind when both contend
Which is the mightier. In his lawless fit,
Behind the arras hearing something stir,
Whips out his rapier, cries "A rat, a rat!" 10
And in this brainish apprehension kills
The unseen good old man.

IV.I. This act division, introduced by ROWE who followed the Q of 1676, is retained by almost all editors, although it does seem to unnecessarily break the
continuity of the action. 1 *matter* meaning. 2 *translate* explain. 4 *Bestow
. . . while* leave us for a little while (Q²; not in F¹). 7 *Mad* Despite Hamlet's
protestation in III.IV.139ff the Queen still believes that he is mad, and that he
was really trying to kill a rat behind the arras. His seeing the Ghost and talking
with it has confirmed this opinion. Thus she can conceal his protestation of
sanity without being false to her husband [K]. 11 *brainish apprehension* insane
notion. 12 *good old man* The regard of the King and Queen for Polonius is
evident throughout the play. It should teach the actor who plays the part that
the old Councillor, though at times ridiculous, is not to be made a mere ancient

KING.   O heavy deed!
          It had been so with us, had we been there.
          His liberty is full of threats to all —
          To you yourself, to us, to every one.   15
          Alas, how shall this bloody deed be answer'd?
          It will be laid to us, whose providence
          Should have kept short, restrain'd, and out of haunt
          This mad young man. But so much was our love
          We would not understand what was most fit,   20
          But, like the owner of a foul disease,
          To keep it from divulging, let it feed
          Even on the pith of life. Where is he gone?

QUEEN.   To draw apart the body he hath kill'd;
          O'er whom his very madness, like some ore   25
          Among a mineral of metals base,
          Shows itself pure. 'A weeps for what is done.

KING.   O Gertrude, come away!
          The sun no sooner shall the mountains touch
          But we will ship him hence; and this vile deed   30
          We must with all our majesty and skill
          Both countenance and excuse. Ho, Guildenstern!

                    Enter Rosencrantz *and* Guildenstern.

          Friends both, go join you with some further aid.
          Hamlet in madness hath Polonius slain,
          And from his mother's closet hath he dragg'd him.   35
          Go seek him out; speak fair, and bring the body
          Into the chapel. I pray you haste in this.

---

buffoon [K].   13 *It had been so with us* The King immediately perceives what
the Queen cannot know — that Hamlet had intended to kill him when he thrust
his sword through the tapestry; and henceforth he has no doubt that Hamlet is
sane and that he is his mortal enemy [K].   16 *answer'd* accounted for, explained
— i.e. to the public [K].   17 *providence* foresight.   18 *short* under control. *out
of haunt* away from association with other people.   22 *divulging* coming to
light, becoming known.   23 *pith* marrow, very substance.   25–6 *some ore . . .
metals base* some vein of gold in a mine (mineral) composed of baser metals.   27
'A Q²; F¹, K: "He."   31–2 *We must . . . excuse* I must defend with all my royal
authority and excuse with all my skill [K].

                        Exeunt [Rosencrantz *and* Guilden-
                        stern].

        Come, Gertrude, we'll call up our wisest friends
        And let them know both what we mean to do
        And what's untimely done. [So haply slander —]   40
        Whose whisper o'er the world's diameter,
        As level as the cannon to his blank,
        Transports his pois'ned shot — may miss our name
        And hit the woundless air. — O, come away!
        My soul is full of discord and dismay.   *Exeunt.* 45

❖❖❖❖❖❖❖❖❖❖❖❖❖❖

        [SCENE II. *Elsinore. A passage in the Castle.*]

        Enter Hamlet.

HAM.   Safely stow'd.

GENTLEMEN. (*within*) Hamlet! Lord Hamlet!

HAM.   But soft! What noise? Who calls on Hamlet? O, here
        they come.

                        Enter Rosencrantz *and* Guilden-
                        stern.

ROS.   What have you done, my lord, with the dead body?   5

HAM.   Compounded it with dust, whereto 'tis kin.

ROS.   Tell us where 'tis, that we may take it thence
        And bear it to the chapel.

HAM.   Do you believe it.

ROS.   Believe what?   10

---

40 *So haply slander* CAPELL; not in Q², F¹.   41 *o'er . . . diameter* across the
whole breadth of the world [K].   42 *level* sure in its aim.   *blank* mark, target.
44 *woundless* invulnerable.   45 *My soul . . . dismay* A sincere expression of
the turmoil in the King's mind. The death of Polonius is, he knows, a serious
matter, likely to shake his throne [K].

    IV.II. 1 *Safely stow'd* Hamlet has not yet recovered from the excited mood in
which we saw him at the very end of the preceding act. Hence the flippancy of
his language [K].   12 *replication* reply.   15 *countenance* favour.   17 *like an*
ape as an ape keeps things which he intends to devour [K] (F¹; Q²: "apple").   22

HAM.   That I can keep your counsel, and not mine own. Besides, to be demanded of a sponge, what replication should be made by the son of a king?

ROS.   Take you me for a sponge, my lord?

HAM.   Ay, sir; that soaks up the King's countenance, his rewards, his authorities. But such officers do the King best service in the end. He keeps them, like an ape, in the corner of his jaw; first mouth'd, to be last swallowed. When he needs what you have glean'd, it is but squeezing you and, sponge, you shall be dry again.   15

ROS.   I understand you not, my lord.   20

HAM.   I am glad of it. A knavish speech sleeps in a foolish ear.

ROS.   My lord, you must tell us where the body is and go with us to the King.

HAM.   The body is with the King, but the King is not with the body. The King is a thing —   25

GUIL.   A thing, my lord?

HAM.   Of nothing. Bring me to him. Hide fox, and all after.

Exeunt.

❖❖❖❖❖❖❖❖❖❖❖❖❖

[SCENE III. *Elsinore. A room in the Castle.*]

Enter King.

KING.   I have sent to seek him and to find the body.
How dangerous is it that this man goes loose!
Yet must not we put the strong law on him.

---

sleeps in is not understood by.   25-6 *The body . . . body* Mere nonsense, designed to carry out Hamlet's pretense of madness [K].   28 *Of nothing* Cf. the Prayer Book version of Psalm CXLIV, 4: "Man is like a thing of naught: his time passeth away like a shadow." *Hide . . . after* Doubtless the formula of a child's game similar to hide-and-seek. One person (the fox) hides, and the other players are to find him if they can. As he speaks, Hamlet runs off as if he were the fox ("Catch me if you can!"), and is followed by Rosencrantz and Guildenstern [K] (F¹; not in Q²).

He's lov'd of the distracted multitude,
Who like not in their judgment, but their eyes;   5
And where 'tis so, th' offender's scourge is weigh'd,
But never the offence. To bear all smooth and even,
This sudden sending him away must seem
Deliberate pause. Diseases desperate grown
By desperate appliance are reliev'd,   10
Or not at all.

Enter Rosencrantz.

How now? What hath befall'n?

ROS.   Where the dead body is bestow'd, my lord,
            We cannot get from him.

KING.   But where is he?

ROS.   Without, my lord; guarded, to know your pleasure.

KING.   Bring him before us.   15

ROS.   Ho, Guildenstern! Bring in my lord.

Enter Hamlet *and* Guildenstern [*with*
Attendants].

KING.   Now, Hamlet, where's Polonius?

HAM.   At supper.

KING.   At supper? Where?

HAM.   Not where he eats, but where 'a is eaten. A certain con-   20
            vocation of politic worms are e'en at him. Your worm is
            your only emperor for diet. We fat all creatures else to
            fat us, and we fat ourselves for maggots. Your fat king
            and your lean beggar is but variable service — two dishes,
            but to one table. That's the end.   25

IV.III. 4 *distracted* turbulent.   6 *scourge* punishment.   7 *bear* manage.   9
Deliberate pause the outcome of careful thought rather than of impulse.   9–11
Diseases . . . at all A common proverbial statement.   12 *bestow'd* deposited,
hidden.   14 *Without* outside.   20 *'a* Q²; F¹, K: "he."   21 *politic* skilled in statecraft. There may be an allusion to the Diet of Worms.   24 *variable service* two
ways of serving the same food [K].   26–8 *Alas . . . worm* Q²; not in F¹.   30 *progress* a journey of state undertaken by a monarch from one part of his realm to
another. Queen Elizabeth and James I were fond of such progresses [K].   35 *if*,
indeed Q²; F¹, K: "indeed, if."   36 *nose* smell.   38 *'A* Q²; F¹, K: "He."   40 *Which*

KING.   Alas, alas!

HAM.   A man may fish with the worm that hath eat of a king,
        and eat of the fish that hath fed of that worm.

KING.   What dost thou mean by this?

HAM.   Nothing but to show you how a king may go a progress   30
        through the guts of a beggar.

KING.   Where is Polonius?

HAM.   In heaven. Send thither to see. If your messenger find
        him not there, seek him i' th' other place yourself. But
        if, indeed, you find him not within this month, you   35
        shall nose him as you go up the stairs into the lobby.

KING.   Go seek him there.   [*To* Attendants.]

HAM.   'A will stay till you come.   [*Exeunt* Attendants.]

KING.   Hamlet, this deed, for thine especial safety, —
        Which we do tender as we dearly grieve   40
        For that which thou hast done, — must send thee hence
        With fiery quickness. Therefore prepare thyself.
        The bark is ready and the wind at help,
        Th' associates tend, and everything is bent
        For England.

HAM.   For England?

KING.   Ay, Hamlet.

HAM.   Good.   45

KING.   So is it, if thou knew'st our purposes.

HAM.   I see a cherub that sees them. But come, for England!
        Farewell, dear mother.

. . . *grieve* which we hold at as high a rate as we deeply grieve.   42 *With fiery
quickness* F¹; not in Q². 43 *at help* favourable.   44 *Th' associates tend* your
companions are waiting.   *bent* ready (a figure from archery).   47 *I see a
cherub . . . them* A mad-sounding remark, meaning simply "I have some notion
of what they are." Heaven's cherubim, of course, see everything [K].   48 *dear
mother* The maddest speech that Hamlet has yet made. The Queen is not
present. The King corrects Hamlet patiently in his reply, which carries us back
to I.II.64, 110–12 [K].

KING.   Thy loving father, Hamlet.

HAM.   My mother! Father and mother is man and wife; man   50
         and wife is one flesh; and so, my mother. Come, for
         England!   *Exit.*

KING.   Follow him at foot; tempt him with speed aboard.
         Delay it not; I'll have him hence to-night.
         Away! for everything is seal'd and done   55
         That else leans on th' affair. Pray you make haste.

                    [*Exeunt* Rosencrantz *and* Guilden-
                         stern.]

         And, England, if my love thou hold'st at aught, —
         As my great power thereof may give thee sense,
         Since yet thy cicatrice looks raw and red
         After the Danish sword, and thy free awe   60
         Pays homage to us, — thou mayst not coldly set
         Our sovereign process, which imports at full,
         By letters congruing to that effect,
         The present death of Hamlet. Do it, England;
         For like the hectic in my blood he rages,   65
         And thou must cure me. Till I know 'tis done,
         Howe'er my haps, my joys were ne'er begun.   *Exit.*

53 *at foot* at his heels. *tempt* coax.   55-6 *seal'd . . . affair* This makes it clear
enough that Rosencrantz and Guildenstern do not know the contents of the
sealed mandate that they carry to the English king. See note on line 63 [K].
leans on the affair appertains to the business [K].   57 *England* King of England.
58 *sense* a feeling (of the value of my favour).   60-1 *thy free . . . to us* though
technically free, yet thou standest in awe of me and payest homage accordingly
[K].   61 *coldly set* regard indifferently.   62 *process* instructions, mandate.   63
letters a letter (Latin "litterae"). This sealed mandate to the English King is
quite distinct from the "commission" given to Rosencrantz and Guildenstern
(III.III.3). Its contents are a secret. Their commission gives them custody of the
mandate and of Hamlet and directs them to deliver it and him. They are ignorant

❖❖❖❖❖❖❖❖❖❖❖❖❖❖❖

[SCENE IV. *Near Elsinore.*]

Enter Fortinbras *with his* Army *over the stage.*

FOR.   Go, Captain, from me greet the Danish king.
Tell him that by his license Fortinbras
Craves the conveyance of a promis'd march
Over his kingdom. You know the rendezvous.
If that his Majesty would aught with us,   5
We shall express our duty in his eye;
And let him know so.

CAPT.   I will do't, my lord.

FOR.   Go softly on.   *Exeunt [all but the* Captain].

Enter Hamlet, Rosencrantz, [Guilden-
stern,] *and others.*

HAM.   Good sir, whose powers are these?

CAPT.   They are of Norway, sir.   10

HAM.   How purpos'd, sir, I pray you?

CAPT.   Against some part of Poland.

HAM.   Who commands them, sir?

CAPT.   The nephew to old Norway, Fortinbras.

---

of its contents [K]. *congruing to* in agreement with. *effect* purport.   64 *present*
instant, immediate. Thus, for the first time, we learn of the King's purpose [K].
65 *the hectic* a continuous (as opposed to an intermittent) fever [K].   67 *Howe'er
my haps* whatever fortune I may have had or may have in the future [K]. *were
ne'er begun* F¹; Q²: "will nere begin."

    IV.IV. 3 *conveyance* escort. Danish heralds would accompany the troops of
Fortinbras to certify that they came marching through the kingdom by royal
license (see II.II.77–80) [K].   6 *eye* presence.   8 *softly* slowly.   9–66 *Good sir
. . . nothing worth* Q²; not in F¹, probably having been cut for the acting version
on which F¹ is based.   9 *powers* troops.

HAM.	Goes it against the main of Poland, sir,	15
	Or for some frontier?	

CAPT.   Truly to speak, and with no addition,
        We go to gain a little patch of ground
        That hath in it no profit but the name.
        To pay five ducats, five, I would not farm it;   20
        Nor will it yield to Norway or the Pole
        A ranker rate, should it be sold in fee.

HAM.   Why, then the Polack never will defend it.

CAPT.   Yes, it is already garrison'd.

HAM.   Two thousand souls and twenty thousand ducats   25
        Will not debate the question of this straw.
        This is th' imposthume of much wealth and peace,
        That inward breaks, and shows no cause without
        Why the man dies. — I humbly thank you, sir.

CAPT.   God b' wi' you, sir.   [*Exit.*]

ROS.   Will't please you go, my lord?   30

HAM.   I'll be with you straight. Go a little before.

                    [*Exeunt all but* Hamlet.]

        How all occasions do inform against me
        And spur my dull revenge! What is a man,
        If his chief good and market of his time

---

15 *main* entire country.   17 *addition* exaggeration.   19 *the name* Emphatic:
"the mere name of conquest" [K].   20 *To pay . . . farm it* I would not take it on
lease at a rental of five ducats a year [K].   22 *A ranker rate* a higher rate. If
the plot of ground were sold outright (in fee), the price would not yield an annual
income of more than five ducats [K].   26 *debate* fight out; settle by combat [K].
27 *imposthume* internal abscess or ulcer. Hamlet means that such wars are the
result of the corruption which comes from too much peace and luxury. It was an
old theory that war is the natural exercise or gymnastics of the body politic, and
that a country long at peace develops faults in the national character analogous
to the diseases that idle luxury breeds in the human body [K].   32 *inform against*
denounce, accuse.   34 *market of his time* occupation — that for which he sells
his time.   36 *discourse* power of thought, rational faculty.   37 *Looking before*

Be but to sleep and feed? A beast, no more.   35
Sure he that made us with such large discourse,
Looking before and after, gave us not
That capability and godlike reason
To fust in us unus'd. Now, whether it be
Bestial oblivion, or some craven scruple   40
Of thinking too precisely on th' event, —
A thought which, quarter'd, hath but one part wisdom
And ever three parts coward, — I do not know
Why yet I live to say "This thing's to do,"
Sith I have cause, and will, and strength, and means   45
To do't. Examples gross as earth exhort me.
Witness this army of such mass and charge,
Led by a delicate and tender prince,
Whose spirit, with divine ambition puff'd,
Makes mouths at the invisible event,   50
Exposing what is mortal and unsure
To all that fortune, death, and danger dare,
Even for an eggshell. Rightly to be great
Is not to stir without great argument,
But greatly to find quarrel in a straw   55
When honour's at the stake. How stand I then,
That have a father kill'd, a mother stain'd,
Excitements of my reason and my blood,
And let all sleep, while to my shame I see
The imminent death of twenty thousand men   60

---

and after as one must do in reasoning logically — passing from premises to conclusions [ᴋ].   38 *capability and godlike reason* Hendiadys: "that capability of
godlike reason"; godlike since reason makes us akin to the gods and distinguishes
us from beasts [ᴋ].   39 *fust* grow musty from lack of use [ᴋ].   40 *Bestial oblivion*
forgetfulness like that of the beasts (which do not remember their parents long)
[ᴋ].   41 *thinking . . . event* considering too carefully what the outcome may be
[ᴋ].   45 *Sith* since.   46 *gross* obvious (literally, "large").   47 *charge* expense.   50
Makes mouths at makes faces at; holds in contempt [ᴋ].   *event* outcome, result.
53–6 *Rightly . . . stake* true nobility of soul is to restrain one's self unless there
is a great cause for resentment, but nobly to recognize even a trifle as such a
cause when honour is involved [ᴋ].   58 *blood* passions.

That for a fantasy and trick of fame
Go to their graves like beds, fight for a plot
Whereon the numbers cannot try the cause,
Which is not tomb enough and continent
To hide the slain? O, from this time forth,   65
My thoughts be bloody, or be nothing worth!   *Exit.*

❖❖❖❖❖❖❖❖❖❖❖❖❖❖❖❖

[SCENE V. *Elsinore. A room in the Castle.*]

Enter Horatio, Queen, *and a* Gentleman.

QUEEN.   I will not speak with her.

GENT.   She is importunate, indeed distract.
          Her mood will needs be pitied.

QUEEN.   What would she have?

GENT.   She speaks much of her father; says she hears
          There's tricks i' th' world, and hems, and beats her heart;   5
          Spurns enviously at straws; speaks things in doubt,
          That carry but half sense. Her speech is nothing,
          Yet the unshaped use of it doth move
          The hearers to collection; they aim at it,
          And botch the words up fit to their own thoughts;   10
          Which, as her winks and nods and gestures yield them,
          Indeed would make one think there might be thought,
          Though nothing sure, yet much unhappily.

HOR.   'Twere good she were spoken with; for she may strew

---

61 *fantasy* mere whim. *trick of fame* trifle of reputation; a matter affecting one's
reputation in the very slightest degree [ᴋ].   63 *Whereon . . . cause* not big
enough to hold the men needed to settle the case by combat [ᴋ].   64 *continent*
container, receptacle.

IV.v. 2 *distract* out of her mind.   5 *tricks* plots and deceits, trickery.   6 *Spurns*
enviously at straws takes offence angrily at trifles [ᴋ].   8 *unshaped use* disordered
manner.   9 *aim* guess (ꜰ¹; Q²: "yawne").   10 *botch . . . thoughts* patch the
words together so as to adapt them to their own ideas, i.e. to the suspicions they
already have about the sudden death of Polonius [ᴋ].   11 *Which* The antecedent
is "words" [ᴋ].   15 *ill-breeding* breeding evil; prone to evil thoughts [ᴋ].   16
Let . . . in ꜰ¹; Q² gives the line to Horatio.   18 *toy* trifle. *amiss* calamity.   19

Dangerous conjectures in ill-breeding minds. 15

QUEEN. Let her come in. [*Exit* Gentleman.]
[*Aside*] To my sick soul (as sin's true nature is)
Each toy seems prologue to some great amiss.
So full of artless jealousy is guilt
It spills itself in fearing to be spilt. 20

Enter Ophelia *distracted.*

OPH. Where is the beauteous Majesty of Denmark?

QUEEN. How now, Ophelia?

OPH. (*sings*) How should I your true-love know
From another one?
By his cockle hat and staff 25
And his sandal shoon.

QUEEN. Alas, sweet lady, what imports this song?

OPH. Say you? Nay, pray you mark.

(*Sings*) He is dead and gone, lady,
He is dead and gone; 30
At his head a grass-green turf,
At his heels a stone.

O, ho!

QUEEN. Nay, but Ophelia —

OPH. Pray you mark.

(*Sings*) White his shroud as the mountain snow — 35

Enter King.

---

artless jealousy unreasonable and unwise suspicion [K]. 20 *spills* destroys. The
excessive suspicion which guilt brings with it often causes the guilty person to
act in a way that rouses suspicion in others. Thus the Queen's avoidance of
Ophelia might have caused that very suspicion which she wishes to avoid [K].
23–6 *How should . . . . shoon* Although the ballad snatches which Ophelia sings
seem to be well-known popular songs, only three lines appear elsewhere. See
Supplementary Notes. 25 *cockle hat and staff* The signs of a pilgrim. A cockle
shell stuck in the hat was originally a sign that the wearer had been on a
pilgrimage to the famous shrine of St. James at Compostela in Spanish Galicia
[K]. 27 *imports* means. 28 *Say you* is that what you want me to say (or sing)?

QUEEN. Alas, look here, my lord!

OPH. (*sings*)　Larded all with sweet flowers;
　　　　　Which bewept to the grave did not go
　　　　　With true-love showers.

KING. How do you, pretty lady? 40

OPH. Well, God dild you! They say the owl was a baker's
daughter. Lord, we know what we are, but know not
what we may be. God be at your table!

KING. Conceit upon her father.

OPH. Pray let's have no words of this; but when they ask you 45
what it means, say you this:

(*Sings*)　To-morrow is Saint Valentine's day,
　　　　　All in the morning betime,
　　　　　And I a maid at your window,
　　　　　To be your Valentine. 50

　　　　　Then up he rose and donn'd his clo'es
　　　　　And dupp'd the chamber door,
　　　　　Let in the maid. that out a maid,
　　　　　Never departed more.

KING. Pretty Ophelia! 55

OPH. Indeed, la, without an oath, I'll make an end on't!

(*Sings*)　By Gis and by Saint Charity,
　　　　　Alack, and fie for shame!
　　　　　Young men will do't if they come to't
　　　　　By Cock, they are to blame. 60

---

37 *Larded* bedecked.　38 *did not go* All the Quartos and Folios have "not." We
are to regard it as Ophelia's insertion in the verse. She suddenly remembers that
the words of the song do not agree with the facts of her father's burial, which
was hasty and without the usual ceremonies. See lines 81–2, 208–10 [K].　41 *God
dild you* God yield (i.e. repay) you [K].　41–2 *owl . . . daughter* According to an
old folktale a baker's daughter was turned into an owl for her lack of gen-
erosity when Christ came to her father's shop to ask for bread.　43 *God be at
your table.* In her madness Ophelia uses a form of blessing that might be spoken
by one who enters and finds company at dinner [K].　44 *Conceit* imagination.
47 *Tomorrow . . . day* Everybody knows what happens in the way of indecorous
speech when delirium stirs up the dregs of memory and puts an end to reticence

    Quoth she, "Before you tumbled me,
     You promis'd me to wed."
  He answers:
    "So would I'a done, by yonder sun,
     An thou hadst not come to my bed."   65

KING. How long hath she been thus?

OPH. I hope all will be well. We must be patient; but I can-
    not choose but weep to think they would lay him i' th'
    cold ground. My brother shall know of it; and so I thank
    you for your good counsel. Come, my coach! Good night, 70
    ladies. Good night, sweet ladies. Good night, good night.
                Exit.

KING. Follow her close; give her good watch, I pray you.

             [*Exit* Horatio.]

  O, this is the poison of deep grief; it springs
  All from her father's death — and now behold!
  O Gertrude, Gertrude,   75
  When sorrows come, they come not single spies,
  But in battalions! First, her father slain;
  Next, your son gone, and he most violent author
  Of his own just remove; the people muddied,
  Thick and unwholesome in their thoughts and whispers 80
  For good Polonius' death, and we have done but greenly
  In hugger-mugger to inter him; poor Ophelia
  Divided from herself and her fair judgment,
  Without the which we are pictures or mere beasts;
  Last, and as much containing as all these,   85

[K]. The bawdiness of Ophelia's song is thus quite natural. The song is based on
the ancient custom by which the first girl seen by a man on the morning of St.
Valentine's day was considered his Valentine or true-love. 52 *dupp'd* opened.
57 *By Gis* by Jesus (a common oath). 60 *Cock* A vulgar substitute for "God" in
oaths [K]. 68 *choose but weep* help weeping. 74 *and now behold* Q²; not
in F¹, K. 76 *spies* scouts — single soldiers. 78 *author* cause. 79 *muddied* The
muddy bottoms of the people's minds have been stirred up by angry suspicions,
and their thoughts are roiled and turbid [K]. 81 *we* I (the royal "we"). *done
but greenly* acted with childish folly [K]. 82 *In hugger-mugger* in haste and
secrecy. Polonius had been buried without the ceremonies that befit his rank.
See lines 208–10 [K].

Her brother is in secret come from France;
Feeds on his wonder, keeps himself in clouds,
And wants not buzzers to infect his ear
With pestilent speeches of his father's death,
Wherein necessity, of matter beggar'd,   90
Will nothing stick our person to arraign
In ear and ear. O my dear Gertrude, this,
Like to a murd'ring piece, in many places
Gives me superfluous death.   *A noise within.*

QUEEN.   Alack, what noise is this?

KING.   Where are my Switzers? Let them guard the door.   95

                    Enter a Messenger.

What is the matter?

MESS.   Save yourself, my lord:
The ocean, overpeering of his list,
Eats not the flats with more impiteous haste
Than young Laertes, in a riotous head,
O'erbears your officers. The rabble call him lord;   100
And, as the world were now but to begin,
Antiquity forgot, custom not known,
The ratifiers and props of every word,
They cry "Choose we! Laertes shall be king!"

---

87 *Feeds . . . clouds* Instead of trying to discover the facts about his father's
death, Laertes does nothing but wonder about it, making such wonder his only
food for thought. Thus he keeps himself in a state of willful uncertainty and
confusion of mind [K]. *Feeds on his* JOHNSON; Q²: "Feeds on this"; F¹: "Keepes on
his."   88 *wants* lacks. *buzzers* whisperers, scandalmongers.   90 *necessity* the
need (to make up a good story). *of matter beggar'd* being unprovided with
facts.   91 *nothing stick* by no means hesitate. *our person* me, the King, as per-
sonally responsible for the death of Polonius — as his actual murderer [K].   92
In ear and ear now in one of his ears, now in the other. These "buzzers" surround him [K].   93 *a murd'ring piece* a kind of mortar loaded with a variety of
missiles and intended to scatter its shot [K].   94 *Alack . . . this* F¹; not in Q².   95
Switzers hired Swiss guards, used in Shakespeare's time as bodyguards by many
European kings.   97 *overpeering of his list* when it towers (literally, looks) above
its boundary or limit (high-water mark) [K].   98 *flats* low country by the sea.
impiteous without pity, impetuous (Q², F¹; Q³, K: "impetuous"). The two words are
actually doublets of similar meaning, but Shakespeare's spelling preserves the
association with "pity."   99 *head* armed band.   101 *as the world . . . begin* as
though we were at the beginning of time, before human institutions had been

| | Caps, hands, and tongues applaud it to the clouds, | 105 |
| | "Laertes shall be king! Laertes king!" *A noise within.* |

QUEEN. How cheerfully on the false trail they cry!
O, this is counter, you false Danish dogs!

KING. The doors are broke.

Enter Laertes *with others.*

LAER. Where is this king? — Sirs, stand you all without.   110

ALL. No, let's come in!

LAER.   I pray you give me leave.

ALL. We will, we will!

LAER. I thank you. Keep the door. [*Exeunt his* Followers.] O
thou vile king,
Give me my father!

QUEEN.   Calmly, good Laertes.

LAER. That drop of blood that's calm proclaims me bastard;   115
Cries cuckold to my father; brands the harlot
Even here between the chaste unsmirched brows
Of my true mother.

KING.   What is the cause, Laertes,
That thy rebellion looks so giantlike?
Let him go, Gertrude. Do not fear our person.   120

---

established.   102 *Antiquity . . . known* forgetting ancient institutions and ig-
noring established customs.   103 *The ratifiers . . . word* the support (ratifiers)
of all human promises or engagements. "Word" in the sense of "promise" is
common.   107–8 *How cheerfully . . . dogs* In this terrifying situation the Queen
appears as a fearless and high-spirited woman, passionately in love with her guilty
husband; and Claudius himself meets the furious mob with calm dignity and
splendid courage [K]. *counter* A hound "hunts counter" when he follows the scent
backward — away from the animal pursued [K].   111 *give me leave* leave me and
let me go in alone [K].   112 *We will* The fact that Laertes has the mob under
control makes him all the more terrifying and emphasizes the King's fortitude
[K].   114 *Give me my father* Henceforth Laertes appears as the typical avenger.
He serves as a complete foil to Hamlet in this regard. He assumes that the King
is somehow guilty of Polonius' death and acts accordingly, without weighing the
evidence. Then, informed that Hamlet was the slayer, he joins in the King's plot
without scruple and violates his own code of honour. Witness his confession in
V.ii.299*ff* [K].   116 *brands . . . harlot.* Harlots were branded.   120 *fear* be
afraid for.

There's such divinity doth hedge a king
That treason can but peep to what it would,
Acts little of his will. Tell me, Laertes,
Why thou art thus incens'd. Let him go, Gertrude.
Speak, man.   125

LAER.   Where is my father?

KING.   Dead.

QUEEN.   But not by him!

KING.   Let him demand his fill.

LAER.   How came he dead? I'll not be juggled with:
To hell, allegiance! vows, to the blackest devil!
Conscience and grace, to the profoundest pit!   130
I dare damnation. To this point I stand,
That both the worlds I give to negligence,
Let come what comes; only I'll be reveng'd
Most throughly for my father.

KING.   Who shall stay you?

LAER.   My will, not all the world's!   135
And for my means, I'll husband them so well
They shall go far with little.

KING.   Good Laertes,
If you desire to know the certainty
Of your dear father's death, is't writ in your revenge
That swoopstake you will draw both friend and foe,   140
Winner and loser?

LAER.   None but his enemies.

---

122 *peep to* look at from a distance. Traitors can get no nearer a king than the
hedge or protecting barrier which "divine right" builds about him; through this
they can "peep," but that is all. The word and the figure are intentionally grotesque, expressing contempt [K].   123 *his* its.   130 *grace* regard for God's laws
[K].   132 *both the worlds* He cares not what may happen to him, either in this
world or the next, if only he can avenge his father's death. Contrast Hamlet's
scruple in II.ii.584*ff* [K].   134 *throughly* thoroughly.   135 *world's* world's will
(Q²: "worlds"; F¹, K: "world").   136 *husband* use economically.   139 *father's
death* F¹; Q²: "father."   140-1 *That swoopstake . . . loser* that you are determined
to include in your revenge both friend and foe, as if, in gaming, you were to
sweep from the board all the money in sight, whether it belonged to the winner
or to the loser [K].   *swoopstake* DYCE; Q², F¹: "soopstake."   144 *pelican* The

KING.   Will you know them then?

LAER.   To his good friends thus wide I'll ope my arms
         And, like the kind life-rend'ring pelican,
         Repast them with my blood.

KING.   Why, now you speak   145
         Like a good child and a true gentleman.
         That I am guiltless of your father's death.
         And am most sensibly in grief for it,
         It shall as level to your judgment 'pear
         As day does to your eye.
                    A noise within: "Let her come in."   150

LAER.   How now? What noise is that?

                    Enter Ophelia.

         O heat, dry up my brains! Tears seven times salt
         Burn out the sense and virtue of mine eye!
         By heaven, thy madness shall be paid with weight
         Till our scale turn the beam. O rose of May!   155
         Dear maid, kind sister, sweet Ophelia!
         O heavens! is't possible a young maid's wits
         Should be as mortal as an old man's life?
         Nature is fine in love, and where 'tis fine,
         It sends some precious instance of itself   160
         After the thing it loves.

OPH.   (*sings*)
                    They bore him barefac'd on the bier
                    (Hey non nony, nony, hey nony)

---

mother pelican supposedly fed her young with blood from her own breast.   145
Repast feed, banquet.   148 *sensibly* feelingly.   149 *level* clear, obvious.   *'pear*
appear (Q²; F¹, ᴋ: "pierce").   152 *O heat . . . brains* We get the impression that
this is the first time Laertes has seen Ophelia since she went mad. At all events,
her entrance at this crisis revives and intensifies his rage against the unknown
murderer, and threatens to undo all that Claudius has accomplished in the way
of controlling him [ᴋ].   153 *virtue* faculty.   154 *with* Q²; F¹, ᴋ: "by."   155 *beam*
the bar of a scale.   159–61 *Nature . . . loves* human nature is made most pure
and exquisite (fine) by love, and when it is so refined (fine), it sends some token
of itself, some part of its own being (instance), to follow the object which it loves
(F¹; not in Q²).   163 *Hey . . . nony* F¹; not in Q².

And in his grave rain'd many a tear.

Fare you well, my dove! 165

LAER. Hadst thou thy wits, and didst persuade revenge,
It could not move thus.

OPH. You must sing "A-down a-down, and you call him
a-down-a." O, how the wheel becomes it! It is the false
steward, that stole his master's daughter. 170

LAER. This nothing's more than matter.

OPH. There's rosemary, that's for remembrance. Pray you,
love, remember. And there is pansies, that's for thoughts.

LAER. A document in madness! Thoughts and remembrance
fitted. 175

OPH. There's fennel for you, and columbines. There's rue for
you, and here's some for me. We may call it herb of
grace o' Sundays. O, you must wear your rue with a
difference! There's a daisy. I would give you some
violets, but they wither'd all when my father died. They 180
say 'a made a good end.

[*Sings*] For bonny sweet Robin is all my joy.

LAER. Thought and affliction, passion, hell itself,
She turns to favour and to prettiness.

OPH. (*sings*)

And will 'a not come again? 185

168–9 *A-down . . . a-down-a* A common refrain or "burden" in Elizabethan
songs.   169 *the wheel* the spinning wheel, to whose rhythmic motion songs and
ballads were often sung [K].   *becomes it* suits the ballad and its tune [K].   169–70
false steward . . . daughter The song tells the story of the false steward. The
ballad is unknown [K].   171 *This . . . matter* this random talk of hers is more
significant (of what she has suffered) than sane speech could be [K].   172 *rosemary* The smell of this herb was believed to strengthen the memory. Each of the
flowers and herbs which Ophelia distributes has a special meaning. See Supplementary Notes.   173 *pansies . . . thoughts* "Pansy" comes from the French
"pensée."   174 *document in madness* piece of instruction given to me in this
mad talk. What the instruction is we learn from the next sentence: "Thoughts
and remembrance would indeed be fitting for me now" [K].   176 *fennel* a symbol
of flattery and deceit [K].   *columbines* symbols of thanklessness.   *rue* Since rue is
bitter, and since its name coincides with the verb "rue," the herb became a symbol

And will 'a not come again?
No, no, he is dead;
Go to thy deathbed;
He never will come again.

His beard was as white as snow,   190
All flaxen was his poll.
He is gone, he is gone,
And we cast away moan.
God 'a' mercy on his soul!

And of all Christian souls, I pray God. God b' wi' you.   195
                                              Exit.

LAER.   Do you see this, O God?

KING.   Laertes, I must commune with your grief,
Or you deny me right. Go but apart,
Make choice of whom your wisest friends you will,
And they shall hear and judge 'twixt you and me.   200
If by direct or by collateral hand
They find us touch'd, we will our kingdom give,
Our crown, our life, and all that we call ours,
To you in satisfaction; but if not,
Be you content to lend your patience to us,   205
And we shall jointly labour with your soul
To give it due content.

LAER.   Let this be so.
His means of death, his obscure funeral —

---

for sorrow or repentance. Its name "herb of grace" was associated with the idea
of repentance for one's sins. Hence Ophelia thinks it a good Sunday name for the
herb [K].   178-9 *with a difference* An heraldic term for a variation (usually
slight) in a family coat of arms, indicating that the wearer belonged to a younger
branch of the family. Ophelia means merely that the Queen's cause of sorrow
differs from hers; but the Queen, and the audience, feel that rue should mean
"grief" in Ophelia's case, "repentance for sin" in the Queen's [K].   179 *daisy*
symbol of dissembling.   180 *violets* symbol of faithfulness.   181, 185, 186 *'a* Q²;
F¹, K: "he."   182 *For . . . joy* A line from a well-known ballad mentioned also
by the Jailer's daughter in THE TWO NOBLE KINSMEN (IV.I.108).   183 *Thought* sorrow.   184 *favour* beauty, charm.   195 *And . . . souls* An old formula for prayer
[K].   201 *collateral* indirect.   202 *touch'd* i.e. with guilt in the death of Polonius
[K].

No trophy, sword, nor hatchment o'er his bones,
No noble rite nor formal ostentation, —   210
Cry to be heard, as 'twere from heaven to earth,
That I must call't in question.

KING.   So you shall;
And where th' offence is let the great axe fall.
I pray you go with me.   *Exeunt.*

◇◇◇◇◇◇◇◇◇◇◇◇◇◇◇◇◇◇

[SCENE VI.
Elsinore. Another room in the Castle.]

Enter Horatio *with an* Attendant.

HOR.   What are they that would speak with me?

SERVANT. Seafaring men, sir. They say they have letters for you.

HOR.   Let them come in.   [*Exit* Attendant.]
I do not know from what part of the world
I should be greeted, if not from Lord Hamlet.   5

Enter Sailors.

SAILOR.   God bless you, sir.

HOR.   Let him bless thee too.

SAILOR.   'A shall, sir, an't please him. There's a letter for you,
sir, — it comes from th' ambassador that was bound for
England — if your name be Horatio, as I am let to know   10
it is.

HOR.   (*reads the letter*) "Horatio, when thou shalt have overlook'd this, give these fellows some means to the King.

---

209 *trophy* anything that serves as a memorial or as a mark of honour [K]. *hatchment* a tablet, with coat of arms and mourning emblems, set up on a tomb or a
house-front or over a gate [K].   210 *formal ostentation* due and proper ceremony
[K].   211 *as . . . earth* as if by a direct summons from God [K].   213 *the great
axe* the axe of vengeance [K].

    IV.VI. 12–13 *overlook'd* read over.   13 *means* of access.   15 *appointment* equip-

They have letters for him. Ere we were two days old at
sea, a pirate of very war-like appointment gave us chase.   15
Finding ourselves too slow of sail, we put on a compelled
valour, and in the grapple I boarded them. On the instant they got clear of our ship; so I alone became their
prisoner. They have dealt with me like thieves of mercy;
but they knew what they did: I am to do a good turn   20
for them. Let the King have the letters I have sent, and
repair thou to me with as much speed as thou wouldest
fly death. I have words to speak in thine ear will make
thee dumb; yet are they much too light for the bore of
the matter. These good fellows will bring thee where I   25
am. Rosencrantz and Guildenstern hold their course for
England. Of them I have much to tell thee. Farewell.

> "He that thou knowest thine, HAMLET."

Come, I will give you way for these your letters,
And do't the speedier that you may direct me   30
To him from whom you brought them.   *Exeunt.*

<><><><><><><><><><><><>

[SCENE VII.
Elsinore. Another room in the Castle.]

Enter King *and* Laertes.

KING.   Now must your conscience my acquittance seal,
And you must put me in your heart for friend,
Sith you have heard, and with a knowing ear,
That he which hath your noble father slain
Pursued my life.

LAER.   It well appears. But tell me   5

---

ment.   19 *thieves of mercy* merciful robbers.   20 *they knew what they did* they
knew what they were doing — that it would serve their own interests.   24-5 *too
light . . . matter* A figure from gunnery: "not weighty enough to do the subject
justice" [K].   29 *give you way* procure you access (to the King).

IV.VII. 1 *my acquittance seal* finally approve my acquittal (of guilt in Polonius'
death).   3 *Sith* since.

Why you proceeded not against these feats
So crimeful and so capital in nature,
As by your safety, greatness, wisdom, all things else,
You mainly were stirr'd up.

KING.   O, for two special reasons,
Which may to you, perhaps, seem much unsinew'd,   10
But yet to me th' are strong. The Queen his mother
Lives almost by his looks; and for myself, —
My virtue or my plague, be it either which, —
She's so conjunctive to my life and soul
That, as the star moves not but in his sphere,   15
I could not but by her. The other motive
Why to a public count I might not go
Is the great love the general gender bear him,
Who, dipping all his faults in their affection,
Would, like the spring that turneth wood to stone,   20
Convert his gyves to graces; so that my arrows,
Too slightly timber'd for so loud a wind,
Would have reverted to my bow again,
And not where I had aim'd them.

LAER.   And so have I a noble father lost;   25
A sister driven into desp'rate terms,
Whose worth, if praises may go back again,
Stood challenger on mount of all the age
For her perfections. But my revenge will come.

KING.   Break not your sleeps for that. You must not think 30

---

6 *proceeded* i.e. by bringing Hamlet to trial for murder and treason [K]. *feats*
acts.   7 *crimeful* F¹; Q²: "criminall."   8 *safety* regard for safety. *greatness* Q²; not
in F¹, K. But Alexandrine lines are common in Shakespeare.   9 *mainly* strongly.
two special reasons These two reasons were obviously genuine. The Queen's love
for her son and the King's love for the Queen are strong motives in the drama,
and the necessity of taking the Danish people into account has just been proved
by their insurrection under the lead of Laertes [K].   10 *much unsinew'd* very
weak.   11 *th' are* Q²; F¹, K: "they are."   13 *be it either which* whichever of the
two you may choose to call it [K].   14 *conjunctive* closely joined.   15 *in his
sphere* in its hollow crystalline sphere, concentric with the earth (in accordance
with the Ptolemaic astronomy) [K].   17 *count* trial, accounting.   18 *general
gender* common people.   19 *dipping . . . affection* gilding over his faults with
their love. The figure is from the plating of base metals by dipping them in gold.

That we are made of stuff so flat and dull
That we can let our beard be shook with danger,
And think it pastime. You shortly shall hear more.
I lov'd your father, and we love ourself,
And that, I hope, will teach you to imagine —   35

Enter a Messenger *with letters.*

How now? What news?

MESS.   Letters, my lord, from Hamlet:
These to your Majesty; this to the Queen.

KING. From Hamlet? Who brought them?

MESS. Sailors, my lord, they say; I saw them not.
They were given me by Claudio; he receiv'd them   40
Of him that brought them.

KING.   Laertes, you shall hear them.
Leave us.   *Exit* Messenger.

[*Reads*] "High and Mighty, — You shall know I am set
naked on your kingdom. To-morrow shall I beg leave to
see your kingly eyes; when I shall (first asking your   45
pardon thereunto) recount the occasion of my sudden
and more strange return.

"HAMLET."

What should this mean? Are all the rest come back?
Or is it some abuse, and no such thing?   50

LAER. Know you the hand?

KING.   'Tis Hamlet's character. "Naked!"

---

20 *Would* F¹; Q²: "Worke." *spring . . . stone* Certain English springs are so full
of lime that they will coat with stone any log placed in them.   21 *Convert . . .
graces* make honours out of his fetters.   22 *timber'd* shafted. A light arrow could
not fly against a strong (loud) wind. *loud a wind* F¹; Q²: "so loued Arm'd."   26
terms condition.   28-9 *Stood challenger . . . perfections* was exalted above the
whole contemporary world, challenging it to bring forward any other woman to
equal her in excellence [K].   31 *flat and dull* tame and without spirit; incapable
of resenting an injury [K].   36 *How . . . Hamlet* F¹; not in Q².   37 *These to*
Q²; F¹, K: "This to."   41 *Of him . . . them* Q²; not in F¹.   44 *naked* destitute.   45
your kingly eyes A formal and courtly phrase (like "high and mighty") masking
Hamlet's scorn and hatred [K].   46 *pardon* permission.   47 *and more strange* F¹;
not in Q².   50 *abuse* deceit, delusion.   *no such thing* not what it appears to be.
51 *character* handwriting.

And in a postscript here, he says "alone."
Can you devise me?

LAER.   I am lost in it, my lord. But let him come!
It warms the very sickness in my heart   55
That I shall live and tell him to his teeth,
"Thus didest thou."

KING.   If it be so, Laertes
(As how should it be so? how otherwise?),
Will you be rul'd by me?

LAER.   Ay, my lord,
So you will not o'errule me to a peace.   60

KING.   To thine own peace. If he be now return'd,
As checking at his voyage, and that he means
No more to undertake it, I will work him
To an exploit now ripe in my device,
Under the which he shall not choose but fall;   65
And for his death no wind of blame shall breathe,
But even his mother shall uncharge the practice
And call it accident.

LAER.   My lord, I will be rul'd;
The rather, if you could devise it so
That I might be the organ.

KING.   It falls right.   70
You have been talk'd of since your travel much,
And that in Hamlet's hearing, for a quality
Wherein they say you shine. Your sum of parts
Did not together pluck such envy from him

---

53 *devise* explain to (Q²; F¹, K: "advise").   59 *Will you . . . me* Even in his horrified perplexity, the mind of Claudius works with its usual clearness and promkti-
tude. He has already formed another plan to destroy Hamlet [K].   60 *So* provided
that.   62 *checking at* refusing to continue, turning aside from (as a falcon in flight
that turns away from its prey).   65 *choose but fall* help falling.   67 *uncharge the
practice* acquit the plot of being a plot [K].   70 *organ* instrument, agent. *It falls
right* the circumstances fit your wish [K].   72 *quality* accomplishment.   73 *Your
sum of parts* all your accomplishments combined.   76 *siege* rank (literally, seat).
77 *A very riband . . . youth* a mere ornament of youth. It was the fashion for
courtiers to wear a jewel or ribbon on the cap [K].   78–81 *youth no less . . .
graveness* In modern English we should invert the phrase: "The light and trivial

> As did that one; and that, in my regard,   75
> Of the unworthiest siege.

LAER.   What part is that, my lord?

KING.   A very riband in the cap of youth —
> Yet needful too; for youth no less becomes
> The light and careless livery that it wears
> Than settled age his sables and his weeds,   80
> Importing health and graveness. Two months since
> Here was a gentleman of Normandy.
> I have seen myself, and serv'd against, the French,
> And they can well on horseback; but this gallant
> Had witchcraft in't. He grew unto his seat,   85
> And to such wondrous doing brought his horse
> As had he been incorps'd and demi-natur'd
> With the brave beast. So far he topp'd my thought
> That I, in forgery of shapes and tricks,
> Come short of what he did.

LAER.   A Norman was't?   90

KING.   A Norman.

LAER.   Upon my life, Lamound.

KING.   The very same.

LAER.   I know him well. He is the brooch indeed
> And gem of all the nation.

KING.   He made confession of you;   95
> And gave you such a masterly report
> For art and exercise in your defence,
> And for your rapier most especially,

---

sports that characterize youth are just as becoming to the young as the serious
and dignified pursuits of sober years are to their elders [K].   80 *sables* dignified
robes of sable fur. *weeds* attire.   81 *Importing health and graveness* signifying
due care for health and a proper regard for dignity [K].   84 *can well* are accomplished.   87 *incorps'd* made one body. *demi-natur'd* so united as to form
with the animal a Centaur — half man and half horse [K].   88 *brave* noble.
topp'd my thought surpassed anything that I could even think [K].   89 *forgery*
invention, imagination.   95 *made confession of you* unwillingly acknowledged
that you (a Dane) were superior to him (a Frenchman).   97 *art and exercise*
skill in both theory and practice [K]. *defence* fencing.

That he cried out 'twould be a sight indeed
If one could match you. The scrimers of their nation   100
He swore had neither motion, guard, nor eye,
If you oppos'd them. Sir, this report of his
Did Hamlet so envenom with his envy
That he could nothing do but wish and beg
Your sudden coming o'er to play with you.   105
Now, out of this —

LAER.   What out of this, my lord?

KING.   Laertes, was your father dear to you?
          Or are you like the painting of a sorrow,
          A face without a heart?

LAER.   Why ask you this?

KING.   Not that I think you did not love your father;   110
          But that I know love is begun by time,
          And that I see, in passages of proof,
          Time qualifies the spark and fire of it.
          There lives within the very flame of love
          A kind of wick or snuff that will abate it;   115
          And nothing is at a like goodness still;
          For goodness, growing to a plurisy,
          Dies in his own too-much. That we would do,
          We should do when we would; for this "would" changes,
          And hath abatements and delays as many   120
          As there are tongues, are hands, are accidents;
          And then this "should" is like a spendthrift sigh,

100–2 *The scrimers . . . them* Q²; not in F¹. *scrimers* fencers.   103 *envenom*
poison, make bitter.   107 *was your father dear to you* The treacherous revenge
which the King is about to propose is so abhorrent to what he knows to be the
feelings of a gentleman that he fears some urging may be necessary. The savage
exclamation "To cut his troat i' th' church!" convinces him that Laertes will
have no scruples (line 126) [K].   111 *begun by time* created by circumstance.
112 *passages of proof* facts of experience [K].   113 *qualifies* weakens.   114–23
There lives . . . ulcer Q²; not in F¹.   114–15 *There lives . . . it* the very intensity
of love serves to abate it, as the flame of a lamp makes the snuff (the charred
piece of wick) that deadens the flame and reduces the light [K].   116 *still* forever.   117 *plurisy* excess, plethora — used especially of an excess of blood in the
system [K].   118 *too-much* excess.   *That* what.   119 *this "would"* our will to
act [K].   122 *spendthrift* wasteful. Each sigh was believed to draw a drop of blood
from the heart and thus to weaken it.   126 *To cut . . . church* The readiness of

That hurts by easing. But to the quick o' th' ulcer!
Hamlet comes back. What would you undertake
To show yourself your father's son in deed   125
More than in words?

LAER.   To cut his throat i' th' church!

KING.   No place indeed should murder sanctuarize;
Revenge should have no bounds. But, good Laertes,
Will you do this? Keep close within your chamber.
Hamlet return'd shall know you are come home.   130
We'll put on those shall praise your excellence
And set a double varnish on the fame
The Frenchman gave you; bring you in fine together
And wager on your heads. He, being remiss,
Most generous, and free from all contriving,   135
Will not peruse the foils; so that with ease,
Or with a little shuffling, you may choose
A sword unbated, and, in a pass of practice,
Requite him for your father.

LAER.   I will do't!
And for that purpose I'll anoint my sword.   140
I bought an unction of a mountebank,
So mortal that, but dip a knife in it,
Where it draws blood no cataplasm so rare,
Collected from all simples that have virtue
Under the moon, can save the thing from death   145
That is but scratch'd withal. I'll touch my point
With this contagion, that, if I gall him slightly,

---

this reply is welcome to the King; but its crude ferocity produces in his mind
that contempt which an intellectual villain must feel for mere brute rage. Yet he
suppresses his disgust, and with admirable suavity assents to the principle of
unscrupulous vengeance [K]. The contrast of Laertes with Hamlet, who had
refused to kill the King at prayer, is further maintained here.   131 *put on*
incite, instigate.   133 *in fine* finally.   134 *remiss* careless; unsuspicious by nature [K].   135 *generous* noble-minded.   *contriving* plotting, treachery.   136
peruse scrutinize.   137 *shuffling* trickery, sleight of hand [K].   138 *unbated* not
blunted. Rapiers for practice were blunted but had no button on the point [K].
pass of practice (a) treacherous thrust (b) bout for exercise.   141 *unction* ointment.   *mountebank* quack doctor.   143 *cataplasm* poultice.   144 *Collected from*
composed of.   *simples* medicinal plants.   146 *withal* with it.   147 *gall* scratch;
break the skin; draw blood [K].

It may be death.

KING.   Let's further think of this,
Weigh what convenience both of time and means
May fit us to our shape. If this should fail,   150
And that our drift look through our bad performance,
'Twere better not assay'd. Therefore this project
Should have a back or second, that might hold
If this did blast in proof. Soft! let me see.
We'll make a solemn wager on your cunnings —   155
I ha't!
When in your motion you are hot and dry —
As make your bouts more violent to that end —
And that he calls for drink, I'll have prepar'd him
A chalice for the nonce; whereon but sipping,   160
If he by chance escape your venom'd stuck,
Our purpose may hold there. — But stay, what noise?

Enter Queen.

How now, sweet queen?

QUEEN.   One woe doth tread upon another's heel,
So fast they follow. Your sister's drown'd, Laertes.   165

LAER.   Drown'd! O, where?

QUEEN.   There is a willow grows aslant a brook,
That shows his hoar leaves in the glassy stream.
There with fantastic garlands did she come
Of crowflowers, nettles, daisies, and long purples,   170

---

150 *fit us to our shape* adapt us (in our actions) to our plans [K].   151 *that . . . performance* if our intention should show itself because of our failure to carry it out adroitly [K].   154 *did blast in proof* should burst (fail) when put to the test [K]. The metaphor is from the practice of testing cannons.   155 *cunnings* skills.   157 *dry* thirsty.   158 *bouts* sword thrusts (in offence).   159 *prepar'd* F¹; Q²: "prefard (preferr'd)," accepted by some editors.   160 *the nonce* that purpose.   161 *stuck* thrust.   162 *But . . . noise* Q²; not in F¹.   163 *How . . . queen* F¹; not in Q².   167 *aslant a* F¹; Q²: "ascaunt the."   168 *hoar* grey — as the leaves of the willow are on the under side [K].   169 *There with* F¹; Q²: "Therewith." *come* F¹; Q²: "make."   170 *crowflowers* Two or three different flowers are so called [K]. *long purples* orchids.   171 *liberal* coarser in speech. *grosser* more vulgar.   172 *cold* chaste.   173 *coronet* woven into wreaths for the head [K].   174 *envious*

That liberal shepherds give a grosser name,
But our cold maids do dead men's fingers call them.
There on the pendent boughs her coronet weeds
Clamb'ring to hang, an envious sliver broke,
When down her weedy trophies and herself   175
Fell in the weeping brook. Her clothes spread wide
And, mermaid-like, awhile they bore her up;
Which time she chaunted snatches of old tunes,
As one incapable of her own distress,
Or like a creature native and indued   180
Unto that element; but long it could not be
Till that her garments, heavy with their drink,
Pull'd the poor wretch from her melodious lay
To muddy death.

LAER.   Alas, then she is drown'd?

QUEEN.   Drown'd, drown'd.   185

LAER.   Too much of water hast thou, poor Ophelia,
And therefore I forbid my tears; but yet
It is our trick; nature her custom holds,
Let shame say what it will. When these are gone,
The woman will be out. Adieu, my lord.   190
I have a speech of fire, that fain would blaze
But that this folly drowns it.   *Exit.*

KING.   Let's follow, Gertrude.
How much I had to do to calm his rage!
Now fear I this will give it start again;
Therefore let's follow.   *Exeunt.* 195

malicious.   178 *tunes* F¹; Q²: "laudes," preferred by some editors as meaning
"hymns of praise."   179 *incapable of* insensible to, having no feeling of.   180
indued adapted by nature.   181 *that element* the water.   186–7 *Too much . . .
my tears* This speech seemed far less artificial to Shakespeare's contemporaries
than it does to us, for such punning expressions had come to be natural in
Elizabethan style and were by no means inconsistent with deep feeling [K].   188
our trick our natural human trait (to shed tears when one is sad).   190 *The
woman will be out* all the womanish qualities of my nature will have spent
themselves, and I shall be remorseless in my vengeance [K].   192 *this folly* this
natural weakness (weeping). Laertes rushes from the stage in tears. *drowns* Q²; F¹:
"doubts"; KNIGHT, K: "douts," meaning "puts out" or "extinguishes." There is no
real reason to depart from the Q² reading.

[Act Five

◇◇◇

SCENE I. *Elsinore. A churchyard.*]

Enter two Clowns, [*with spades and pickaxes*].

CLOWN. Is she to be buried in Christian burial when she wilfully
seeks her own salvation?

OTHER. I tell thee she is; therefore make her grave straight. The
crowner hath sat on her, and finds it Christian burial.

CLOWN. How can that be, unless she drown'd herself in her own   5
defence?

OTHER. Why, 'tis found so.

CLOWN. It must be *se offendendo;* it cannot be else. For here lies
the point: if I drown myself wittingly, it argues an act;
and an act hath three branches — it is to act, to do, and   10
to perform; argal, she drown'd herself wittingly.

OTHER. Nay, but hear you, Goodman Delver!

CLOWN. Give me leave. Here lies the water; good. Here stands
the man; good. If the man go to this water and drown
himself, it is, will he nill he, he goes — mark you that.   15

V.I. s.d. *Clowns* rustics, boors — an elderly sexton and his young helper [K].   1–2
when she . . . salvation when she wilfully seeks to go to heaven before her time
[K].   3 *straight* (a) immediately (b) narrow.   4 *crowner* coroner — a regular
pronunciation, not a blunder.   *sat on her* considered her case.   5–6 *in her own
defence* The Clown knows that self-defence is a justification for homicide, and
he ludicrously infers that it may justify suicide also [K].   8 *se offendendo* in
self-offence — the Clown's blunder for "se defendendo," in self-defence [K] (F¹; Q²:
"so offended").   8–9 *For here lies the point* Shakespeare here burlesques the
language used in the famous contemporary law-suit of Hales *v.* Petit, which

142

But if the water come to him and drown him, he drowns
not himself. Argal, he that is not guilty of his own death
shortens not his own life.

OTHER.   But is this law?

CLOWN.   Ay, marry, is't — crowner's quest law.   20

OTHER.   Will you ha' the truth an't? If this had not been a
gentlewoman, she should have been buried out o' Christian burial.

CLOWN.   Why, there thou say'st! And the more pity that great
folk should have count'nance in this world to drown   25
or hang themselves more than their even-Christen. Come,
my spade! There is no ancient gentlemen but gard'ners,
ditchers, and grave-makers. They hold up Adam's pro-
fession.

OTHER.   Was he a gentleman?   30

CLOWN.   'A was the first that ever bore arms.

OTHER.   Why, he had none.

CLOWN.   What, art a heathen? How dost thou understand the
Scripture? The Scripture says Adam digg'd. Could he
dig without arms? I'll put another question to thee. If   35
thou answerest me not to the purpose, confess thyself —

OTHER.   Go to!

CLOWN.   What is he that builds stronger than either the mason,
the shipwright, or the carpenter?

OTHER.   The gallows-maker; for that frame outlives a thousand   40
tenants.

CLOWN.   I like thy wit well, in good faith. The gallows does well.

---

established the law regarding suicide. See Supplementary Notes.   11 *argal* therefore (a corrupt form of "ergo") (F¹; Q²: "or all").   20 *crowner's quest* coroner's
inquest.   24 *there thou say'st* you are right about that.   25 *count'nance* au-
thorization. The Clown ludicrously speaks of the liberty to commit suicide as
one more unfair advantage which the aristocracy have over the common people
[ĸ].   26 *even-Christen* fellow Christian.   28 *hold up* support.   31 *bore arms*
had a coat of arms — the sign of a gentleman.   33-5 *What, art . . . without arms*
F¹; not in Q².   40 *frame* structure (F¹; not in Q²).

But how does it well? It does well to those that do ill.
Now, thou dost ill to say the gallows is built stronger
than the church. Argal, the gallows may do well to thee.   45
To't again, come!

OTHER.   Who builds stronger than a mason, a shipwright, or a
carpenter?

CLOWN.   Ay, tell me that, and unyoke.

OTHER.   Marry, now I can tell!   50

CLOWN.   To't.

OTHER.   Mass, I cannot tell.

Enter Hamlet *and* Horatio *afar off.*

CLOWN.   Cudgel thy brains no more about it, for your dull ass
will not mend his pace with beating; and when you are
ask'd this question next, say "a grave-maker." The   55
houses he makes lasts till doomsday. Go, get thee to
Yaughan; fetch me a stoup of liquor.

[*Exit* Second Clown.]

[Clown *digs and*] *sings.*

In youth when I did love, did love,
    Methought it was very sweet;
To contract — O — the time for — a — my behove,   60
    O, methought there — a — was nothing — a — meet.

HAM.   Has this fellow no feeling of his business, that 'a sings
at grave-making?

HOR.   Custom hath made it in him a property of easiness.

---

43 *does well* is a pretty good answer to my conundrum [K].   49 *unyoke* unyoke
your team of oxen; call it a day's work [K].   52 *Mass* by the mass (a common
oath).   56–7 *to Yaughan* to Yohan, Johan, some alehouse keeper in the neigh-
borhood (F¹; Q²: "in and").   *stoup* a big cup or mug.   58 *In youth* The three
stanzas which the Sexton sings are a garbled version of "The aged lover re-
nounceth love," a poem by Thomas, Lord Vaux, first printed in Tottel's
MISCELLANY of 1557.   60 *contract* shorten, make it pass pleasantly [K].   *behove*
behoof, advantage.   62 *'a* Q²; F¹, K: "he."   64 *hath made . . . easiness* has made
for it (has given it) an easy quality in his case; has made it a commonplace
occupation which leaves his mind at ease [K].   65–6 *The hand . . . sense* the

HAM.   'Tis e'en so. The hand of little employment hath the 65
         daintier sense.

CLOWN.   (sings)
                    But age with his stealing steps
                       Hath clawed me in his clutch,
                    And hath shipped me intil the land,
                       As if I had never been such.   70

                                      [*Throws up a skull.*]

HAM.   That skull had a tongue in it, and could sing once. How
         the knave jowls it to the ground, as if 'twere Cain's jaw-
         bone, that did the first murder! This might be the pate
         of a politician, which this ass now o'erreaches; one that
         would circumvent God, might it not?   75

HOR.   It might, my lord.

HAM.   Or of a courtier, which could say "Good morrow, sweet
         lord! How dost thou, good lord?" This might be my
         Lord Such-a-one, that prais'd my Lord Such-a-one's horse
         when 'a went to beg it — might it not?   80

HOR.   Ay, my lord.

HAM.   Why, e'en so! and now my Lady Worm's, chapless, and
         knock'd about the mazzard with a sexton's spade. Here's
         fine revolution, an we had the trick to see't. Did these
         bones cost no more the breeding but to play at loggets 85
         with 'em? Mine ache to think on't.

CLOWN.   (sings)
                    A pickaxe and a spade, a spade,
                       For and a shrouding sheet;

---

hand that is unaccustomed to manual labour has more sensitiveness, is less
callous [K].   68 *clawed* seized.   69 *hath . . . land* has stopped my voyage and
sent me ashore [K].   *intil* in to (F¹; Q²: "into").   72 *jowls* dashes.   73 *that* Cain
is the antecedent.   74 *o'erreaches* gets the better of.   74-5 *one . . . God* one who
was clever enough, while he lived, to disregard God's law and apparently to escape
unscathed [K].   80 *'a went* Q²; F¹, K: "he meant."   82 *chapless* without the
lower jaw (chap).   83 *mazzard* Like "pate" an old cant word for "head" [K].
84 *trick* knack, special skill.   85 *loggets* little logs — a game in which the
players throw pieces of hard wood at a stake or wooden wheel [K].

> O, a pit of clay for to be made
> For such a guest is meet. 90

Throws up [another skull].

HAM. There's another. Why may not that be the skull of a lawyer? Where be his quiddities now, his quillets, his cases, his tenures, and his tricks? Why does he suffer this rude knave now to knock him about the sconce with a dirty shovel, and will not tell him of his action of bat- 95 tery? Hum! This fellow might be in's time a great buyer of land, with his statutes, his recognizances, his fines, his double vouchers, his recoveries. Is this the fine of his fines, and the recovery of his recoveries, to have his fine pate full of fine dirt? Will his vouchers vouch him no 100 more of his purchases, and double ones too, than the length and breadth of a pair of indentures? The very conveyances of his lands will scarcely lie in this box; and must th' inheritor himself have no more, ha?

HOR. Not a jot more, my lord. 105

HAM. Is not parchment made of sheepskins?

HOR. Ay, my lord, and of calveskins too.

HAM. They are sheep and calves which seek out assurance in that. I will speak to this fellow. Whose grave 's this, sirrah? 110

CLOWN. Mine, sir.

---

90 *meet* fitting. 92 *quiddities* subtle arguments, fine distinctions (Q²; F¹, K: "Quiddits"). *quillets* quibbles, subtle distinctions. Hamlet strings out a series of expressions used by lawyers. 93 *tenures* titles to property. *tricks* deceit, trickery. *suffer* permit. 94 *rude* F¹; Q²: "madde." *sconce* Another cant term for "head" [K]. 96 *in's time* during his lifetime. 96–7 *buyer of land* There are constant references in Elizabethan and older literature to the ambitions of persons not belonging to the "landed gentry" to purchase estates and thus make themselves gentlemen. In this case it is a successful lawyer that Hamlet imagines as the purchaser [K]. 97–8 *his statutes . . . his recoveries* his various legal documents pertaining to the holding and transfer of estates. 98–9 *Is this . . . recoveries* is this the final outcome of his fines and the total acquired by his recoveries? "Fine and recovery" was a legal process for changing an entailed estate into an estate in fee simple (absolute possession) [K] (F¹; not in Q²). 100 *vouchers*

[*Sings*] O, a pit of clay for to be made
For such a guest is meet.

HAM.   I think it be thine indeed, for thou liest in't.

CLOWN. You lie out on't, sir, and therefore 'tis not yours. For 115
my part, I do not lie in't, yet it is mine.

HAM.   Thou dost lie in't, to be in't and say it is thine. 'Tis for
the dead, not for the quick; therefore thou liest.

CLOWN. 'Tis a quick lie, sir; 'twill away again from me to you.

HAM.   What man dost thou dig it for?   120

CLOWN. For no man, sir.

HAM.   What woman then?

CLOWN. For none neither.

HAM.   Who is to be buried in't?

CLOWN. One that was a woman, sir; but, rest her soul, she's dead. 125

HAM.   How absolute the knave is! We must speak by the card,
or equivocation will undo us. By the Lord, Horatio,
this three years I have taken note of it, the age is grown
so picked that the toe of the peasant comes so near the
heel of the courtier he galls his kibe. — How long hast 130
thou been a grave-maker?

CLOWN. Of all the days i' th' year, I came to't that day that our
last king Hamlet overcame Fortinbras.

HAM.   How long is that since?

---

guarantors of the legality of a title to land. A "double voucher" was a guarantee
sworn by two persons.   102 *indentures* contracts. These were drawn up in
duplicate on a single sheet of paper or parchment and were then cut apart in a
zigzag (indented) line. Their fitting together at this line was proof of genuineness
[K].   103 *conveyances* deeds.   104 *inheritor* possessor, owner.   113 *For . . .
meet* F[1]; not in Q[2].   118 *quick* living. The Sexton makes the obvious pun.   126
absolute insistent on accuracy in language.   *by the card* by the compass, observing every point; punctiliously [K].   127 *equivocation* ambiguity. Such deliberate ambiguity was a common source of Elizabethan humour.   129 *picked*
choice, refined.   130 *galls his kibe* follows him so closely that he rubs and
irritates the chilblain on the courtier's heel [K]. The peasant has come to imitate
the language and manners of the courtier.

CLOWN.   Cannot you tell that? Every fool can tell that. It was 135
          that very day that young Hamlet was born — he that is
          mad, and sent into England.

HAM.   Ay, marry, why was he sent into England?

CLOWN.   Why, because 'a was mad. 'A shall recover his wits there;
          or, if 'a do not, 'tis no great matter there.   140

HAM.   Why?

CLOWN.   'Twill not be seen in him there. There the men are as
          mad as he.

HAM.   How came he mad?

CLOWN.   Very strangely, they say.   145

HAM.   How strangely?

CLOWN.   Faith, e'en with losing his wits.

HAM.   Upon what ground?

CLOWN.   Why, here in Denmark. I have been sexton here, man
          and boy, thirty years.   150

HAM.   How long will a man lie i' th' earth ere he rot?

CLOWN.   Faith, if 'a be not rotten before 'a die (as we have many
          pocky corses now-a-days that will scarce hold the laying
          in), 'a will last you some eight year or nine year. A tan-
          ner will last you nine year.   155

HAM.   Why he more than another?

CLOWN.   Why, sir, his hide is so tann'd with his trade that 'a
          will keep out water a great while; and your water is a
          sore decayer of your whoreson dead body. Here's a skull
          now. This skull hath lien you i' th' earth three-and-   160
          twenty years.

---

136 *that very* Q²; F¹, K: "the very."   142–3 *as mad as he* The supposed eccentricity
of Englishmen gave rise to the notion on the Continent that they were a nation of
madmen [K].   150 *thirty years* This figure and the "three-and-twenty" in lines
160–1 involve a problem as to Hamlet's age [K]. Much has been made of the matter
by critics, but Shakespeare was not always consistent in minor details, and he did
not usually use his clowns to indicate the ages of his major characters.   153 *pocky*
corrupted by venereal disease (the pox).   *now-a-days* F¹; not in Q².   159 *whoreson*
bastard.   160 *you* The "ethical dative," which gives a colloquial touch to the
style but adds nothing to the sense [K].   168 *Yorick* Futile attempts have been

HAM.   Whose was it?

CLOWN.   A whoreson mad fellow's it was. Whose do you think it was?

HAM.   Nay, I know not.   165

CLOWN.   A pestilence on him for a mad rogue! 'A pour'd a flagon of Rhenish on my head once. This same skull, sir, was Yorick's skull, the King's jester.

HAM.   This?

CLOWN.   E'en that.   170

HAM.   Let me see. [*Takes the skull.*] Alas, poor Yorick! I knew him, Horatio. A fellow of infinite jest, of most excellent fancy. He hath borne me on his back a thousand times. And now how abhorred in my imagination it is! My gorge rises at it. Here hung those lips that I have kiss'd 175 I know not how oft. Where be your gibes now? your gambols? your songs? your flashes of merriment that were wont to set the table on a roar? Not one now, to mock your own grinning? Quite chapfall'n? Now get you to my lady's chamber, and tell her, let her paint an inch 180 thick, to this favour she must come. Make her laugh at that. Prithee, Horatio, tell me one thing.

HOR.   What's that, my lord?

HAM.   Dost thou think Alexander look'd o' this fashion i' th' earth?   185

HOR.   E'en so.

HAM.   And smelt so? Pah!   [*Puts down the skull.*]

HOR.   E'en so, my lord.

HAM.   To what base uses we may return, Horatio! Why may

---

made to explain this name as Danish; but, until it can be shown that Polonius, Claudius, Ophelia, Marcellus, and Bernardo are also Danish names, we need not trouble about the matter [K].   171 *Let me see* F¹; not in Q².   173 *fancy* imagination.   175 *it* the mere thought of it, i.e. of his bearing me on his back [K]. 179 *chapfall'n* lacking the lower jaw; with a pun on the sense of "down in the mouth," "disconcerted" [K].   180 *chamber* Q¹, F¹; Q²: "table."   181 *favour* (a) facial appearance (b) token to be granted to a lover. The pun is a bitter one: all that the lady finally can present to her lover is the grinning face of a skull.

not imagination trace the noble dust of Alexander till 190
'a find it stopping a bunghole?

HOR.   'Twere to consider too curiously, to consider so.

HAM.   No, faith, not a jot; but to follow him thither with
modesty enough, and likelihood to lead it; as thus: Alexander died, Alexander was buried, Alexander returneth 195
into dust; the dust is earth; of earth we make loam; and
why of that loam (whereto he was converted) might they
not stop a beer barrel?

Imperious Cæsar, dead and turn'd to clay,
Might stop a hole to keep the wind away.   200
O, that that earth which kept the world in awe
Should patch a wall t' expel the winter's flaw!
But soft! but soft awhile! Here comes the King —

> *Enter* [Priests *with*] *a coffin* [*in funeral*
> *procession*], King, Queen, Laertes,
> *with* Lords *attendant.*

The Queen, the courtiers. Who is this they follow?
And with such maimed rites? This doth betoken   205
The corse they follow did with desp'rate hand
Fordo it own life. 'Twas of some estate.
Couch we awhile, and mark.   [*Retires with* Horatio.]

LAER.   What ceremony else?

HAM.   That is Laertes,
A very noble youth. Mark.   210

LAER.   What ceremony else?

---

191 *'a* Q²; F¹, ᴋ: "he." *bunghole* hole in a beer or wine cask.   192 *curiously*
with unreasonable ingenuity [ᴋ].   194 *modesty* moderation, reasonableness [ᴋ].
as thus Q¹, F¹; not in Q².   196 *loam* a mixture of sand and clay used in masonry.
199 *Imperious* imperial.   201 *earth* body (being composed of earth).   202
winter's F¹; Q²: "waters." *flaw* blast.   203 *awhile* Q²; F¹, ᴋ: "aside."   204 *Who
is this* Hamlet has not heard of Ophelia's death or even of her madness, and
this fact must be remembered in judging his passionate behaviour at the grave.
There is nothing strange in his ignorance. He has not yet gone to court, and
Horatio would not blurt out the sad news as soon as he met him at the pier [ᴋ].
205 *maimed* curtailed.   207 *Fordo* destroy. *estate* rank.   208 *Couch we* let us
conceal ourselves [ᴋ].   210 *noble* referring not to the character of Laertes but
to his rank [ᴋ].   212 *Priest* F¹; Q²: "Doct." Also at line 221.   212-13 *Her obse-*

PRIEST. Her obsequies have been as far enlarg'd
     As we have warranty. Her death was doubtful;
     And, but that great command o'ersways the order,
     She should in ground unsanctified have lodg'd   215
     Till the last trumpet. For charitable prayers,
     Shards, flints, and pebbles should be thrown on her.
     Yet here she is allow'd her virgin crants,
     Her maiden strewments, and the bringing home
     Of bell and burial.   220

LAER.   Must there no more be done?

PRIEST.   No more be done.
     We should profane the service of the dead
     To sing a requiem and such rest to her
     As to peace-parted souls.

LAER.   Lay her i' th' earth;
     And from her fair and unpolluted flesh   225
     May violets spring! I tell thee, churlish priest,
     A minist'ring angel shall my sister be
     When thou liest howling.

HAM.   What, the fair Ophelia?

QUEEN. Sweets to the sweet! Farewell.   [*Scatters flowers.*]
     I hop'd thou shouldst have been my Hamlet's wife;   230
     I thought thy bride-bed to have deck'd, sweet maid,
     And not have strew'd thy grave.

LAER.   O, treble woe
     Fall ten times treble on that cursed head

---

quies . . . *warranty* her funeral rites have been made as complete as we are permitted to make them.   213 *doubtful* Though Ophelia fell into the stream by
accident (IV.VII.174), yet her demeanour, and the fact that she did not call for aid
or attempt to save herself, had made the clergy fear that she had committed
suicide [K].   214 *great . . . order* The King's command has prevailed against
the usual rule of the church [K].   216 *For* instead of.   217 *shards* bits of
broken pottery.   218 *crants* wreaths of flowers, carried to the grave and afterwards hung up in church, as signs that she had died a virgin.   219 *maiden
strewments* flowers strewn upon the grave of a virgin.   219–20 *bringing . . .
burial* laying in the grave (her final home) to the sound of the passing bell.   228
liest howling in hell.   233 *times treble* F¹; Q²: "times double."

Whose wicked deed thy most ingenious sense
Depriv'd thee of! Hold off the earth awhile,   235
Till I have caught her once more in mine arms.

Leaps in the grave.

Now pile your dust upon the quick and dead
Till of this flat a mountain you have made
T' o'ertop old Pelion or the skyish head
Of blue Olympus.   240

HAM.   [*comes forward*] What is he whose grief
Bears such an emphasis? whose phrase of sorrow
Conjures the wand'ring stars, and makes them stand
Like wonder-wounded hearers? This is I,
Hamlet the Dane.   *Leaps in after* Laertes.

LAER.   The devil take thy soul!   245

[*Grapples with him.*]

HAM.   Thou pray'st not well.
I prithee take thy fingers from my throat;
For, though I am not splenitive and rash,
Yet have I in me something dangerous,
Which let thy wisdom fear. Hold off thy hand!   250

KING.   Pluck them asunder.

QUEEN.   Hamlet, Hamlet!

ALL.   Gentlemen!

HOR.   Good my lord, be quiet.

---

234 *thy most ingenious sense* thy mind, endowed by nature with the finest
faculties [K].   236 s.d. *Leaps in the grave* F¹; not in Q². On the Elizabethan
stage the grave was represented by the open trap door.   237 *quick* living.   239
Pelion the lofty mountain upon which the Giants piled Mount Ossa in their
attempt to scale Mount Olympus, which rose to the home of the gods in the
sky [K].   243 *Conjures* lays a spell upon. The word may be accented on either
syllable [K]. *wand'ring stars* planets.   245 s.d. *Leaps in after Laertes* Q¹; not in
Q², F¹. Although the bad quarto stage directions are generally reliable, it is just
as likely that Laertes leaps out of the grave to grapple with Hamlet, thus providing
a much fuller view for the audience.   248 *splenitive and rash* Synonymous:
"excitable and quick-tempered" [K].   254 *wag* move up and down — such motion
being the last sign of life in a dying man [K].   255 *what theme* The Queen

[*The* Attendants *part them, and they come out of the grave.*]

HAM. Why, I will fight with him upon this theme
Until my eyelids will no longer wag.

QUEEN. O my son, what theme? 255

HAM. I lov'd Ophelia. Forty thousand brothers
Could not (with all their quantity of love)
Make up my sum. What wilt thou do for her?

KING. O, he is mad, Laertes.

QUEEN. For love of God, forbear him! 260

HAM. 'Swounds, show me what thou't do.
Woo't weep? woo't fight? woo't fast? woo't tear thyself?
Woo't drink up esill? eat a crocodile?
I'll do't. Dost thou come here to whine?
To outface me with leaping in her grave? 265
Be buried quick with her, and so will I.
And if thou prate of mountains, let them throw
Millions of acres on us, till our ground,
Singeing his pate against the burning zone,
Make Ossa like a wart! Nay, an thou'lt mouth, 270
I'll rant as well as thou.

QUEEN.   This is mere madness;
And thus a while the fit will work on him.
Anon, as patient as the female dove
When that her golden couplets are disclos'd,
His silence will sit drooping.

---

regards Hamlet as raving mad. His language, however, shows no incoherency until line 277 [K]. 258 *for her* to prove your love for her. 260 *forbear him* Addressed to Laertes: "Let him alone," "Do not harm him" [K]. 261 *'Swounds* by God's wounds. 262 *Woo't* wilt. 263 *drink up esill* drain bumpers of vinegar. The word "esill" (Old French "aisil") was associated, in everybody's mind, with the draught of vinegar and gall given to Christ at his crucifixion (MATTHEW, XXVII, 34). This, though intended as an anesthetic, was regarded as an additional torment [K]. 266 *quick* alive. 269 *the burning zone* that zone or belt of the celestial sphere that is bounded by the Tropics of Cancer and Capricorn [K]. 270 *mouth* rant. 271 *mere* utter, stark. 273 *patient* calm. 274 *golden couplets* The pigeon lays two eggs which hatch into young birds covered with golden down. *disclos'd* hatched.

HAM.　　　　　　　　　　　　Hear you, sir!　　　275
What is the reason that you use me thus?
I lov'd you ever. But it is no matter.
Let Hercules himself do what he may,
The cat will mew, and dog will have his day.　　*Exit.*

KING.　　I pray thee, good Horatio, wait upon him.　　280

　　　　　　　　　　　　Exit Horatio.

[*To* Laertes] Strengthen your patience in our last night's
　　speech.
We'll put the matter to the present push. —
Good Gertrude, set some watch over your son. —
This grave shall have a living monument.
An hour of quiet shortly shall we see;　　　　285
Till then in patience our proceeding be.　　*Exeunt.*

◇◇◇◇◇◇◇◇◇◇◇◇◇◇◇◇

[SCENE II.　*Elsinore. A hall in the Castle.*]

Enter Hamlet *and* Horatio.

HAM.　　So much for this, sir; now shall you see the other.
You do remember all the circumstance?

---

277 *But it is no matter* At this point Hamlet recollects himself. In his excitement
he had quite forgotten that madness is his cue and he does not realize that his
words to Laertes have seemed insane to the hearers. Hence he now reverts to his
habitual style of counterfeiting insanity. Lines 278–9, therefore, are not to be
brought into logical connection with what precedes or with the situation at all
[K].　　279 *The cat . . . day* A familiar proverb. The King may or may not regard
Hamlet's words as a veiled threat [K].　　281 *patience* calm endurance under
stress of emotion [K].　　*in . . . speech* by thinking of what we said last night
(with regard to your revenge). See IV.VII.123ff [K].　　282 *to the present push* to
the immediate attack or onset; into immediate action [K].　　284 *a living monument* If the Queen hears this, she will take "living" in the sense of "lifelike." To
Laertes, however, the words mean that Hamlet shall be sacrificed as an offering
to Ophelia's memory [K].

　　V.II. 1 *this* Hamlet has just finished telling Horatio certain early incidents of
the voyage [K].　　*the other* the rest of the story.　　2 *circumstance* details.　　6

HOR.   Remember it, my lord!

HAM.   Sir, in my heart there was a kind of fighting
         That would not let me sleep. Methought I lay   5
         Worse than the mutines in the bilboes. Rashly —
         And prais'd be rashness for it; let us know,
         Our indiscretion sometime serves us well
         When our deep plots do pall; and that should learn us
         There's a divinity that shapes our ends,   10
         Rough-hew them how we will —

HOR.   That is most certain.

HAM.   Up from my cabin,
         My sea-gown scarf'd about me, in the dark
         Grop'd I to find out them; had my desire,
         Finger'd their packet, and in fine withdrew   15
         To mine own room again; making so bold
         (My fears forgetting manners) to unseal
         Their grand commission; where I found, Horatio
         (O royal knavery!), an exact command,
         Larded with many several sorts of reasons,   20
         Importing Denmark's health, and England's too,
         With, hoo! such bugs and goblins in my life —
         That, on the supervise, no leisure bated,
         No, not to stay the grinding of the axe,
         My head should be struck off.

HOR.   Is't possible?   25

---

mutines mutineers. *bilboes* a kind of portable stocks carried on board ship.
They consisted of a heavy horizontal bar of iron, to which were attached rings
for the ankles [K]. *Rashly* obeying a sudden impulse [K]. 7 *know* recognize as
a fact. 8 *indiscretion* unthinking action. 9 *pall* fail. *learn* teach. 10 *ends*
outcome of our plans [K]. 11 *Rough-hew them as we may* no matter how we
roughly shape them in trial form. He is saying that human designs, although
begun by man, are finished by God. 15 *Finger'd* laid hold on. *in fine* finally,
at last. 17 *to* as to. *unseal* F¹; Q²: "vnfold." 20 *Larded* garnished. 21 *Importing* signifying. *health* welfare. 22 *hoo* An interjection expressing fright [K].
such bugs . . . life interspersed with such outbursts as to the danger of leaving a
terrible creature like me alive [K]. *bugs* bugbears. 23 *on the supervise* immediately upon its being read. *no leisure bated* no time for delay being sub-
tracted from the immediacy of the execution. The idea is expressed from an odd
point of view, and indeed, the whole speech is in a vein of fierce and bitter
humour [K]. 24 *stay* wait for. *grinding* sharpening.

HAM.   Here's the commission; read it at more leisure.
        But wilt thou hear now how I did proceed?

HOR.   I beseech you.

HAM.   Being thus benetted round with villainies,
        Or I could make a prologue to my brains,   30
        They had begun the play. I sat me down;
        Devis'd a new commission; wrote it fair.
        I once did hold it, as our statists do,
        A baseness to write fair, and labour'd much
        How to forget that learning; but, sir, now   35
        It did me yeoman's service. Wilt thou know
        Th' effect of what I wrote?

HOR.   Ay, good my lord.

HAM.   An earnest conjuration from the King,
        As England was his faithful tributary,
        As love between them like the palm might flourish,   40
        As peace should still her wheaten garland wear
        And stand a comma 'tween their amities,
        And many such-like as's of great charge,
        That, on the view and knowing of these contents,
        Without debatement further, more or less,   45
        He should those bearers put to sudden death,
        Not shriving time allow'd.

HOR.   How was this seal'd?

---

27 *now how* Q²; F¹, ᴋ: "me how."   30 *Or* A by-form of "ere." Hamlet means that before he could prepare his brains, they had begun to act in carrying out a plan [ᴋ].   32 *fair* in legible script.   33 *statists* politicians.   34 *A baseness* a plebeian accomplishment [ᴋ].   36 *yeoman's service* substantial service, though in a humble capacity [ᴋ].   37 *effect* purport.   39–42 *As England . . . amities* Hamlet burlesques the words of his own document, which he had composed in the formal and stately style used by the King in the original [ᴋ].   41 *wheaten garland* since agriculture can flourish only in time of peace [ᴋ].   42 *a comma* as a connecting link. The language is scornfully grotesque [ᴋ].   43 *as's of great charge* A standard pun on "ass" and "as." "Charge" means "burden" (as applied to the "asses") and "earnest conjuration" (as applied to the "as's") [ᴋ].   45 *debatement* discussion or consideration.   46 *those* Q²; F¹, ᴋ: "the." *sudden* instant.   47 *shriving time* time for confession.   48 *ordinant* operative in controlling events; practically equivalent to "foreordaining." Hamlet recurs to the thought of the "divinity that shapes our ends" (line 10) [ᴋ].   50 *model* copy.   51 *writ* writing, document.   52 *impression* of the seal.   53 *changeling* Spoken with bitter

HAM. Why, even in that was heaven ordinant.
      I had my father's signet in my purse,
      Which was the model of that Danish seal;   50
      Folded the writ up in the form of th' other,
      Subscrib'd it, gave't th' impression, plac'd it safely,
      The changeling never known. Now, the next day
      Was our sea-fight; and what to this was sequent
      Thou know'st already.   55

HOR. So Guildenstern and Rosencrantz go to't.

HAM. Why, man, they did make love to this employment!
      They are not near my conscience; their defeat
      Does by their own insinuation grow.
      'Tis dangerous when the baser nature comes   60
      Between the pass and fell incensed points
      Of mighty opposites.

HOR.   Why, what a king is this!

HAM. Does it not, think thee, stand me now upon —
      He that hath kill'd my king, and whor'd my mother;
      Popp'd in between th' election and my hopes;   65
      Thrown out his angle for my proper life,
      And with such coz'nage — is't not perfect conscience
      To quit him with this arm? And is't not to be damn'd
      To let this canker of our nature come
      In further evil?   70

---

humour. A "changeling" is an elf or imp, often hideously ugly and always ill-tempered and malicious, substituted by the fairies for a baby stolen from the cradle. In the present instance Hamlet's changeling is fair to look upon, but its character is evil enough [ĸ].   56 *to't* to their death.   57 *Why man . . . employment* F¹; not in Q².   58 *defeat* destruction.   59 *their own insinuation* their own act in worming themselves into this affair [ĸ].   60 *baser* Hamlet speaks as a prince, conscious of his royalty and convinced of the difference between kings and common men. "Baser" is not used in a moral sense, but refers to rank and dignity. These lines indicate the proper position of Claudius in the drama. He is the "mighty opposite," the great antagonist of Hamlet, and no contemptible foe. The struggle between him and his stepson is a battle of giants [ĸ].   61 *pass* thrust. *fell* fierce.   63 *think thee* does it seem to thee (Q²; F¹, ĸ: "thinkst thee"). *stand me now upon* be now my duty.   66 *proper* own.   67 *coz'nage* trickery, deceit.   68–80 *To quit . . . comes here* F¹; not in Q².   *quit him* pay him off.   69 *canker* eating sore, cancer or ulcer [ĸ].

HOR.   It must be shortly known to him from England
   What is the issue of the business there.

HAM.   It will be short; the interim is mine,
   And a man's life 's no more than to say "one."
   But I am very sorry, good Horatio,   75
   That to Laertes I forgot myself;
   For by the image of my cause I see
   The portraiture of his. I'll court his favours.
   But sure the bravery of his grief did put me
   Into a tow'ring passion.

HOR.   Peace! Who comes here? 80

Enter young Osric, *a courtier.*

OSR.   Your lordship is right welcome back to Denmark.

HAM.   I humbly thank you, sir. [*Aside to* Horatio] Dost know
   this waterfly?

HOR.   [*aside to* Hamlet] No, my good lord.

HAM.   [*aside to* Horatio] Thy state is the more gracious; for 'tis 85
   a vice to know him. He hath much land, and fertile.
   Let a beast be lord of beasts, and his crib shall stand at
   the king's mess. 'Tis a chough; but, as I say, spacious in
   the possession of dirt.

OSR.   Sweet lord, if your lordship were at leisure, I should im- 90
   part a thing to you from his Majesty.

71–2 *It must . . . there* Horatio, tacitly accepting Hamlet's argument, suggests
that immediate action is necessary and will be merely self-defence [K]. 76
I forgot myself Hamlet's own account of his behaviour refutes the theories both
of those critics who think he was then acting the madman, and those who think
that he was really insane [K]. 77–8 *For by . . . his* A clear indication that Laertes
the revenger was meant to be the foil to Hamlet the revenger [K]. 78 *court*
ROWE; F¹: "Count." 79 *bravery* ostentation. 80 s.d. *Osric* The language and
manners of Osric are a good-natured satire on the affectations of many young
gentlemen at the English court. One of the peculiarities of his style is the use of
words in a forced or unusual sense. Polonius has a touch of the same affectation
[K]. Shakespeare ridicules also his elaborate clothes, and particularly the large
hat which he flourishes as he speaks. 83 *waterfly* an unsubstantial creature, all
wings and iridescence, skimming along the surface of life [K]. 85 *state* condition. *gracious* virtuous. 87–8 *his crib . . . mess* A disrespectful way of saying "He will be sure to be admitted to the King's table" [K]. 88 *chough* jackdaw,
or any similar noisy, chattering bird. *spacious* owning much ground, wealthy. 93

HAM.   I will receive it, sir, with all diligence of spirit. Put your
        bonnet to his right use. 'Tis for the head.

OSR.   I thank your lordship, it is very hot.

HAM.   No, believe me, 'tis very cold; the wind is northerly.   95

OSR.   It is indifferent cold, my lord, indeed.

HAM.   But yet methinks it is very sultry and hot for my com-
        plexion.

OSR.   Exceedingly, my lord; it is very sultry, as 'twere — I can-
        not tell how. But, my lord, his Majesty bade me signify 100
        to you that 'a has laid a great wager on your head. Sir,
        this is the matter —

HAM.   I beseech you remember.

                [Hamlet *moves him to put on his hat.*]

OSR.   Nay, good my lord; for mine ease, in good faith. Sir,
        here is newly come to court Laertes; believe me, an ab- 105
        solute gentleman, full of most excellent differences, of
        very soft society and great showing. Indeed, to speak
        feelingly of him, he is the card or calendar of gentry;
        for you shall find in him the continent of what part a
        gentleman would see.   110

HAM.   Sir, his definement suffers no perdition in you; though,

---

bonnet Osric has removed his large hat.   96 *indifferent* rather.   97–8 *complexion*
temperament (literally, the peculiar combination of the four humours of the
body).   101 *'a has* Q²; F¹: "he ha's"; κ: "he has."   104 *for mine ease* A common
phrase when one politely insists on standing hat in hand [κ].   105–32 *here is
. . . Well, sir* Q²; not in F¹, which substitutes a single sentence: "Sir, you are not
ignorant of what excellence Laertes is at his weapon."   105–6 *absolute* perfect,
finished.   106 *differences* qualities or talents that distinguish him from others;
accomplishments [κ].   107 *soft society* agreeable manners [κ].   *great showing*
splendid appearance.   108 *feelingly* with a due sense of his merits [κ] (Q³; Q²:
"sellingly").   *card . . . gentry* a guide or model of courtly manners. As one con-
sults a card (compass) or a calendar for accurate information and sure guidance,
so every gentleman may learn how to behave by observing Laertes [κ].   109–10
the continent . . . see the sum total of whatever qualities one gentleman would
like to find in another. A "continent" is literally "that which contains" [κ].
111 *definement* definition.   *perdition* loss.

I know, to divide him inventorially would dozy th'
arithmetic of memory, and yet but yaw neither in respect of his quick sail. But, in the verity of extolment,
I take him to be a soul of great article, and his infusion   115
of such dearth and rareness as, to make true diction of
him, his semblable is his mirror, and who else would
trace him, his umbrage, nothing more.

OSR.   Your lordship speaks most infallibly of him.

HAM.   The concernancy, sir? Why do we wrap the gentleman   120
in our more rawer breath?

OSR.   Sir?

HOR.   [*aside to* Hamlet] Is't not possible to understand in another tongue? You will to't, sir, really.

HAM.   What imports the nomination of this gentleman?   125

OSR.   Of Laertes?

HOR.   [*aside*] His purse is empty already. All's golden words are
spent.

HAM.   Of him, sir.

OSR.   I know you are not ignorant —   130

HAM.   I would you did, sir; yet, in faith, if you did, it would
not much approve me. Well, sir?

OSR.   You are not ignorant of what excellence Laertes is —

112–14 *to divide . . . sail* to make an inventory of his fine qualities would stagger
the reckoning power of one's memory, and yet, after all, the inventory would
come far short of his real excellence. The excellence of Laertes is a fast boat
which sails steadily on; the inventory is another boat, which tries to overtake the
leader, but "yaws" continually and thus falls far behind. A boat "yaws" when
she steers badly, so that she does not hold her course but swings her bow from
side to side and thus loses headway [K].   112 *dozy* confuse.   113 *neither* after
all.   113–14 *respect of* comparison with.   114 *in . . . extolment* to give him due
praise.   115 *article* scope, importance.   *his infusion* the nature with which he
is infused or endowed [K].   116 *dearth and rareness* rare excellence.   117 *his
semblable is his mirror* the only person who resembles him is his own image
in the looking-glass [K].   117–18 *who else . . . more* anybody else who wishes to
keep pace with him can do so only as the shadow follows the substance [K].   120
concernancy purport, meaning.   120–1 *Why . . . breath* why do we attempt to
describe the gentleman in our words, which are too crude to do him justice [K]?
124 *to't* go to it; be able to tackle it (Q²; JOHNSON, K: "do't").   125 *nomination*

HAM.   I dare not confess that, lest I should compare with him
        in excellence; but to know a man well were to know him- 135
        self.

OSR.   I mean, sir, for his weapon; but in the imputation laid
        on him by them, in his meed he's unfellowed.

HÁM.   What's his weapon?

OSR.   Rapier and dagger.   140

HAM.   That's two of his weapons — but well.

OSR.   The King, sir, hath wager'd with him six Barbary horses;
        against the which he has impawn'd, as I take it, six
        French rapiers and poniards, with their assigns, as girdle,
        hangers, and so. Three of the carriages, in faith, are very 145
        dear to fancy, very responsive to the hilts, most delicate
        carriages, and of very liberal conceit.

HAM.   What call you the carriages?

HOR.   [*aside to* Hamlet] I knew you must be edified by the
        margent ere you had done.   150

OSR.   The carriages, sir, are the hangers.

HAM.   The phrase would be more germane to the matter if
        we could carry cannon by our sides. I would it might
        be hangers till then. But on! Six Barbary horses against
        six French swords, their assigns, and three liberal-con- 155
        ceited carriages: that's the French bet against the Danish.
        Why is this all impawn'd, as you call it?

---

naming.   131-2 *yet . . . approve me* if you, who are yourself a fool, supposed me
to be ignorant, that belief of yours would not be much evidence in my favour [K].
134-8 *I dare . . . unfellowed* Q²; not in F¹.   134-5 *I dare not . . . excellence* I
dare not say that I know how excellent Laertes is, for such an assertion would
be an implied claim to equal excellence on my own part, since only the excellent
can judge of excellence [K].   137 *imputation* reputation.   138 *meed* excellence.
unfellowed without peer.   143 *impawn'd* placed in pawn, staked (Q²; F¹, K:
"impon'd").   144 *assigns* appurtenances.   145 *hangers* straps by which the
sword hung from the belt.   146 *dear to fancy* tastefully designed.   *responsive*
harmonious in design.   147 *liberal conceit* elegant conception, fine design.   149-50
I knew . . . done Q²; not in F¹.   *edified by the margent* instructed by a marginal
note [K].   151 *carriages* This use is an affectation of Osric's and, as such, is
humourously criticised by Hamlet, to whom the word suggests a gun carriage,
the wheeled frame that "carries" a cannon [K].   152 *germane* related.   157
impawn'd WILSON; not in Q²; F¹, K: "impon'd."

OSR.   The King, sir, hath laid that, in a dozen passes between
      yourself and him, he shall not exceed you three hits; he
      hath laid on twelve for nine, and it would come to im-   160
      mediate trial if your lordship would vouchsafe the an-
      swer.

HAM.   How if I answer no?

OSR.   I mean, my lord, the opposition of your person in trial.

HAM.   Sir, I will walk here in the hall. If it please his Majesty,   165
      it is the breathing time of day with me. Let the foils be
      brought, the gentleman willing, and the King hold his
      purpose, I will win for him if I can; if not, I will gain
      nothing but my shame and the odd hits.

OSR.   Shall I redeliver you e'en so?   170

HAM.   To this effect, sir, after what flourish your nature will.

OSR.   I commend my duty to your lordship.

HAM.   Yours, yours. [*Exit* Osric.] He does well to commend it
      himself; there are no tongues else for's turn.

HOR.   This lapwing runs away with the shell on his head.   175

HAM.   'A did comply with his dug before 'a suck'd it. Thus has
      he, and many more of the same bevy that I know the
      drossy age dotes on, only got the tune of the time and
      outward habit of encounter — a kind of yesty collection,
      which carries them through and through the most fann'd   180

---

158 *laid* wagered. *passes* bouts.   161-2 *vouchsafe the answer* kindly consent to
meet Laertes in this match. Hamlet purposely misunderstands Osric and thus
forces him to explain [K].   166 *the breathing . . . me* the time of day when I
take my exercise. To "breathe" or to "breathe one's self" was common in this
sense [K].   170 *redeliver you e'en so* carry back that as your reply (F¹; Q²: "deliver
you so").   171 *flourish* elaborate language.   172 *I commend my duty* I offer
my devoted service; I declare myself your humble servant. Hamlet puns on
"commend," which means also (as nowadays) "to praise" [K].   174 *for's turn*
for his purpose.   175 *This lapwing . . . head* A mere joust at Osric's juvenile
self-sufficiency: "This young fellow is as forward as the lapwing, which begins to
run before it is fairly out of the shell." The lapwing was proverbially precocious
[K]. The "shell" refers also to Osric's hat.   176 *'A* Q²; F¹, K: "He." *comply* use
compliments, i.e. ceremonious language [K].   *'a* Q²; F¹, K: "he."   177 *bevy* F¹; Q²:
"breede."   177-8 *the drossy age* the degenerate present, in contrast with the
Golden Age. In this sentence Hamlet more or less unconsciously continues to
speak in the style that he has adopted in his talk with Osric [K].   179 *outward*

and winnowed opinions; and do but blow them to their
trial — the bubbles are out.

Enter a Lord.

LORD.   My lord, his Majesty commended him to you by young
Osric, who brings back to him, that you attend him in
the hall. He sends to know if your pleasure hold to play 185
with Laertes, or that you will take longer time.

HAM.   I am constant to my purposes; they follow the King's
pleasure. If his fitness speaks, mine is ready; now or
whensoever, provided I be so able as now.

LORD.   The King and Queen and all are coming down. 190

HAM.   In happy time.

LORD.   The Queen desires you to use some gentle entertainment
to Laertes before you fall to play.

HAM.   She well instructs me. [*Exit* Lord.]

HOR.   You will lose this wager, my lord. 195

HAM.   I do not think so. Since he went into France I have been
in continual practice. I shall win at the odds. But thou
wouldst not think how ill all's here about my heart. But
it is no matter.

HOR.   Nay, good my lord — 200

HAM.   It is but foolery; but it is such a kind of gaingiving as
would perhaps trouble a woman.

---

habit (a) fashionable habits (b) showy clothes (F¹; Q²: "out of an habit"). *en-counter* society (literally, "meeting"). *yesty* frothy (F¹; Q²: "misty"). *collection* of words and phrases.   180–1 *fann'd and winnowed* choicest and most refined. The words are virtually identical in meaning (HANMER; Q²: "prophane and tren-nowned"; F¹: "fond and winnowed").   181 *opinions* judgments.   181–2 *and do . . . are out* one puff of breath, and the froth is gone. The metaphor of the passage is probably based upon the frothy bubbles which appear in the vat when beer is brewed.   183–94 *My lord . . . instructs me* Q²; not in F¹.   188 *if his fitness speaks* if his convenience calls for the match [K].   191 *In happy time* opportunely.   192 *to use . . . entertainment* to meet Laertes in a cordial and friendly way [K].   193 *fall to play* begin fencing.   197 *in continual practice* Very significant. Cf. II.II.292 [K].   198 *how ill . . . heart* how uneasy I feel. Hamlet has a presentiment of evil. "Ill" is regularly used of any uneasy or un-comfortable physical feeling. As everybody knows, such presentiments are often accompanied by physical symptoms [K].   201 *gaingiving* misgiving.

HOR.   If your mind dislike anything, obey it. I will forestall
        their repair hither and say you are not fit.

HAM.   Not a whit, we defy augury; there's a special providence   205
        in the fall of a sparrow. If it be now, 'tis not to come;
        if it be not to come, it will be now; if it be not now,
        yet it will come: the readiness is all. Since no man
        knows aught of what he leaves, what is't to leave be-
        times? Let be.   210

                    Enter King, Queen, Laertes, [Osric],
                    and Lords, *with other* Attendants *with*
                    foils and gauntlets. A Table and flag-
                    ons of wine on it.

KING.   Come, Hamlet, come, and take this hand from me.

                    [*The* King *puts* Laertes' *hand into*
                    Hamlet's.]

HAM.   Give me your pardon, sir. I have done you wrong;
        But pardon't, as you are a gentleman.
        This presence knows,
        And you must needs have heard, how I am punish'd   215
        With a sore distraction. What I have done
        That might your nature, honour, and exception
        Roughly awake, I here proclaim was madness.
        Was't Hamlet wrong'd Laertes? Never Hamlet.
        If Hamlet from himself be ta'en away,   220
        And when he's not himself does wrong Laertes,

---

205 *augury* omens (in which a good Christian would not believe).   206 *sparrow*
Cf. MATTHEW X, 29: "Are not two sparrows sold for a farthing? and one of them
shall not fall on the ground without your father." Cf. also LUKE, XII, 6 [K].   *it* i.e.
death.   208 *readiness* for death.   209 *knows aught . . . leaves* has any knowledge of what life would have been like had he continued to live (K; Q²: "of ought
he leaues, knows"; F¹: "ha's ought of what he leaues"). The passage in Q² is obviously corrupt, and F¹ represents an attempt at editorial emendation.   209–10
what is't . . . betimes of what importance is it when a man dies. The statement,
which some critics have regarded as the clearest expression of Shakespeare's
philosophical position in the play, is a Stoic commonplace: "It is not the time
of a man's death that is important, but the manner in which he dies."   210
Let be let it go. Do not try to dissuade me [K].   214 *This presence* the King
and Queen.   216 *a sore* Q²; F¹: "sore." · 217 *exception* objection, resentment.

Then Hamlet does it not, Hamlet denies it.
Who does it, then? His madness. If't be so,
Hamlet is of the faction that is wrong'd;
His madness is poor Hamlet's enemy.   225
Sir, in this audience,
Let my disclaiming from a purpos'd evil
Free me so far in your most generous thoughts
That I have shot my arrow o'er the house
And hurt my brother.

LAER.   I am satisfied in nature,   230
Whose motive in this case should stir me most
To my revenge. But in my terms of honour
I stand aloof, and will no reconcilement
Till by some elder masters of known honour
I have a voice and precedent of peace   235
To keep my name ungor'd. But till that time
I do receive your offer'd love like love,
And will not wrong it.

HAM.   I embrace it freely,
And will this brother's wager frankly play.
Give us the foils. Come on.

LAER.   Come, one for me.   240

HAM.   I'll be your foil, Laertes. In mine ignorance
Your skill shall, like a star i' th' darkest night,
Stick fiery off indeed.

LAER.   You mock me, sir.

---

224 *faction* party.   226 *Sir, in this audience* F¹; not in Q². 228 *Free me* absolve
me.   230 *in nature* in so far as my natural feelings are concerned (as opposed to
the demands of my honour).   234 *masters* experts in these questions [K].   235
a voice . . . peace a decision that may serve as a precedent for reconciliation [K].
236 *ungor'd* unscathed; free from disgrace [K].   236–8 *But . . . wrong it* The
monstrous hypocrisy of these words, spoken as they are by a young nobleman
whose instinct and training are honourable, shows the blind ruthlessness of the
doctrine of revenge and stands in marked contrast to Hamlet's caution and conscience in his own case [K].   239 *frankly* freely, without rancour.   240 *Come on*
F¹; not in Q².   241 *your foil* A courteous pun. "Foil" often means "a bit of
tinsel placed under a gem to enhance its brilliancy," and so, "that which sets
off something by contrast" [K].   243 *Stick fiery off* stand out in brilliant contrast [K].

HAM.	No, by this hand.	
KING.	Give them the foils, young Osric. Cousin Hamlet,	245
	You know the wager?	
HAM.	Very well, my lord.	
	Your Grace has laid the odds o' th' weaker side.	
KING.	I do not fear it, I have seen you both;	
	But since he is better'd, we have therefore odds.	
LAER.	This is too heavy; let me see another.	250
HAM.	This likes me well. These foils have all a length?	

Prepare to play.

OSR.	Ay, my good lord.	
KING.	Set me the stoups of wine upon that table.	
	If Hamlet give the first or second hit,	
	Or quit in answer of the third exchange,	255
	Let all the battlements their ordnance fire;	
	The King shall drink to Hamlet's better breath,	
	And in the cup an union shall he throw	
	Richer than that which four successive kings	
	In Denmark's crown have worn. Give me the cups;	260
	And let the kettle to the trumpet speak,	
	The trumpet to the cannoneer without,	
	The cannons to the heavens, the heaven to earth,	
	"Now the King drinks to Hamlet." Come, begin.	
	And you the judges, bear a wary eye.	265
HAM.	Come on, sir.	
LAER.	Come, my lord. *They play.*	
HAM.	One.	

---

247 *odds* i.e. in the value of the stake. The King's stake is much greater than
that of Laertes [K].   249 *is better'd* has improved (since he went to France).
odds i.e. in terms of the wager. Laertes may score two points more than Hamlet
and still lose the match [K].   250 *let me see another* Laertes picks out the unbated and poisoned foil [K].   251 *likes* pleases.   253 *stoups* large cups.   255
quit . . . exchange repay Laertes (score a hit) in the third bout [K].   258 *an
union* a great and flawless pearl [K] (F¹; Q²: "Vnice").   261 *kettle* kettledrum.
272 *A touch, a touch* F¹; not in Q².   273 *fat* not in perfect training [K], or
sweaty, since perspiration was regarded as melting body fat. The word certainly

LAER.	No.
HAM.	Judgment!
OSR.	A hit, a very palpable hit.
LAER.	Well, again!
KING.	Stay, give me drink. Hamlet, this pearl is thine; Here's to thy health.

Drum; trumpets sound; a piece goes off [*within*].

Give him the cup.

HAM.	I'll play this bout first; set it by awhile.	270
	Come. (*They play.*) Another hit. What say you?	
LAER.	A touch, a touch; I do confess't.	
KING.	Our son shall win.	
QUEEN.	He's fat, and scant of breath.	
	Here, Hamlet, take my napkin, rub thy brows.	
	The Queen carouses to thy fortune, Hamlet.	275
HAM.	Good madam!	
KING.	Gertrude, do not drink.	
QUEEN.	I will, my lord; I pray you pardon me. *Drinks.*	
KING.	[*aside*] It is the poison'd cup; it is too late.	
HAM.	I dare not drink yet, madam; by-and-by.	
QUEEN.	Come, let me wipe thy face.	280
LAER.	My lord, I'll hit him now.	
KING.	I do not think't.	

does not mean "corpulent," and there is no reason to suppose that Shakespeare would call attention to the excessive girth of Richard Burbage, who played the part.   274 *napkin* handkerchief.   275 *carouses* drinks a full draught [K].   276 *Good madam* With a gesture, in courteous acknowledgment of the Queen's toast [K]. There is no reason to regard the line as Hamlet's attempting to warn his mother from drinking.   277 s.d. *Drinks* Q¹; not in Q², F¹.   279 *dare not* Hamlet has no suspicion that the cup is poisoned. He means that he does not think it wise to drink (in response to the Queen's toast) until the match is over [K].

LAER.　[*aside*] And yet it is almost against my conscience.

HAM.　Come for the third, Laertes! You do but dally.
　　　I pray you pass with your best violence;
　　　I am afeard you make a wanton of me.　　　285

LAER.　Say you so? Come on.　　　　　　　　*Play.*

OSR.　Nothing neither way.

LAER.　Have at you now!

　　　　　　[Laertes *wounds* Hamlet; *then,*] *in*
　　　　　　scuffling, they change rapiers, [*and*
　　　　　　Hamlet *wounds* Laertes].

KING.　　　　　Part them! They are incens'd.

HAM.　Nay come! again!　　　　*The* Queen *falls.*

OSR.　　　　　Look to the Queen there, ho!

HOR.　They bleed on both sides. How is it, my lord?　　290

OSR.　How is't, Laertes?

LAER.　Why, as a woodcock to mine own springe, Osric.
　　　I am justly kill'd with mine own treachery.

HAM.　How does the Queen?

KING.　　　　　She sounds to see them bleed.

QUEEN.　No, no! the drink, the drink; O my dear Hamlet!　　295
　　　The drink, the drink! I am poison'd.　　[*Dies.*]

HAM.　O villainy! Ho! let the door be lock'd.
　　　Treachery! Seek it out.　　　　[Laertes *falls.*]

LAER.　It is here, Hamlet. Hamlet, thou art slain;
　　　No med'cine in the world can do thee good.　　300
　　　In thee there is not half an hour of life.

---

282 *almost . . . conscience* This aside makes the confession of Laertes in lines
299–306, 313–17, sound less like too sudden a conversion [K].　283 *you do but* Q²;
F¹, K: "you but."　284 *pass* thrust.　285 *make a wanton of me* treat me in-
dulgently; play with me (instead of doing your best to win). A wanton is "a
spoiled child" [K].　292 *as a woodcock . . . springe* like a fool, caught in my
own snare. A woodcock, in its stupid curiosity, was supposed to fumble with the
snare and thus achieve its own capture [K].　294 *sounds* swounds, swoons.　303

The treacherous instrument is in thy hand,
Unbated and envenom'd. The foul practice
Hath turn'd itself on me. Lo, here I lie,
Never to rise again. Thy mother 's poison'd.   305
I can no more. The King, the King 's to blame.

HAM.   The point envenom'd too?
Then, venom, to thy work.   *Hurts the* King.

ALL.   Treason! treason!

KING.   O, yet defend me, friends! I am but hurt.   310

HAM.   Here, thou incestuous, murd'rous, damned Dane,
Drink off this potion! Is thy union here?
Follow my mother.   King *dies.*

LAER.   He is justly serv'd.
It is a poison temper'd by himself.
Exchange forgiveness with me, noble Hamlet.   315
Mine and my father's death come not upon thee,
Nor thine on me!   *Dies.*

HAM.   Heaven make thee free of it! I follow thee.
I am dead, Horatio. Wretched queen, adieu!
You that look pale and tremble at this chance,   320
That are but mutes or audience to this act,
Had I but time (as this fell sergeant, Death,
Is strict in his arrest) O, I could tell you —
But let it be. Horatio, I am dead;
Thou liv'st; report me and my cause aright   325
To the unsatisfied.

HOR.   Never believe it.
I am more an antique Roman than a Dane.
Here's yet some liquor left.

HAM.   As th'art a man,

---

practice plot.   310 *hurt* wounded.   312 *thy union* F¹; Q²: "the Onixe."   314
temper'd mixed, compounded.   316 *come not upon thee* are not upon thy
head.   318 *make thee free of* forgive thee for.   321 *mutes* players who have
no part in the drama [K].   322 *fell* fierce, cruel.   *sergeant* a sheriff's officer.   326
the unsatisfied those who are uninformed.   327 *antique Roman* Ancient Romans,
like Cato and Brutus, often committed suicide rather than live in such a world
as Horatio envisages with Hamlet gone.

Give me the cup. Let go! By heaven, I'll ha't.
O God, Horatio, what a wounded name   330
(Things standing thus unknown) shall live behind me!
If thou didst ever hold me in thy heart,
Absent thee from felicity awhile,
And in this harsh world draw thy breath in pain,
To tell my story.   *March afar off, and shot within.*
                    What warlike noise is this?   335

OSR.   Young Fortinbras, with conquest come from Poland,
To the ambassadors of England gives
This warlike volley.

HAM.   O, I die, Horatio!
The potent poison quite o'ercrows my spirit.
I cannot live to hear the news from England,   340
But I do prophesy th' election lights
On Fortinbras. He has my dying voice.
So tell him, with th' occurrents, more and less,
Which have solicited — the rest is silence.   *Dies.*

HOR.   Now cracks a noble heart. Good night, sweet prince,   345
And flights of angels sing thee to thy rest!

                              [*March within.*]

Why does the drum come hither?

                    Enter Fortinbras *and English* Am-
                    bassadors, *with Drum, Colours, and*
                    Attendants.

---

330 *O God* Q²; F¹, ᴋ: "O good," which almost certainly represents an attempt to remove profanity from the play on the orders of the Master of the Revels.   339 *o'ercrows* overcomes. The figure is from cockfighting, and the word (like the sport) was common in Elizabethan times [ᴋ]. *spirit* vital force, vitality, life [ᴋ]. 341 *election* as King of Denmark.   342 *voice* suffrage, vote. The crown of Denmark was elective (within limits), but nomination by the reigning king had much influence in determining his successor, and Hamlet is, for a moment, practically King of Denmark. We may infer that Fortinbras is related to the Danish royal family. Cf. lines 375–6 [ᴋ].   343 *occurrents* occurrences.   344 *solicited* brought on (this tragedy) [ᴋ].   350 *This . . . havoc* these dead bodies proclaim that a massacre has taken place. "Quarry" is the regular word for the game killed in a hunt. "Havoc" was the old battle cry for "No quarter." "Cries on" means simply

FORT.   Where is this sight?

HOR.   What is it you would see?
         If aught of woe or wonder, cease your search.

FORT.   This quarry cries on havoc. O proud Death,   350
         What feast is toward in thine eternal cell
         That thou so many princes at a shot
         So bloodily hast struck?

AMBASSADOR.   The sight is dismal;
         And our affairs from England come too late.
         The ears are senseless that should give us hearing   355
         To tell him his commandment is fulfill'd,
         That Rosencrantz and Guildenstern are dead.
         Where should we have our thanks?

HOR.   Not from his mouth,
         Had it th' ability of life to thank you.
         He never gave commandment for their death.   360
         But since, so jump upon this bloody question,
         You from the Polack wars, and you from England,
         Are here arriv'd, give order that these bodies
         High on a stage be placed to the view;
         And let me speak to th' yet unknowing world   365
         How these things came about. So shall you hear
         Of carnal, bloody, and unnatural acts;
         Of accidental judgments, casual slaughters;
         Of deaths put on by cunning and forc'd cause;

"cries out," "shouts," not "calls for" or "exclaims against" [K].   351 *toward* in
preparation. Scandinavian warriors believed that, if slain in battle, they were
translated to Valhalla, Odin's palace in the sky, where they were to spend their
time in feasting and fighting. Though Shakespeare may have known nothing
about this pagan creed, the present passage accords with it and sounds appropriate
in the mouth of young Fortinbras [K].   361 *jump* exactly, opportunely. *question*
matter.   368 *accidental judgments* judgments of God brought about by means
apparently accidental. This refers particularly to the death of the Queen and of
Laertes. Cf. line 293. "Casual slaughters" merely repeats the idea [K].   369 *put
on* instigated, prompted [K]. If the deaths here referred to are those of Rosencrantz and Guildenstern, as is usually believed, "cunning" would refer to Hamlet's
cleverness and "forc'd cause" to the fact that he acted in self-defence.

And, in this upshot, purposes mistook   370
Fall'n on th' inventors' heads. All this can I
Truly deliver.

FORT.   Let us haste to hear it,
And call the noblest to the audience.
For me, with sorrow I embrace my fortune.
I have some rights of memory in this kingdom,   375
Which now to claim my vantage doth invite me.

HOR.   Of that I shall have also cause to speak,
And from his mouth whose voice will draw on more.
But let this same be presently perform'd,
Even while men's minds are wild, lest more mischance   380
On plots and errors happen.

FORT.   Let four captains
Bear Hamlet like a soldier to the stage;
For he was likely, had he been put on,
To have prov'd most royal; and for his passage
The soldiers' music and the rites of war   385
Speak loudly for him.
Take up the bodies. Such a sight as this
Becomes the field, but here shows much amiss.
Go, bid the soldiers shoot.

> *Exeunt marching; after the which a*
> *peal of ordinance are shot off.*

370–1 *purposes . . . heads* This must refer to the deaths of Laertes and the
King, brought about by their own devices having gone wrong.   372 *deliver* report.   375 *rights of memory* unforgotten rights.   376 *my vantage* my presence
(with troops) at this opportune moment [K].   378 *voice . . . more* vote will draw
on more votes.   379 *presently* at once.   381–9 *Let four . . . shoot* In Elizabethan tragedy, the person of highest rank among the survivors regularly makes
the speech which brings the play to a formal close. This necessity, indeed, ac-
counts for the presence of Fortinbras in HAMLET. But for him, there would be
no one left of sufficient rank to fulfill this office [K]. But we must not neglect his
importance also as a foil by which the conduct of Hamlet may be set off in
contrast.   383 *put on* advanced to the kingship, and so put to the test [K].   384
To have prov'd most royal to have shown himself every inch a king. This tribute
from a fighter like Fortinbras should be a sufficient answer to those critics who
regard Hamlet as a weak creature [K].   *royal* Q²; F¹, K: "royally."   *passage* death.
388 *shows* appears.

SUPPLEMENTARY NOTES

G. L. Kittredge devoted more attention to HAMLET than to any other of Shakespeare's plays, and his notes to this play — although modern scholars may not always agree with them — represent a contribution to an understanding of the drama which is of permanent value. Even those critics who do not share Kittredge's basic attitude towards HAMLET must recognize these notes as classic statements of a critical position of great historical importance. A selection of those important notes which could not conveniently be placed at page bottoms therefore follows:

I.II. 1–39 *Though yet . . . your duty* This speech deserves careful study with reference to the character of Claudius, which is often misconceived. Its artificial style and balanced antithesis are not the effects of hypocrisy, but merely of ceremony. Being the King's first speech from the throne since his coronation, it is formal and dignified, especially so through line 16 — the end of the King's acknowledgment of the aid of his advisers. Then follows, in a style still dignified but less stilted, an account of the business for which this particular Council has been assembled. Lines 17–25 sum up facts already known to the Council, and the rest of the speech concerns the dispatching of Voltemand and Cornelius as ambassadors to Norway. The whole address is appropriate, skillfully constructed, and even eloquent. It gives the audience a high idea of the intellectual powers of the King, whom we as yet have no reason to suspect or to dislike.

109–17 *the most immediate . . . our son* Thus the King solemnly proclaims Hamlet his heir; and, even in this elective monarchy, such an announcement would go far to determine the succession. Cf. III. II. 325–8. We must not regard his words as hypocritical. He loves the Queen passionately, and she is devoted to her son. Besides, Claudius is not an habitual or hardened criminal, nor does he wish to increase his guilt by further offences. He hopes to live at peace with Hamlet and to atone for past wrongs by kindness in the days to come. That this cannot be, is a part of the tragedy. It is the King's nemesis that the good he purposes turns to evil in his hands.

I.III. 10 *No more but so* Not spoken in plaintive accents; for Ophelia does not doubt Hamlet, nor, gentle as she is, has she any lack of spirit. Her question is merely an acknowledgment that she is listening to her brother's sermon, much as if she had said "Ah?" "Indeed?" or "Well?" The actress's foreknowledge of Ophelia's doom should not overshadow this scene. Ophelia is full of the joy of living; and she is rather more than a match for her brother, as we shall see presently (lines 45–51).

I.IV. 27 *the o'er-growth of some complexion* A man's "complexion" (temperament) was thought to be determined by the proportion of the four humours that existed in his physical make-up. These were called blood, phlegm, bile (red bile or choler), and black bile (or melancholy). According as one or another of these substances predominated, the man was sanguine, phlegmatic, choleric, or melancholy. If one of these four tendencies increased to an excessive degree, a fault might be the result — rashness, sloth, irascibility, or moroseness.

44–5 *Hamlet . . . Dane* There is no climax in these words. Hamlet the scholar knows that a supernatural being should be called upon by all known names that may belong to it. The theory was that the right name would force or induce it to speak. The same idea is the basis of all such invocations as that which begins the third book of PARADISE LOST: "Hail, holy Light," etc. *royal Dane* Hamlet pauses for a moment after these words; but the Ghost says nothing, and he calls upon it passionately for an answer.

I.v. 116 *Hillo . . . bird, come* The halloo of Marcellus reminds Hamlet of the falconer's call in summoning a hawk. In what follows he speaks flippantly of the Ghost and its errand. This does not mean that he wishes to conceal the seriousness of the whole matter from his friends; for that would be idle, and the end of the scene shows that he has no such intention. Nor is this light tone a symptom of madness. It is merely revulsion of feeling after an emotional crisis. The fearful strain to which Hamlet has been subjected demands relief, and in such cases the relief may come either in tears or in laughter and reckless jesting. When he recovers his self-possession, he speaks soberly and coherently (lines 165*ff*).

II.i. 96 *That done, he lets me go* It is at this moment that Hamlet decides that he must renounce Ophelia and give up all thought of marriage and happiness. To involve an innocent girl in such a revenge as he contemplates would have been a crime. His study of Ophelia's face is but the long look in which he says farewell to his hopes. Some critics, however, imagine that he is trying to discover whether Ophelia is strong enough to stand by him in his plans, and that, reading weakness in her countenance, he renounces her for ever. Such a theory ignores the obvious fact that Hamlet cannot for a moment have wished to make Ophelia his accomplice in a deed of blood.

II.ii. 5–10 *So call it . . . dream of* The King's language shows that Hamlet's appearance and behaviour since he has begun to play the madman are very different from what they were in Scene ii of the First Act. Then he was merely sorrowful; now he looks and acts like a lunatic. The distinction was doubtless made much more striking on the Elizabethan stage than it usually is in our modern theatres. Cf. line 150.

18 *open'd* if it is disclosed. The King has a bad conscience, and may feel somewhat uneasy about Hamlet's madness; but we are not called upon to see anything in his words beyond their plain meaning. The Queen is distressed at her son's condition, and Claudius is anxious to make her happy. Her request to Rosencrantz and Guildenstern, we observe, is precisely the same as his.

26–34 *Both your majesties . . . gentle Rosencrantz* Shakespeare has purposely made Rosencrantz and Guildenstern, who always hunt in couples, indistinguishable in character, manners, and language. Their close likeness is amusingly shown in their replies, which are almost antiphonic: Rosencrantz utters a half-line, two whole lines, and a half-line; Guildenstern continues in a speech of exactly the same length and the same metrical arrangement. We note, too, the carefully regulated form of the thanks of the King and Queen, in which the names are so arranged that neither Rosencrantz nor Guildenstern shall feel that either has been more honoured than the other.

109–24 *To the celestial,* etc. Hamlet's love letter was written before he began to play the madman. Its stilted style has done him much harm in the esteem of modern readers. However, he is but following the fashion of Shakespeare's time.

No suitor would have dreamed of beginning with so unceremonious a phrase as "Dear Ophelia."

II.II. 438 *The rugged Pyrrhus* etc. Whether the passages that follow are actually quotations from some lost tragedy is an insoluble question. Probably not. At all events, there is no satire involved. To make the recited passages sound like histrionic recitation ("a fiction and a dream of passion") they must be sharply distinguished from the blank-verse speeches in HAMLET itself; and this effect of declamation (as contrasted with natural passion) is produced by overcharging the style. The contrast is strengthened by putting the actual dialogue of the scene in prose.

556 *Am I a coward* Hamlet rages against himself for stupid inactivity — not for hesitation or weakness of will. He has done nothing to avenge his father and seems incapable of doing anything. Why? Not, surely, because he is a coward! Yet even *that,* he exclaims, with bitter irony, is possible: otherwise he must have killed his uncle long ago. Thus he relieves his excitement by railing until, at the end of the soliloquy, he grows calm and expresses in the plainest language what the matter really is: *he needs evidence.* He must not kill a man on the word of an apparition, and thus far no other testimony has been procurable. He is angry at what he thinks his own stupidity and he calls upon his brains to go to work. They have, indeed, obeyed him before he spoke: "The play's the thing!" It will force the King to confession, and then Hamlet can act when once he "knows his course."

III.I. 49–54 *'tis . . . burden* This remark of the King's is an aside and is therefore perfectly sincere: it is, in fact, a thought, not a speech. Claudius, like Macbeth, has sinned hideously under the influence of temptation, and his conscience, like Macbeth's, torments him incessantly. Herein he differs from such deliberate villains as Iago (in OTHELLO) and Edmund (in KING LEAR). His words prepare us for the wonderful scene (III. III) in which he tries in vain to repent and makes a hopeless attempt to pray.

56–88 *To be, or not to be . . . of action* In this famous soliloquy Hamlet is often thought to be dallying with the purpose of suicide as a means of escape from his duty. But this view overlooks the facts of the situation and does violence to Hamlet's own words. He has formed his plan to make the King betray himself, has written his "dozen or sixteen lines," and is eager to try the crucial experiment. Meanwhile there is a wearisome interval in which he can do nothing but wait for nightfall. Inaction brings depression of spirits, and the thought recurs to him that death would be a relief. All men have such thoughts at such moments, and to all men — as to Hamlet — they lead to the further reflection that every one has the power of life or death in his own hands. But reflections are not purposes. By *the question* Hamlet does not mean "the question for me to decide now, in my own case," but rather the question which, as it seems to him, must sooner or later force itself upon every man: "Is it nobler to live miserably or to end one's troubles by a single stroke?" The answer, he says, would be obvious if death were only a sleep. The whole course of his argument is general, not personal. He is not suffering from the scorn of the world, the law's delay, or the insolence of office.

III.I. 95–6 *No, not I . . . you aught* From this point Hamlet talks as insanely as he knows how. Ophelia replies with the gentle firmness which one might use to a refractory child, until Hamlet's feigned madness grows so distressing that she can only pray to heaven for his relief. No doubt Hamlet suspects that somebody is listening, and he cannot afford to take chances. Whether or not Ophelia is acting under instructions, it is necessary that she should share the general opinion that he has lost his mind. Indeed, it is far more merciful to her to confirm that impression than to let her think that he is sane and does not love her. As for taking her into his confidence, that is manifestly impossible. He cannot think for a moment of making her his accomplice in a deed of blood. Love and marriage are not for him until his revenge is accomplished. If ever he emerges triumphant from the difficulties that surround him and takes his seat upon the throne of Denmark, explanation will be easy enough.

130 *Where's your father* An awkward question for Ophelia, but she does not hesitate to give the only possible answer. She must not reply, "My lord, he is behind the arras." Hamlet, she thinks, is insane, and she is acting under the orders of those whom she regards as most interested in his cure. Hence she does not scruple to treat him, in this matter of telling the truth, as madmen must often be treated. Nor has Hamlet any reason to be angry with Ophelia, even if he knows that Polonius is behind the arras; for, by counterfeiting lunacy, he has forfeited the right to be treated as sane. It is possible that he has seen the arras shake, or even that he has caught sight of Polonius for a moment. Note, however, that in what follows he treats Ophelia no more harshly than before. Indeed, he merely follows the train of thought already begun in line 121 ("Get thee to a nunnery!"). As to the stage action, however, one thing is certain. Polonius undoubtedly shows his head for a moment to the audience; for such is the regular convention when a character is in hiding — whether behind the hangings, or behind a screen, or in a chest. And he must withdraw his head precipitately when he hears Hamlet's question — to the amusement of the audience, who are further diverted by realizing that the old courtier must hear himself called a fool. The comic effect would be heightened if Hamlet had his back turned to Polonius when the head appeared. On the whole, then, we may feel reasonably certain that Hamlet does not see Polonius but has merely a vague suspicion that he is within earshot.

III.II. 129 s.d. *dumb show* It has caused remark that after Hamlet's fling at "inexplicable dumb shows" (lines 11–12) he should have allowed such a pantomime in this play. There are three good reasons. First, the dumb show suits the old-fashioned and stilted character of THE MURDER OF GONZAGO (see note on lines 146*ff*). The second reason is even more important. The centre and focus of interest during the acting of THE MURDER OF GONZAGO must be — for Shakespeare's audience — not the actors in that play, but the guilty Claudius. We should therefore be enabled to follow the plot without attending too much to the players — and in this we are assisted by the dumb show, which is by no means "inexplicable" but gives a clear summary of the plot. Finally, the dumb show is meant to torture King Claudius, and thus to help in making him reveal his "occulted guilt." It is the first turn of the thumbscrew.

130 *What means this* Ophelia may need enlightenment, but King Claudius cannot fail to perceive that the play will come close to the facts of his crime. Yet he must not betray himself by objecting or by leaving the hall: he must stand the torture, if he can, without wincing. And, indeed, he shows amazing self-control. He does not flinch until the very moment when Lucianus uses the poison, and even then his actions do not reveal his secret, except to Hamlet and Horatio, who already know it.

223 *the argument* an outline of the plot. When a play was presented at

court, it was customary to submit such an outline beforehand in order to avoid incidents that might be offensive. The King's question shows how well he is controlling himself. He knows what torture the play has in store for him (for he has seen the dumb show), but he does not betray himself, even by a tone or a look. To the courtiers his question seems to concern merely some resemblance between the play and the Queen's second marriage. Hamlet's reply is meant to give another turn to the screw, but even then Claudius shows no distress. He merely asks (line 226), with an air of polite interest, what the *title* of the play is.

253 *rises* The King has endured the dumb show without flinching, and also the whole course of the play until this moment. Even now, when the details of his secret crime are enacted before his eyes, he does not betray himself except to Hamlet and Horatio, who have learned the facts already. To the others (including the Queen) Claudius seems merely to be suddenly indisposed. Cf. lines 285-9.

370-81 *'Tis now . . . consent* Hamlet's imaginative nature pictures him to himself as capable of any atrocity in the way of revenge. We are not, however, to suppose that there was any danger of his killing his mother. Indeed, the Ghost has expressly warned him not to harm her (I, v, 84-8). One purpose of this speech is to enlighten the audience, so that, when Hamlet threatens the Queen in Scene IV (lines 18-21), they may know that he does not mean to do her any harm.

III.III. **68** *limed soul* The figure is that of a bird caught by alighting upon a twig smeared with the sticky substance called birdlime. The harder it struggles, the more it is besmeared and ensnared ("engag'd"). Thus the King's soul, in its efforts to find some escape from guilt, merely succeeds in convincing itself that no escape is possible — since he can neither pray nor repent. Cf. Ariosto, ORLANDO FURIOSO, XXIII, 105: "Like the heedless bird that finds itself caught in a net or in birdlime: the more it beats its wings and strives to get loose, the more it entangles itself."

IV.V. **23-6** *How should . . . shoon* The fragments that Ophelia sings appear to be bits that would be familiar to the Elizabethan audience, but only three lines (23, 24, 182) have been found that antedate the play. Coleridge rightly bids us note "the conjunction here of these two thoughts that had never subsisted in conjunction, the love for Hamlet and her filial love, and the guileless floating on the surface of her pure imagination of the cautions so lately expressed and the fears not too delicately avowed by her father and brother concerning the dangers to which her honour lay exposed" (SHAKESPEARE CRITICISM, ed. Raysor, I, 33, 34).

73-4 *this is the poison . . . death* That it is Claudius who speaks must not blind us to the fact that this sentence is meant to sum up for us — the audience — the meaning of the madness that precedes, as the Gentleman's "She speaks much of her father" (line 4) prepares us to understand it. Laertes agrees with the King's diagnosis (lines 154ff). Disappointed love and Hamlet's madness had no doubt made Ophelia "deject and wretched" (III, I, 155), but it is the mysterious tragedy of her father's death that has driven her mad. In her madness, thoughts of love and marriage of course recur and take strange shapes in their utterance.

75-94 *O Gertrude . . . death* The King feels genuine sorrow for Polonius and Ophelia; and, besides, their fate has involved him in such difficulties that he seems to be hemmed in by troubles which are ever drawing nearer.

IV.V. **172ff** Whether Ophelia actually brings flowers and herbs on the stage or simply imagines them, nobody can tell for certain. That she has culled precisely those that she mentions is out of the question. There is no indication in the old stage directions how the distribution (real or imagined) was made. Editors are pretty well agreed, however, that she gives rosemary and pansies to Laertes (as if he were her true-love), fennel and columbines to the King, and rue to the Queen — saving some for herself. The daisy remains in doubt. Perhaps she gave it to the King or the Queen. Wilson thinks she kept it (as well as the pansies) for herself. For the old "language of flowers" see Clement Robinson, A HANDFUL OF PLEASANT DELITES, 1584, and the first few pages of Greene's A QUIP FOR AN UPSTART COURTIER, 1592 (ed. Grosart, XI, 213*ff*).

V.I. 8–9 *For here lies the point* The Sexton's logic (as Sir John Hawkins suggests) may be an echo of arguments elaborated in a lawsuit of 1554 — a case resulting from the death of Sir James Hales, who had committed suicide by walking into a river.

"Walsh [one of the counsel] said that the Act [of self-destruction] consists of three Parts. The first is the Imagination, which is a Reflection or Meditation of the Mind, whether or no it is convenient for him to destroy himself, and what Way it can be done. The second is the Resolution, which is a Determination of the Mind to destroy himself, and to do it in this or that particular Way. The third is the Perfection, which is the Execution of what the Mind has resolved to do. And this Perfection consists of two Parts, viz. the Beginning and the End. The Beginning is the doing of the Act which causes the death, and the End is the Death, which is only a Sequel to the Act (Plowden's REPORTS, translation, 1779, p. 259)."

In summing up, the judge remarked:

"Sir James Hales was dead, and how came he to his Death? It may be answered, by drowning; and who drowned him? Sir James Hales. And when did he drown him? In his Lifetime. So that Sir James Hales being alive caused Sir James Hales to die; the Act of the living, was the Death of the dead Man. And for this Offence it is reasonable to punish the living Man, who committed the Offence, and not the dead Man (p. 262)."

V.II. 158 *a dozen passes* The terms of the wager seem clear enough. There are to be a dozen passes, or "bouts," and the King bets that the total score of Laertes shall not exceed Hamlet's by three hits. Thus if the score stood 7 for Laertes and 5 for Hamlet, the King would win; so also if it stood 6 to 6, or 6 to 4 with two draws. But if it stood Laertes 8, Hamlet 4, the King would lose; so also if it stood 7 to 4, with one draw. "Twelve for nine," however, cannot by any twist be brought into accord with these terms. Many attempts have been made to clear up the passage, but they are not worth repeating. As Dr. Johnson sensibly remarks, "The passage is of no importance; it is sufficient that there was a wager."

V.II. 203 *obey it* Neither Hamlet nor Horatio suspects a plot; for, although they distrust the King, they believe Laertes to be a man of honour, and the presence of the Queen is additional security. Yet Horatio, the philosopher, urges Hamlet to obey his instinctive reluctance of mind; for he knows that such feelings sometimes come from ideas that are well-founded; though too indistinct to be expressed at the moment.

212–30 *Give me your pardon . . . my brother* "I wish Hamlet had made some other defence; it is unsuitable to the character of a good or a brave man to shelter himself in falsehood" (Johnson). It is odd that Dr. Johnson failed to see that Hamlet's particular falsehood here is inseparable from the general falsehood involved in his counterfeiting madness. If his conduct here is to be reprehended, the blame should go farther back and attach itself to his whole stratagem, and no one has ever taken ethical ground against that.